ADVANCE PRAISE FOR

GOOD VIDEO GAMES + GOOD LEARNING

"Gee is at his masterful best in this brilliant collection. No one speaks with more insight and clarity when it comes to the learning potential of videogames. Gee seeks nothing short of a revolution; we will do well to follow his lead."

Katie Salen, Associate Professor, Parsons the New School for Design; Executive Director, Gamelab Institute of Play

"*Good Video Games and Good Learning* is packed with deep insight about games and learning. If you are creating games or studying them, if you are using games to educate or just want a sneak peek at the future of learning, then you must read this book.

Gee doesn't focus on educational games: he shows how any good game is a context for learning—and conversely, what educators can learn from games. His aim is not to tell teachers how to teach, or to tell game creators how to make better games—but instead to bridge the gap between the two. In doing so, Gee presents essential ideas about game design and game experience, cognition and pleasure, and learning both in and out of the classroom—all with the playful rigor and clear thinking we have come to expect from this eminent scholar (and expert player) of games.

If you read one book on games and learning this year, read *Good Video Games and Good Learning*. It will change the way you think about—and play—games."

Eric Zimmerman, Co-Founder & CEO, Gamelab; and Co-Author, Rules of Play & The Game Design Reader

GOOD VIDEO GAMES
+ GOOD LEARNING

Colin Lankshear, Michele Knobel,
Chris Bigum, and Michael Peters
General Editors

Vol. 27

PETER LANG
New York • Washington, D.C./Baltimore • Bern
Frankfurt am Main • Berlin • Brussels • Vienna • Oxford

JAMES PAUL GEE

GOOD VIDEO GAMES
+ GOOD LEARNING

Collected Essays on Video Games, Learning and Literacy

PETER LANG
New York • Washington, D.C./Baltimore • Bern
Frankfurt am Main • Berlin • Brussels • Vienna • Oxford

Library of Congress Cataloging-in-Publication Data

Gee, James Paul.
Good video games and good learning: collected essays on video games,
learning and literacy / James Paul Gee.
p. cm. — (New literacies and digital epistemologies; v. 27)
Includes bibliographical references and index.
1. Video games—Psychological aspects.
2. Computer games—Psychological aspects.
3. Learning, Psychology of. 4. Visual literacy.
5. Video games and children. I. Title.
GV1469.3.G438   794.8—dc22   2006101455
ISBN 978-0-8204-9734-1 (hardcover)
ISBN 978-0-8204-9703-7 (paperback)
ISSN 1523-9543

Bibliographic information published by **Die Deutsche Bibliothek**.
Die Deutsche Bibliothek lists this publication in the "Deutsche
Nationalbibliografie"; detailed bibliographic data is available
on the Internet at http://dnb.ddb.de/.

FSC
Mixed Sources
Product group from well-managed
forests, controlled sources and
recycled wood or fiber
Cert no. SCS-COC-002464
www.fsc.org
©1996 Forest Stewardship Council

Cover design by Lisa Barfield

The paper in this book meets the guidelines for permanence and durability
of the Committee on Production Guidelines for Book Longevity
of the Council of Library Resources.

© 2007 Peter Lang Publishing, Inc., New York
29 Broadway, 18th floor, New York, NY 10006
www.peterlang.com

Printed in the United States of America

Acknowledgements

I went down the games path, as I have other paths in my career, because it looked very promising and interesting, but I had no idea who I would meet down the road. I had feared that people who had lived longer in this new territory than me would resent me as an interloper. I have been wildly pleased to find out how many generous and wonderful people there were there, who welcomed me, helped me, and made me feel at home.

Henry Jenkins called me before my first book on video games even appeared in print—he had gotten hold of a draft—and has been amazingly supportive ever since, as he has been for so many others. He is a titan as a scholar and a human being. Kurt Squire came to the University of Wisconsin after the initial book appeared and has been a fellow traveler ever since, though it is clear, too, that he will soon pass me on the road (truth be told, he already has). When I was writing the initial book I day dreamed about being invited to talk at the annual Game Developers

Conference (GDC). Jason Della Rocca, Executive Director of the International Game Developers' Association (IGDA), made that dream come true, not once but several times. Jason was a truly welcoming, helpful, and brilliant guide into the game developers' community. Through GDC I met Eric Zimmerman, co-founder (with Peter Lee) of Gamelab in New York. Eric has become a colleague and a friend—he is surely one of smartest and most creative humans I have ever met. Through Eric I met Katie Salen, Executive Director, Gamelab Institute of Play, and have since worked closely with her on a joint project. Like everyone else, I admire Katie and wish I had one half the talent and charisma she has.

I have been on lots of different paths in my academic career since I left theoretical linguistics to deal with the messy world of language, learning, and literacy in their social and cultural contexts. I have met a great many academics on those roads and over the years, alas, become more and more disappointed with academic institutions. Every time I have wanted to give up, to turn back, my friend Colin Lankshear has shown up to encourage me and push me on. He has had the guts, through his whole career, to play the "game" of academics on his own terms. This book would not exist without him—it was his idea and he put it together. In fact, without his inspiration—and the work he and Michele Knobel had done before me on new literacies and digital literacies—I doubt I would have pursued my work on games in the first place. This book is dedicated to him (thanks, brother).

I wish to acknowledge permissions granted by publishers for me to use work for which they hold copyright, as follows:

James Paul Gee, *Games and Culture* Vol. 1, No. 1, 58–61, copyright 2006 by Sage Publications. Reprinted by Permission of Sage Publications.

James Paul Gee, "Learning and Gaming" in *Situated Language and Learning*, 57-76, Routledge, 2004.

James Paul Gee, "Affinity Spaces" in *Situated Language and Learning*, 77–90, Routledge, 2004.

Contents

Introduction

Today, culture sometimes goes backwards. We adults pick it up from our children, rather than the other way round. That's how I became a gamer. Five years ago I had no real interest in video games. Today I play them and write about them a good deal because of my son, Sam. When he was three, Sam played games like *Dr. Seuss's Cat in the Hat* and *Winnie the Pooh*, eventually moving on to games like *Pajama Sam* and *Spy Fox*. I played *Pajama Sam* myself so that I could help him play it and found the game fascinating. It involved a colorful and entertaining world, lots of humor—including lots of play on words—and thought-provoking problems. Of course, I discovered that Sam didn't really need my help and often had to help me.

I decided to try an adult game, just to see what such games were like. I was 53 when I started and was amazed at how long, challenging, and complex good games like *Deus Ex* or *Half-Life* were. Yet millions of people pay a lot of money to buy these games and they learn them very well, including kids who wouldn't spend twelve concentrated minutes really learning algebra in school and certainly wouldn't pay for the experience. Game companies face an interesting problem, a problem that schools face, as well: how to get someone to learn something that is challenging and requires persistence. Game companies need to sell games that are long, hard, and require an extended commitment. They can't dumb them down, because most players don't want and won't accept short or easy games. If people can't learn to play a company's games, the company goes broke. So game designers have no choice, they have to make games that are very good at getting themselves learned.

As I played—confronting my own learning and how atrophied my learning muscles had become when forced to learn something entirely new and unable simply to rest on the laurels of my past experience—it dawned on me that good games are learning machines. Good learning principles are built into their very designs. As someone who had worked for years in the areas of learning and literacy, I realized that these principles were supported, in fact, by cutting-edge research in the Learning Sciences. Many of these principles—with or without a game—could well be used in schools to get students to learn things like science, but, too often today schools are centered on skill-and-drill and multiple-choice tests that kill deep learning. If we don't soon use these principles in our schools, other countries will use them to their advantage and business will see them as forms of "just in time" and "on demand" 24/7 learning in competition with our public schools.

My interest in video games, however, goes beyond worries about schools and schooling. Good video games reverse a lot of our cherished beliefs. They show that pleasure and emotional involvement are central to thinking and learning. They show that language has its true home in action, the world, and dialogue, not in dictionaries and texts alone. They show that all types of young people—regardless of class and whether they are "ADHD" or not—can master complex stuff at a very high level of skill. They show that collaboration and participation with others is essential to engaged thinking and learning. They show that most young people want to live in worlds outside of and beyond their own cultural groups, they don't want to be trapped with someone else's single label. They want to be both African-American and a *Pokémon* fan and many other things as well. They show that for our young people it is and ever has been a global world—where they are as liable to draw their own Japanese anime as watch a Disney cartoon and will effortlessly consume both together in a game like *Kingdom Hearts*. It is a global world in which they are often more at home than either their parents or our politicians.

But of course, it is not learning, but violence that dominates the public discussion of video games, despite the fact that the best selling video game of all time, *The Sims*, is not violent and that a great many non-violent games are made each year. But then, if you play games, you know that even violent games require more attention to strategy—to finding patterns and solving problems—than to the images, violent or not, on the screen.

At the same time, the power of video games is not in their present state just as it is, but in their potential: what we can do with them if we want to innovate. The video game industry is, like so many other parts of our economy, narrowing down to a few big powerful companies. Innovation wanes as each company seeks to imitate the last big blockbuster. In my view, we have made to date 1% of the types of games that could be made. Nonetheless, innovation does occur, as games like *Shadow of the Colossus* and *Okami*, for instance, demonstrate.

If the media has missed the fact that there are many non-violent games (e.g., *The Sims*, *Zoo Tycoon*, *Animal Crossing*, and *Harvest Moon*) and games with fighting where strategic thinking far outweighs violence of any sort (e.g., *Age of Mythology*, *Rise of Nations*, and *Civilization*), it has even more crucially missed the fact that video games—like any other technology—are neither good nor bad all by themselves. It all depends on how they are played and the social contexts in which they are played. Effects (good or bad) flow not from the game but from game + context. Played strategically, with reflective interactions with parents and peers, they have good cognitive effects for children. Played as babysitters by children from violent homes, they are bad.

Before writing about video games I wrote a good deal about language and literacy and I am by training a linguist and that is what I have remained through all my transformations. Schools hand people books full of words; things like a textbook in biology. The language in these books is often very technical and highly complex. The theory is that kids can understand the books just by reading them.

But these school books are about worlds—and the world of the biologist is not the same as the world of the physicist and, in turn, not the same as the world of the social scientist, artist, urban planner, or literary critic. Unfortunately, many students have not visited these worlds, not played in them. Giving them the book, then, is akin to giving them the manual to a game without the game. The manual is boring and makes no sense all by itself. It is hard to read until you have played the game for a while; then it becomes easy to read, because now you have an image, action, experience, or dialogue to associate with each word in the manual, not just "dictionary definitions." The words in the manual now have "situated meanings," real ones, ones you can use.

School gives kids manuals without games. The kids who have played the game at home—thanks to the resources their parents can muster—can sometimes give the texts situated meanings, while the other kids cannot. Often, however, no one can really give the texts situated meanings—it's just that some kids can answer paper-and-pencil multiple choice tests about the words and others cannot. Next to no one can actually apply their knowledge to solve actual problems. Next to no one knows why people use such words, what identities they take on when they recruit such words to their purposes and goals. I don't want to give kids video games in schools, I want to give them worlds that make words meaningful, whether these worlds are virtual, real, or a mixture of the two.

So, let me overview the contents of the book. The first chapter—"Why Video Games Are Good for Your Soul: Pleasure and Learning"—is about the sense of ownership, agency, and control good video games can give people and the ways in which, in doing so, they marry pleasure, mastery, and learning.

The second chapter—"Video Games, Violence, and Effects: Good and Bad"—is a short statement on the issue of violence and the effects games can have (e.g., Will they make Johnny shoot people at school?). When I wrote *What Video Games Have to Teach Us About Learning and Literacy* (2003) I took a lot of heat for not discussing the violence issue. I argued then, and still argue now, that the vast majority of the literature is already devoted to this topic and, given that there are lots and lots of other topics about games worth discussing, someone has to move on. That doesn't mean the topic isn't important, it just means that I trust others to discuss it in more depth so I can concentrate on learning about other things than violence (and there are plenty of things that teach violence in our culture that are not video games).

Suffice it to say that infinitely more violence has been done because people thought the Bible or God told them to do it than because of all video games combined—yet we can find other things to discuss about both God and the Bible. But, at the same time, yes, let's most certainly stop violence in the name of religion. Then we can worry about games.

Chapter 3—"Notes on Content and Technological Determinism"—is another short piece meant simply to clear some ground for better understanding later. People tend to think school is about "content" (facts, information) and games are just about actions. In fact, games have lots of content, but "teach" it in ways radically different from school. The piece also takes up the issue of what effects games have or do not have. The issue of "content" is dealt with at much greater length in Chapter 10.

Chapter 4—"Good Video Games, the Human Mind, and Good Learning"— argues that the way in which current research in the Learning Sciences looks at the human mind—how the mind works—is much like a video game. Humans think and learn through experiences they have had and via simulations they run in their heads based on those experiences, much as if they were playing video games in their heads. Good video games can externalize good thinking and problem solving. This will be a theme throughout the book. This chapter also discusses a number of principles of good learning that good video games use to get themselves—and their "content"—mastered.

Chapter 5—"Learning About Learning from a Video Game: *Rise of Nations*"— is a meditation on my own learning in regard to the real-time strategy game *Rise of Nations*. Real-time strategy games (like *Age of Mythology, Age of Empires, Company of Heroes*) are the most complex games made and when I began playing them I found them difficult enough and had had enough bad experiences with them that by the time I came to *Rise of Nations* I considered myself a "disabled learner." *Rise of Nations* dealt with me far differently than schools do with such learners. Rather than being sent to "Special Ed," I was rehabilitated as a player and learner.

Chapter 6—"Pleasure and 'Being a Professional': Learning and Video Games"—puts two things together than don't seem at first sight to fit together, namely pleasure and learning to be a professional (e.g., an urban planner or a scientist of a certain sort). But a certain class of video games does just this. While these games usually concentrate on things like being a SWAT team member or a soldier, the principles they recruit can and have been used for other sorts of "content." Such games show us the crucial ties between identity, values, content, and learning.

Chapter 7—"Why Games Studies Now? Video Games: A New Art Form"— is a bit of a break from learning and enters the debate over whether or not video games are "art." I think they are an art form, but one of a very different type than literature and movies. Video games place the emphasis on the "player's story," not on the finely tuned top-down intricate architecture of an "author" designing an intricate plot for someone else. In fact, the way in which games are art is closely tied to how and why they recruit learning (so not a total break here).

Chapter 8—"Affinity Spaces: From *Age of Mythology* to today's Schools"— takes up the new forms of affiliation and social interaction in which many young people are engaged today. I contrast these forms both with school and with the popular notion "communities of practice." I mentioned above that games have effects only in terms of the contexts in which they are used and one of those contexts—a context that goes far beyond the game as a piece of software—is the ways in which fans interact together on Internet sites devoted to a given game. Such interactions are forming new ways for people to produce knowledge, participate in social interactions, and create learning.

Chapter 9—"Reading, Specialist Language Development, and Video Games"— deals directly with literacy in schools. It takes off from debates about how to teach reading—a very contentious issue these days—and argues that the real problem in school is the way in which many kids who pass reading tests in early grades later on in school cannot read to learn complex content (e.g., in science, math, of social studies). I argue that this problem is caused by how complex and technical language eventually becomes in school. But then I raise the issue that children today deal with complex and technical language in their popular culture all the time without difficulty, but are thrown by such language in school. The problem has to be in the school and not the children.

Chapter 10—"Games and Learning: Issues, Perils, and Potentials"—is very long and is the main piece in the book. It sums up my view of games and learning since writing the book *What Video Games Have to Teach Us About Learning and Literacy* (2003). I hope it takes the discussion much further. The chapter deals with many of the issues dealt with in the other chapters and tries to put them all into a "big picture."

Sam is 11 now. He still plays games and we regularly compare notes on the games we are playing. He helps me and I help him, as gamers do. He said to me recently "I guess I got the game gene from you." Then he thought a moment and remembered that he was the one who turned me on to games: "No, actually, you got the gene from me." Yes, culture—even, perhaps, our biology (certainly my hands and brain work differently today, thanks to Sam)—runs backwards these days. We need to learn from our children.

CHAPTER 1

Why Video Games Are Good for Your Soul

Pleasure and Learning

Good video games are good for your soul. Now there's a statement that begs for some qualifications!

First, what's a video game? What I mean are the sorts of commercial games people play on computers and game platforms like the *PlayStation 2*, the *GameCube*, the *Xbox*, and the handheld *Game Boy*. I mean action, adventure, shooter, strategy, sports, and role-playing games. I mean games like *Castlevania*, *Half-Life*, *Deus Ex*, *Metal Gear Solid*, *Max Payne*, *Return to Castle Wolfenstein*, *Tony Hawk's Underground*, *Rise of Nations*, *Civilization*, *Age of Mythology*, *The Elder Scrolls III: Morrowind*, *Allied Assault*, *Call of Duty*, *Tales of Symphonia*, *ICO*, *Pikmin*, *Zelda: The Wind Waker*, and *Ninja Gaiden* to name some random good games off the top of my head. There are many others.

Second, what does "good for you" mean? Next to nothing is good or bad for you in and of itself and all by itself. It all depends on how it is used and the context in which it is used. Is television good or bad for children? Neither and both. It's good if people around them are getting them to think and talk about what they are watching, bad when they sit there alone, watching passively, being baby-sat by the tube (Greenfield 1984a and b). The same is true of books. Reading reflectively, asking yourself questions, and engaging in a dialogue with others, is good for your head. Believing everything you read uncritically is bad for you and for the rest of us, as well, since you may well become a danger to the world.

So good video games are good for your soul when you play them with thought, reflection, and engagement with the world around you. They are good if, as a player, you begin to think and act like a game designer while you play the game, something good games encourage. After all, players co-author games by playing them, since if the player doesn't interact with the game and make choices about what will happen, nothing will happen. Each page of a book and each scene in a movie is predetermined before you see it and is the same for every reader. Many acts and their order in a video game, however, are open to player choice and are different for different players.

So, then, what's a good, as opposed to a bad, video game? You have to play the games. Good games are the ones gamers come to see as "gaming goodness," "fair," and sometimes even "deep"—all terms of gaming art. Good games are the games that lots of gamers come to agree are good, though they rarely think any one game is perfect.

Some games, like *ICO* or *American McGee's Alice*, get discovered late and become underground classics, while others, like *Half-Life* or *Zelda: The Wind Waker*, nearly everyone agrees from the outset are good. Then there are games like *Anachronox*, which didn't sell well and received some rather tepid reviews, but is, I'm telling you, a darn good game—you see I have my own opinions about these matters. In fact, different gamers like and dislike different games and different types of games.

OK, then, what for heaven's sake is your soul? And what could playing video games have to do with it? Once, years ago, I had the special experience of going back into time and living for several years in the Middle Ages. The details need not detain us—you'll just have to trust me on this—but, believe me, that experience taught me what souls meant in one context. That is not what I mean here.

Too often in the world today people from all sorts of religions believe that those who don't share their beliefs will go to some sort of hell and, worse, they are sometimes willing to make life hell for others here and now to help them, whether they like it or not, avoid going to hell. Or, perhaps, they just make life hell for others to ensure that they themselves will go to heaven, having displayed their merit by removing a suitable number of infidels. While I do retain a certain nostalgia for the Middle Ages, that nostalgia plays no role in this book.

So what could I mean by "soul?" I mean what the poet Emily Dickinson meant (Dickinson 1924):

> *My life closed twice before its close—*
> *It yet remains to see*
> *If Immortality unveil*
> *A third event to me*
> *So huge, so hopeless to conceive*
> *As these that twice befell.*
> *Parting is all we know of heaven,*
> *And all we need of hell.*

What Emily Dickinson is talking about here is not the immortality, heaven, and hell of traditional religion (Dickinson was skeptical of traditional religion at a time and place where that was socially dangerous, especially for women). She is talking about a fact that every human being knows and feels, a fact that defines what it means to be human. This fact is that we each have two parts. One of these parts is our body. If you truly traumatize the body, it will die and it can die but once, which is, indeed, a mercy.

But there is another part of us, a part to which different religions and cultures through the ages have given different names. This part—let's just say it is our "soul"—can be traumatized over and over again and not die, just as in the case of the two emotionally damaging events to which Emily Dickinson alludes. No mercy here, as we all very well know, unless you have been very fortunate, indeed, in your life. The rest of us have, if old enough, already died more than once. This part—this soul—is immortal in the sense that, until the body goes, it can go on suffering grievously over and over again, suffering many deaths, unlike the body which can die but once.

But it is because we have this soul part that events and other people can take on such a charge for human beings. It is because we have this soul part that events and other people can give us what we know of heaven here on earth. It is only because losing a loved one, either by death or parting, as Dickinson is alluding to, can give rise to such pain that loving others can rise to such joy. You can't really have the one without the other. Having the charge, the spark, is heaven and losing it is hell. But you can't have it if there is no chance of losing it, that's the way of life for us humans. That's why we "need" hell. There is no heaven without hell, no positive charges without risk of negative ones.

Emily Dickinson very well knew, then, that it matters hugely whether life here and now for people is heaven or hell. It matters hugely whether we help make life heaven or hell for others, whether we murder or rejoice their other parts, their souls, that part of them that cannot die as long as they have their bodies. It matters. We can be complicit with murder without having killed anyone. The world can murder us several times over long before it takes our bodies.

The Middle Ages saw to it that peasants and the poor died many times before they died. The rich got off more easily; though, by the nature of life itself, they, too, paid their soul dues. Modern life offers more opportunities, but more complexity, as well. For many people—perhaps, all of us at times—modern life offers too much risk and too much complexity (Kelly 1994). We don't really understand what's going on around us, lots of it just doesn't make any good sense, at least as far as we can tell. We can understand why some people turn to fundamentalism to garner secure "truths" without thought and reflection. It is, indeed, an attempt to save their souls, to protect themselves from the traumas of modern life, a life where often the rich get richer, the poor get poorer, and everyone suffers risks created by other people, even people clear across the globe.

If people are to nurture their souls, they need to feel a sense of control, meaningfulness, even expertise in the face of risk and complexity. They want and need to feel like heroes in their own life stories and to feel that their stories make sense. They need to feel that they matter and that they have mattered in other people's stories. If the body feeds on food, the soul feeds on agency and meaningfulness. I argue that good video games are, in this sense, food for the soul, particularly appropriate food in modern times. Of course, the hope is that this food will empower the soul to find agency and meaning in other aspects of life.

Good video games give people pleasures. These pleasures are connected to control, agency, and meaningfulness. But good games are problem-solving spaces that create deep learning, learning that is better than what we often see today in our schools. Pleasure and learning: For most people these two don't seem to go together. But that is a mistruth we have picked up at school, where we have been taught that pleasure is fun and learning is work, and, thus, that work is not fun (Gee 2004). But, in fact, good videos games are hard work and deep fun. So is good learning in other contexts.

Pleasure is the basis of learning for humans and learning is, like sex and eating, deeply pleasurable for human beings. Learning is a basic drive for humans. School has taught people to fear and avoid learning as anorexics fear and avoid food; it has turned some people into mental anorexics. Some of these same people learn deeply in and through games, though they say they are playing, not learning. The other people who often say they are playing when they're working hard at learning are those professionals—scientists, scholars, and craftsmen—who love their work. There is a reason for this kinship between gamers and professionals and that will be one of the things I deal with in this book.

Well, we have to deal with it. We all know the topic is looming over us. What about violence and video games? Does playing video games lead people to be more violent? More ink has been devoted to this topic than any other concerned with video games. But most of that ink has been wasted.

The 19th century was infinitely more violent than the 20th in terms of crime (though not actual warfare) and no one played video games. The politicians who have heretofore sent people to war have not played video games—they're too old. The Japanese play video games more than Americans do, as, indeed, they watch more television, but their society is much less violent than America's. No, as we said above, video games are neither good nor bad all by themselves, they lead neither to violence nor to peace. They can be and do one thing in one family, social, or cultural context, quite another in other such contexts.

If you want to lower violence, then worry about those contexts, which all extend well beyond just playing video games. Politicians who get hot and heavy about violence in video games usually don't want to worry about such contexts—contexts like poverty, bad parenting, and a culture that celebrates greed, war, and winning. Too expensive, perhaps. In my view, the violence and video games question is a silly one and you won't hear much more about it here. I do live in fear of people who would kill someone because they have played a video game, but I know that they would equally kill someone if they had read a book or seen a movie or even overheard another nut, and I would like you first to take their weapons away. Then, too, someone should have taught these people how to play video games, read books, and watch movies critically and reflectively.

In a world in which millions of people across the globe are dying in real wars, many of them civil wars, it is surely a luxury that we can worry about little boys getting excited for ten minutes after playing a shooter. There are much better things to worry about and I just pray that a time comes in the world where such a problem really merits serious attention. Let's stop the killing, for example in Africa, on the part of people who have never played a video game before we ban games, books, and movies to save ourselves from a handful of disturbed teenagers who would have been better served by better families and schools.

On a more positive note, we should realize that the possibilities of video games and the technologies by which they are made are immense. Video games hold out immense economic opportunities for business and for careers. They hold out equally immense possibilities for the transformation of learning inside and outside schools. They hold out immense promise for changing how people think, value, and live. We haven't seen the beginning yet. As I write, all the game platforms are on their last legs, soon to be replaced by more powerful devices. What wonderful worlds will we eventually see? What charged virtual lives will we be able to live?

The Wild West and space were seen as new frontiers. Video games and the virtual worlds to which they give birth are, too, a new frontier and we don't know where they will lead. It would be a shame, indeed, not to find out because, like any frontier, they were fraught with risk and the unknown. But, then, I have already admitted that all of us in the complex modern world are frightened of risk and the unknown. But that, I will argue, is a disease of the soul that good games can help alleviate, though, of course, not cure.

Some people may say, well, he's really arguing it's all about escape from the perils and pitfalls of real life. But, then, I will say there are escapes that lead nowhere, like hard drugs, and escapes like scholarly reflection and gaming that can lead to the imagination of new worlds, new possibilities to deal with those perils and pitfalls, new possibilities for better lives for everyone. Our emotions and imagination—our souls—need food for the journeys ahead.

CHAPTER 2

Video Games, Violence, and Effects

Good and Bad

"Much of the contempt for social conventions for which the rising generation is blamed is due to the reading of this poisonous sort of fiction." "The harm done . . . is simply incalculable. I wish I could label each one of these books 'Explosives! Guaranteed to Blow Your Boy's Brains Out.'" These quotes are from the early 20th century and the dangerous books are books like *The Hardy Boys* and *The Rover Boys* (Rehak 2005, p. 97). No one today, I hope and suspect, finds the *The Hardy Boys* threatening and there is no outcry against Nancy Drew, even when she's in a computer game.

There is, of course, an outcry today against violence in video games. Here, in my view, is what we know from the research on this issue thus far: Under contrived laboratory conditions, people who play, say, *Castle Wolfenstein*, will, afterwards, blast a competitor in a button pushing task with a noise blast .21 seconds longer than someone who played *Myst* (Anderson & Dill 2000: the researchers don't say whether or not the *Myst* players fell asleep or were so becalmed that their energy level was lowered). Additionally, it is pretty clear that video games can make young boys, in particular, aroused for a short period of time after play, an effect that seems to follow from pretend-play as super heroes as well, if schools that ban super-hero shirts are to be trusted (Anderson & Bushman 2001; Sherry, Curtis, & Sparks 2001). Finally, despite some claims to the contrary, the fact of the matter is that the effect size of video-game play on aggression is smaller than the effect size for television (Sherry 2006), thereby rendering the claim that there is something special about the interactivity of games as a source of aggression suspect. None of this is to say that future research won't discover other additional information, pro or con.

However, none of the current research even remotely suggests video games lead to real-life violence in any predictable way. As a good many people already know, since it has been repeatedly pointed out by conservative politicians and policy makers as a sign of the effectiveness of their social policies (e.g., Fukyuama 1999), there has been a pronounced decrease in violent crime since the earlier 1990s, the very time when violent video games were introduced, e.g., *Mortal Kombat, Doom, Quake* (Sherry 2006: p. 231). Even more to the point, if playing violent video games leads to a statistical increase in violence we should see a rise in violent crime, say, after QuakeCon each year, an event which draws thousands of gamers to play violent games. And the streets of L.A. should be awash with violence each year after E3. So far no one has found any such thing. On the other hand, some researchers have argued that video games have beneficial effects in regard to violence: for example, that teens use violent games as a way to manage feelings of anger or as an outlet for feelings of a lack of control (e.g., Gee 2005; Kestenbaum & Weinstein 1985).

Finally, let me point out one problem that stands in the way of keeping M-rated games away from children. Carding purchasers of M-rated games might seem like a good idea, until you realize parents of young children today are fast becoming young enough to be gamers themselves. Indeed, I have found, in giving talks to school children, that often they have access to M-rated games because their parents have purchased them to play them themselves. As this trend continues, carding would be less than fully effective and education will be the most effective tool to solve the problem, as, in reality, it is today and has been in the case of cigarettes. Of course, controls on advertising to young children are intelligent as well.

We know that human beings respond to media—movies, for example—as if what was happening on the screen was actually happening in the world (Reeves & Nass 1996). That's why people cry at movies. People are this way because their evolutionary past had no screens and screens have not been around long enough for people to have evolved a different set of emotional responses to virtual realities as they have to real ones. This effect has long been known, is well studied, and has long been exploited in the market place. It has also long been known that people can choose to suppress this effect and that, of course, poorly designed media can ruin it.

That we respond emotionally to media as if they were real—and that, indeed, this is part of what makes media powerful to us humans—does not imply that people will go so far as to leave the movie theater and act out or respond to the events in the film. If this were so, our streets would be full of movie-inspired sex, violence, and comedy. What is striking, in fact, is how vanishingly few humans actually act out the emotional responses they have had to media. The reason is relatively simple: action requires the cooperation of our affective (emotional) responses and our higher-order thought processes and, at the level of conscious control and awareness, all but the very sick know a movie or a game is not reality. What is equally striking is that certainly a great many more people have acted out their emotional responses to books—at least "sacred" ones like the Bible—in the real world, often in terms of violence, though, of course, also often in terms of doing good, than have ever done so in regard to a movie or a video game (though *Birth of a Nation* comes to mind as an example of a movie that inspired real world violence, perhaps because people "read" it as a documentary).

Here is something else we know. As previously mentioned, movies, books, television, or video games—i.e., technologies—do not have any effects, good or bad, all by themselves. The question as to whether video games (or computers, or television, or what have you) are good for you (or children) or bad for you (or children) is actually meaningless. Technologies have effects—and different ones—**only as they are situated within specific contexts** (e.g., Gee 2004; Greenfield 1984a and b; Gauntlett 1998). So we always have to ask—though reporters rarely do—how the technology was used and in what context it was being used. For example, we have known for some time that television is good for children's cognitive growth if they are watching it in a reflective state of mind; for example, because an adult is interacting with them and discussing what they are watching with them (Greenfield 1984a and b). If the child is just passively consuming the television, then it is not necessarily of any great use. It is also clear that children raised in a culture of violence or abuse may consume media—not to mention their real-world interactions—as fodder for their anger and confusion. In these cases, we would hope, of course, that policy makers would speak to the real-world culture of violence or abuse and not just the virtual images the child sees.

People have the idea that video games are somehow more potent than movies or books because the player does things in the virtual world via his or her avatar. This is akin, I suppose, to the claim that because I have planted lots of corn in *Harvest Moon* I will run out and plant corn in my back yard—in reality we have as little real corn from *Harvest Moon* as we have real killings from *Grand Theft Auto* (which is not to rule out the rare case of either—given enough time even low probability events occur—though, of course, by definition, rarely). In my view, the power of video games is not in operating an avatar *per se*. Rather, it is in situating one's body and mind in a world from the perspective of the avatar, whether this is a policeman in *S.W.A.T.4*, a waitress in *Diner Dash*, or a young farmer in *Harvest Moon*. What video games do—better than any other medium in my view—is let people understand a world from the inside. What does it feel like to be a S.W.A.T. team member? What's it like to act like one? To accept for a time and place the values of one? What do ideas and words mean from the position in which S.W.A.T. team members stand? Do I like this way of looking at and being in the world or not? What all this means is not that I will run out and pretend to be a S.W.A.T. team member—or even sign up for real training— it means, first and foremost that *S.W.A.T. 4* is primarily a tool for *understanding*. The emotional response *S.W.A.T.4* triggers—thanks to our human response to media—deepens that understanding.

This is the source of a video game's great pleasure—for me, it is just exhilarating to be in the world as Solid Snake, actually to see and act on the world as he can and does: to play in the world by his rules. But this is, in my view, also the great potential that video games hold. They are new tools for letting people understand from the inside out the worlds other people inhabit or worlds no one has yet seen (Gee 2003, 2004, 2005). If we have a *Full Spectrum Warrior* that lets me see and be in the world as a soldier, why can't we have a *Full Spectrum Scientist?* Of course, we will never get one as long we demonize and trivialize the medium of video games. Understanding does not lead to acceptance or action— we humans are still choosers, but real understanding can lead to better choices. I enjoyed *Operation Flashpoint* immensely and it made me sure I would never want to be a soldier if I could ethically avoid it. Ditto for *S.W.A.T 4*—I couldn't even take the pressure in my living room, let alone want it in my real life, but it is a great game and I really appreciate and admire S.W.A.T team members now.

There IS a danger here, in my view, though. The danger exists if games show, or kids see, only one world, one world view, only one narrow type of game. Real intellectual and ethical growth comes from having been in many worlds, some of them different enough to get you thinking for yourself. So I would not ban games—ban worlds—but mandate lots and lots of them. Again, too bad, there is no *Full Spectrum Astronaut, Biologist, Urban Planner* (oops, there's *SimCity*), *Community Activist, Doctor, Craftsman,* or *Public Health Official* (scouring the world for viruses before they kill us all). For that matter, there should be a *Full Spectrum Virus*, so we all know what the world looks and feels like from the perspective of a virus. But none of this means we should get rid of *Metal Gear Solid*, *Thief*, *S.W.A.T 4.*, *Grand Theft Auto*, or *Diner Dash*. It does mean, perhaps, that we should all think about how to deepen the moral dimensions of all these games, enrich them yet more as thinking/reflective spaces—my prediction, by the way, is that this will make them more fun. But, then, witness *Shadow the Hedgehog*, where the (even young) player can choose moment-by-moment to support one side or another while seeking to find out what exactly constitutes in this world being good or bad—which, after all, often involves, even in the real world, trying to find out what the "big picture" is.

Good video games are thinking tools. Their deepest pleasures are cognitive. The "drug" the video game industry discovered was learning—humans love it when it's done right. We need to discuss the content of games—just as we do the content of books and movies—as a society. We need to ensure that there are lots of different worlds on offer. We need to educate parents about the good games can do their kids when their content is appropriate for their age and the game is part of effective adult-child interactions—just as with books, television, and movies. We need to educate how, under other conditions, games, like books, television, and movies, can waste their children's time, even if they are not violent. But, the most important thing, in the end, is that we educate ourselves about how to draw the most good from this new and powerful technology, one that has so captured our children and, for some of us, ourselves.

CHAPTER 3

Notes on Content
and Technological Determinism

1. Introduction

Today, children's popular culture is more complex than ever before (Johnson 2005). A game like *Yu-Gi-Oh*—a card game played by children as young as 7, either face-to-face or on a *Game Boy* handheld game machine—involves the sorts of complex language, vocabulary, and thinking skills we associate with the advanced grades in school (Gee 2004). Children today "multi-task" across multiple modalities, playing a video game like *Age of Mythology*, reading and writing about mythology, researching it on the Internet, and, maybe, even contributing to web sites devoted to the game and wider topics in mythology (Jenkins 2006).

Children today often engage in cutting-edge learning in their popular cultural practices, learning of a sort that fits well with what the Learning Sciences have discovered about optimal human learning, but not necessarily well with how current schools operate (Bransford, Brown, and Cocking 2000; Gee 2003, 2004, 2005; Sawyer 2006a). At the same time, good video games—like contemporary research in the Learning Sciences—challenge us to truly integrate cognition, language, literacy, affect, and social interaction in our ideas about learning and the organization of learning inside and outside schools (Gee 1996, 2004; Damasio 1994).

Much of what is true of video games is equally true when comparable games are played face-to-face with no digital technology involved, whether this be *Yu-Gi-Oh* or *Dungeons & Dragons*. However, digital technology does add certain features to the learning, features that are, we will see, reminiscent of how scientists use simulations to learn and to produce new knowledge.

But two key points always seem to come up when we discuss video games and learning: content and technological determinism. So, first, content. As I have already mentioned, media discussions of video games often focus on the content of video games, especially if that content is violent (though as mentioned in a previous chapter many games are not violent, including the best-selling game of all time, *The Sims*). More generally, non-gamers tend to view video games in the same way in which they view films and novels: content is what determines the nature and value of the work. However, in video games—unlike in novels and films—content has to be separated from game play. The two are connected, but, to gamers, game play is the primary feature of video games; it is what makes them good or bad games (Koster 2004; Juul 2005; Salen & Zimmerman 2003).

The content in a game like *Grand Theft Auto: San Andreas* involves poverty, an African-American community, and crime. However, the game play involves solving problems strategically, problems like how to ride a bike through city streets so as to evade pursuing cars and follow a map to end up safely where you need to go. In games like this, elements of content could be changed without changing the game play—for example, in some cases, taking pictures of people instead of shooting them or secretly planting a message rather than a bomb in their car would leave the problem solving and its difficulty pretty much the same. Critics of games need to realize that players, especially strategic and mature players, are often focusing on game play more than they are on content *per se*.

Content in a game sets up, but does not fully determine, game play. It also determines the basic themes, metaphors, and emotional valences of the game, beyond the emotions of challenge, frustration, competition, and accomplishment that are determined by game play. However, the two inter-relate in complex ways, for example, in a role-playing game one's pride in accomplishment or regret for poor decisions can easily be projected onto the character the player is playing in the game. Equivalently, the power, problems, or fascinating features and accomplishments of a character in a game can be transferred as emotions to the player (e.g., feeling "cool" while being Solid Snake in *Metal Gear Solid* or empathy with the main character in *Grand Theft Auto: San Andreas*).

Then, too, video games, like most popular culture media, reflect back to us, in part, the basic themes and even prejudices of our own society. The *Grand Theft Auto* series is made in Scotland, but it clearly recycles U.S. media images from television and film. In this respect, games are no different than popular films and television. Some people think they are more powerful than these other media, because the player acts in games. But the fact is that while humans react emotionally to images (television, film, games, even pictures) in much the way they do to real life (Reeves & Nass 1999), this does not mean they are tempted to act on these emotions in real life—people do, after all, have higher thought processes in terms of which they make decisions and decide what is and is not real.

We also need to realize that video games involve content in a quite broad sense. Video gaming has turned out—despite early predictions to the contrary—to be a deeply social enterprise (Steinkuehler 2006; Taylor 2006). Even single-player gaming often involves young people in joint play, collaboration, competition, sharing, and a myriad of websites, chat rooms, and game guides, many of them produced by players themselves. But the social nature of gaming goes much further. Multiplayer gaming—games where small teams play against each other—is very popular among many young people. And massively-multiplayer games—games where thousands or millions of people play the same game—have recently (thanks, in part, to the tremendous success of *World of WarCraft*) become mainstream forms of social interaction across the globe. Such games are introducing new "states" (6 million people world wide for *World of WarCraft*) or "communities" into the world. In such games, people are learning new identities, new forms of social interaction, and even new values, a broad form of "content," indeed (Steinkuehler 2006; Taylor 2006).

There is, indeed, much space for critique and critical theory in regard to video games, though that is not my topic here. My remarks about content are meant to suggest some of the issues particularly germane to video games as a media form that need to be considered for such critique, not to mistake games for books or films. But there is another issue relevant to anyone who wants to engage in critical theory in regard to games: technological determinism.

The media often discuss video games as if they are inherently good for people or bad for them. This is a form of technological determinism. To repeat: Technologies—including television, computers, and books, as well as games—are neither good nor bad and have no effects all by themselves, though, like all tools, they have certain affordances (Greenfield 1984a and b; Sternheimer 2003). Rather, they have different effects, some good, some bad, some neutral, depending on how they are used and the contexts in which they are used (Hawisher & Selfe 2007). One important aspect of use is, as I have already mentioned, the ways in which the player engages with the game's game play as opposed to its content or graphics ("eye candy"). Players can be more or less reflective, strategic, and focused on game play rather than content or graphics. Critics of games need to consider how games are "consumed" by different people in different contexts. Blanket general claims—either for the good or the bad effects of games—are close to useless.

Finally, let me say that my claims about the powerful ways in which video games can recruit learning as a form of pleasure are as much about the potential of games as we spread them to new contexts and design new types of games as they are about the present of games. Video games are a relatively new form of popular culture and no one should mistake their present state—for example, deeply influenced as it is by a Hollywood blockbuster mentality that often drives out innovation—for their future potential in the context of a diverse array of new technologies, designers, players, and learning and playing situations.

CHAPTER 4

Good Video Games, the Human Mind, and Good Learning

Introduction

This chapter has two main points to make and, in turn, it falls into two main parts. My first point—a point some will find startling at first—is that good video games (by which I mean both computer games and games played on platforms like the *Xbox, Cube,* or *PlayStation*) represent a technology that illuminates how the human mind works. My second point follows, in part, from this first one. It is that good video games incorporate good learning principles and have a great deal to teach us about learning in and out of schools, whether or not a video game is part of this learning.

Video Games and the Mind

Video games are a relatively new technology replete with important, and not yet fully understood, implications (Gee 2003). Scholars have historically viewed the human mind through the lens of a technology they thought worked like the mind. Locke and Hume, for example, argued that the mind was like a blank slate on which experience wrote ideas, taking the technology of literacy as their guide. Much later, modern cognitive scientists argued that the mind worked like a digital computer, calculating generalizations and deductions via a logic-like rule system (Newell & Simon 1972). More recently, some cognitive scientists, inspired by distributed parallel-processing computers and complex adaptive networks, have argued that the mind works by storing records of actual experiences and constructing intricate patterns of connections among them (Clark 1989; Gee 1992). So we get different pictures of the mind: mind as a slate waiting to be written on, mind as software, mind as a network of connections.

Human societies get better through history at building technologies that more closely capture some of what the human mind can do and getting these technologies to do mental work publicly. Writing, digital computers, and networks each allow us to externalize some functions of the mind.

Though they are not commonly thought of in these terms, video games are a new technology in this same line. They are a new tool with which to think about the mind and through which we can externalize some of its functions. Video games of the sort I am concerned with—games like *Half-Life 2, Rise of Nations, Full Spectrum Warrior, The Elder Scrolls III: Morrowind,* and *World of WarCraft*—are what I would call "action-and-goal-directed preparations for, and simulations of, embodied experience." A mouthful, indeed, but an important one.

To make clear what I mean by the claim that games act like the human mind and are a good place to study and produce human thinking and learning, let me first briefly summarize some recent research in cognitive science, the science that studies how the mind works (Bransford, Brown, & Cocking 2000). Consider, for instance, the remarks below [in the quotes below, the word "comprehension" means "understanding words, actions, events, or things"]:

> . . . comprehension is grounded in perceptual simulations that prepare agents for situated action (Barsalou, 1999a: p. 77)

> . . . to a particular person, the meaning of an object, event, or sentence is what that person can do with the object, event, or sentence (Glenberg, 1997: p. 3)

What these remarks mean is this: human understanding is not primarily a matter of storing general concepts in the head or applying abstract rules to experience. Rather, humans think and understand best when they can imagine (simulate) an experience in such a way that the simulation prepares them for actions they need and want to take in order to accomplish their goals (Barsalou 1999b; Clark 1997; Glenberg & Robertson 1999).

Let's take weddings as an example, though we could just as well have taken war, love, inertia, democracy, or anything. You don't understand the word or the idea of weddings by meditating on some general definition of weddings. Rather, you have had experiences of weddings, in real life and through texts and media. On the basis of these experiences, you can simulate different wedding scenarios in your mind. You construct these simulations differently for different occasions, based on what actions you need to take to accomplish specific goals in specific situations. You can move around as a character in the mental simulation as yourself, imaging your role in the wedding, or you can "play" other characters at the wedding (e.g., the minister), imaging what it is like to be that person.

You build your simulations to understand and make sense of things, but also to help you prepare for action in the world. You can act in the simulation and test out what consequences follow, before you act in the real world. You can role-play another person in the model and try to see what motivates their actions or might follow from them before you respond in the real world. So I am arguing that the mind is a simulator, but one that builds simulations to purposely prepare for specific actions and to achieve specific goals (i.e., they are built around win states).

Video games turn out to be the perfect metaphor for what this view of the mind amounts to, just as slates and computers were good metaphors for earlier views of the mind. To see this, let me now turn to a characterization of video games and then I will put my remarks about the mind and games together.

Video games usually involve a visual and auditory world in which the player manipulates a virtual character (or characters). They often come with editors or other sorts of software with which the player can make changes to the game world or even build a new game world. The player can make a new landscape, a new set of buildings, or new characters. The player can set up the world so that certain sorts of actions are allowed or disallowed. The player is building a new world, but is doing so by using and modifying the original visual images (really the code for them) that came with the game. One simple example of this is the way in which players can build new skateboard parks in a game like *Tony Hawk Pro Skater*. The player must place ramps, trees, grass, poles, and other things in space in such a way that players can manipulate their virtual characters to skate the park in a fun and challenging way.

Even when players are not modifying games, they play them with goals in mind, the achievement of which counts as their "win state" (and it's the existence of such win states that, in part, distinguishes games from simulations) These goals are set by the player, but, of course, in collaboration with the world the game designers have created (and, at least in more open-ended games, players don't just accept developer's goals, they make real choices of their own). Players must carefully consider the design of the world and consider how it will or will not facilitate specific actions they want to take to accomplish their goals.

One technical way that psychologists have talked about this sort of situation is through the notion of "affordances" (Gibson 1979). An "affordance" is a feature of the world (real or virtual) that will allow for a certain action to be taken, but only if it is matched by an ability in an actor who has the wherewithal to carry out such an action. For example, in the massive multiplayer game *World of WarCraft* stags can be killed and skinned (for making leather), but only by characters that have learned the Skinning skill. So a stag is an affordance for skinning for such a player, but not for one who has no such skill. The large spiders in the game are not an affordance for skinning for any players, since they cannot be skinned at all. Affordances are relationships between the world and actors.

Playing *World of WarCraft*, or any other video game, is all about such affordances. The player must learn to *see* the game world—designed by the developers, but set in motion in particular directions by the players, and, thus, co-designed by them—in terms of such affordances (Gee 2005). Broadly speaking, players must think in terms of "What are the features of this world that can enable the actions I am capable of carrying out and that I want to carry out in order to achieve my goals?"

So now, after our brief bit about the mind and about games, let's put the two together. The view of the mind I have sketched, in fact, argues, as far as I am concerned, that the mind works rather like a video game. For humans, effective thinking is more like running a simulation than it is about forming abstract generalizations cut off from experiential realities. Effective thinking is about perceiving the world such that the human actor sees how the world, at a specific time and place (as it is given, but also modifiable), can afford the opportunity for actions that will lead to a successful accomplishment of the actor's goals. Generalizations are formed, when they are, bottom up from experience and imagination of experience. Video games externalize the search for affordances, for a match between character (actor) and world, but this is just the heart and soul of effective human thinking and learning in any situation.

As a game player you learn to see the world of each different game you play in a quite different way. But in each case you see the world in terms of how it will afford the sorts of embodied actions you (and your virtual character, your sur-rogate body in the game) need to take to accomplish your goals (to win in the short and long run). For example, you see the world in *Full Spectrum Warrior* as routes (for your squad) between cover (e.g., corner to corner, house to house) because this prepares you for the actions you need to take, namely attacking without being vulnerable to attack yourself. You see the world of *Thief* in terms of light and dark, illumination and shadows, because this prepares you for the different actions you need to take in this world, namely hiding, disappearing into the shadows, sneaking, and otherwise moving unseen to your goal.

When we sense such a match, in a virtual world or the real world, between our way of seeing the world, at a particular time and place, and our action goals—and we have the skills to carry these actions out—then we feel great power and satisfaction. Things click, the world looks as if it were made for us. While com-mercial games often stress a match between worlds and characters like soldiers or thieves, there is no reason why other games could not let players experience such a match between the world and the way a particular type of scientist, for instance, sees and acts on the world (Gee 2004). Such games would involve facing the sorts of problems and challenges that type of scientist does and liv-ing and playing by the rules that type of scientist uses. Winning would mean just what it does to a scientist: feeling a sense of accomplishment through the pro-duction of knowledge to solve deep problems.

I have argued for the importance of video games as "action-and-goal-directed preparations for, and simulations of, embodied experience." They are the new tech-nological arena—just as were literacy and computers earlier—around which we can study the mind and externalize some of its most important features to improve human thinking and learning. But games have two other features that suit them to be good models for human thinking and learning externalized out in the world. These two additional features are: a) they distribute intelligence via the creation of smart tools, and b) they allow for the creation of "cross functional affiliation," a particularly important form of collaboration in the modern world.

Consider first how good games distribute intelligence (Brown, Collins, & Duguid 1989). In *Full Spectrum Warrior*, the player uses the buttons on the controller to give orders to two squads of soldiers. The instruction manual that comes with the game makes it clear from the outset that players, in order to play the game successfully, must take on the values, identities, and ways of thinking of a pro-fessional soldier: "Everything about your squad," the manual explains, "is the result of careful planning and years of experience on the battlefield. Respect that expe-rience, soldier, since it's what will keep your soldiers alive" (p. 2). In the game, that experience—the skills and knowledge of professional military expertise—is distributed between the virtual soldiers and the real-world player. The soldiers in the player's squads have been trained in movement formations; the role of the player is to select the best position for them on the field. The virtual characters (the soldiers) know part of the task (various movement formations) and the player must come to know another part (when and where to engage in such formations). This kind of distribution holds for every aspect of military knowledge in the game.

By distributing knowledge and skills this way—between the virtual characters (smart tools) and the real-world player—the player is guided and supported by the knowledge built into the virtual soldiers. This offloads some of the cognitive burden from the learner, placing it in smart tools that can do more than the learner is currently capable of doing by him or herself. It allows the player to begin to act, with some degree of effectiveness, before being really competent—"performance before competence." The player thereby eventually comes to gain competence through trial, error, and feedback, not by wading through a lot of text before being able to engage in activity. Such distribution also allows players to internalize not only the knowledge and skills of a professional (a professional soldier in this case), but also the concomitant values ("doctrine" as the military says) that shape and explain how and why that knowledge is developed and applied in the world. There is no reason why other professions—scientists, doctors, government officials, urban planners (Shaffer 2004)—could not be modeled and distributed in this fashion as a deep form of value-laden learning (and, in turn, learners could compare and contrast different value systems as they play different games).

Finally, let me turn to the creation of "cross-functional affiliation." Consider a small group partying (hunting and questing) together in a massive multiplayer game like *World of WarCraft*. The group might well be composed of a Hunter, Warrior, Druid, and Priest. Each of these types of characters has quite different skills and plays the game in a different way. Each group member (player) must learn to be good at his or her special skills and also learn to integrate these skills as a team member within the group as a whole. Each team member must also share some common knowledge about the game and game play with all the other members of the group—including some understanding of the specialist skills of other player types—in order to achieve a successful integration. So each member of the group must have specialist knowledge (intensive knowledge) and general common knowledge (extensive knowledge), including knowledge of the other members' functions.

Players—who are interacting with each other, in the game and via a chat system—orient to each other not in terms of their real-world race, class, culture, or gender (these may very well be unknown or if communicated made up as fictions). They must orient to each other, first and foremost, through their identities as game players and players of *World of WarCraft* in particular. They can, in turn, use their real-world race, class, culture, and gender as strategic resources if and when they please, and the group can draw on the differential real-world resources of each player, but in ways that do not force anyone into pre-set racial, gender, cultural, or class categories.

This form of affiliation—what I will call cross-functional affiliation—has been argued to be crucial for the workplace teams in modern "new capitalist" workplaces, as well as in modern forms of social activism (Beck 1999; Gee 2004; Gee, Hull, & Lankshear 1996). People specialize, but integrate and share, organized around a primary affiliation to their common goals and using their cultural and social differences as strategic resources, not as barriers.

Good Video Games and Good Learning

So video games, though a part of popular culture, are, like literacy and computers, sites where we can study and exercise the human mind in ways that may give us deeper insights into human thinking and learning, as well as new ways to engage learners in deep and engaged learning. And, in fact, one of the biggest contributions the study of good video games can make is to illuminate ways in which learning works when it works best for human beings. In part because they externalize the way in which the human mind thinks, good video games often organize learning in deep and effective ways.

Many good computer and video games, games like *Deus Ex, The Elder Scrolls III: Morrowind*, or *Rise of Nations*, are long, complex, and difficult, especially for beginners. As we well know from school, young people are not always eager to do difficult things. When adults are faced with the challenge of getting them to do so, two choices are often available. We can force them, which is the main solution schools use. Or, a temptation when profit is at stake, though not unknown in school either, we can dumb down the product. Neither option is open to the game industry, at least for the moment. They can't force people to play and most avid gamers don't want their games short or easy. Indeed, game reviews regularly damn easy or short games.

For people interested in learning, this raises an interesting question. How do good game designers manage to get new players to learn their long, complex, and difficult games and not only learn them but pay to do so? It won't do simply to say games are "motivating." That just begs the question of "Why?" Why is a long, complex, and difficult video game motivating? I believe it is something about how games are designed to trigger learning that makes them so deeply motivating.

So the question is: How do good game designers manage to get new players to learn long, complex, and difficult games? The answer, I believe, is this: the designers of many good games have hit on profoundly good methods of getting people to learn and to enjoy learning. They have had to, since games that were bad at getting themselves learned didn't get played and the companies that made them lost money. Furthermore, it turns out that these learning methods are similar in many respects to cutting-edge principles being discovered in research on human learning (for details, see Gee 2003, 2004, 2005 and the references therein).

Good game designers are practical theoreticians of learning, since what makes games deep is that players are exercising their learning muscles, though often without knowing it and without having to pay overt attention to the matter. Under the right conditions, learning, like sex, is biologically motivating and pleasurable for humans (and other primates). It is a hook that game designers own to a greater degree—thanks to the interactivity of games—than do movies and books.

But the power of video games resides not just in their present instantiations, but in the promises the technologies by which they are made hold out for the future. Game designers can make worlds where people can have meaningful new experiences, experiences that their places in life would never allow them to have or even experiences no human being has ever had before. These experiences have the potential to make people smarter and more thoughtful.

Good games already do this and they will do it more and more in the future. *Star Wars: Knights of the Old Republic* immerses the player in issues of identity and responsibility: What responsibility do I bear for what an earlier, now transformed, "me" did? *Deus Ex: Invisible War* asks the player to make choices about the role ability and equality will or won't play in society: If we were all truly equal in ability would that mean we would finally have a true meritocracy? Would we want it? In these games, such thoughtful questions are not abstractions; they are part and parcel of the fun and interaction of playing.

I care about these matters both as a cognitive scientist and as a gamer. I believe that we can make school and workplace learning better if we pay attention to good computer and video games. This does not necessarily mean using game technologies in school and at work, though that is something I advocate. It means applying the fruitful principles of learning that good game designers have hit on, whether or not we use a game as a carrier of these principles. My book *What Video Games Have to Teach Us About Learning and Literacy* (2003) lists many of these principles. Science educator Andy diSessa's book *Changing Minds: Computers, Learning, and Literacy* (2000) offers many related principles without ever mentioning video games.

There are many good principles of learning built into good computer and video games. These are all principles that could and should be applied to school learning tomorrow, though this is unlikely given the current trend for skill-and-drill, scripted instruction, and standardized multiple choice testing. The principles are particularly important for so-called "at risk" learners, students who have come to school under-prepared, who have fallen behind, or who have little support for school-based literacy and language skills outside of school.

The principles are neither conservative nor liberal, neither traditionalist nor progressive. They adopt some of each side, reject some of each, and stake out a different space. If implemented in schools they would necessitate significant changes in the structure and nature of formal schooling as we have long known it, changes that may eventually be inevitable anyway given modern technologies.

I list a baker's dozen below. We can view this list as a checklist: The stronger any game is on more of the features on the list, the better its score for learning. The list is organized into three sections: I. Empowered Learners; II. Problem Solving; III. Understanding. Under each item on the list I first give a principle relevant to learning, then a comment on games in regard to that principle, as well as some example games that are strong on that principle. I then discuss the educational implications of the principle. Those interested in more ample citations to research that supports these principles and how they apply to learning things like science in school should consult the references cited in Gee (2003, 2004, 2005). I should point out, as well, that the first part of this chapter has already discussed some of learning principles that we don't need to discuss further below, since distributed knowledge and cross-functional affiliation are themselves powerful forms of social organization for learning and knowledge building. So is the way in which good video games teach players to look for and build affordances into their learning environments.

I. Empowered Learners

1. Co-design

PRINCIPLE: Good learning requires that learners feel like active agents (producers) not just passive recipients (consumers).

GAMES: In a video game, players make things happen. They don't just consume what the "author" (game designer) has placed before them. Video games are interactive. The player does something and the game does something back that encourages the player to act again. In good games, players feel that their actions and decisions—and not just the designers' actions and decisions—are co-creating the world they are in and the experiences they are having. What the player does matters and each player, based on his or her own decisions and actions, takes a different trajectory through the game world.

EXAMPLE: *The Elder Scrolls III: Morrowind* is an extreme example of a game where each decision the player makes changes the game in ways that ensure that each player's game is, in the end, different from any other player's. But at some level this is true of most games. Players take different routes through *Castlevania: Symphony of the Night* and do different things in different ways in *Tony Hawk's Underground*.

EDUCATION: Co-design means ownership, buy in, engaged participation. It is a key part of motivation. It also means learners must come to understand the design of the domain they are learning so that they can make good choices about how to affect that design. Do student decisions and actions make a difference in the classroom curriculum? Are students helping to design their own learning? If the answers are no, what gives students the feeling of being agents in their own learning? Forced and enforced group discussions are about as far as interactivity goes in most classrooms, if it goes that far. The whole curriculum should be shaped by the learners' actions and react back on the learners in meaningful ways.

2. Customize

PRINCIPLE: Different styles of learning work better for different people. People cannot be agents of their own learning if they cannot make decisions about how their learning will work. At the same time, they should be able (and encouraged) to try new styles.

GAMES: Good games achieve this goal in one (or both) of two ways. In some games, players are able to customize the game play to fit their learning and playing styles. In others, the game is designed to allow different styles of learning and playing to work.

EXAMPLE: *Rise of Nations* allows players to customize myriad aspects of the game play to their own styles, interests, and desires. *Deus Ex* and its sequel *Deus Ex: Invisible War* both allow quite different styles of play and, thus, learning, too, to succeed.

EDUCATION: Classrooms adopting this principle would allow students to discover their favored learning styles and to try new ones without fear. In the act of customizing their own learning, students would learn a good deal not only about how and why they learn, but about learning and thinking themselves. Can students engage in such customization in the classroom? Do they get to reflect on the nature of their own learning and learning in general? Are there multiple ways to solve problems? Are students encouraged to try out different learning styles and different problem solutions without risking a bad grade?

3. Identity

PRINCIPLE: Deep learning requires an extended commitment and such a commitment is powerfully recruited when people take on a new identity they value and in which they become heavily invested—whether this be a child "being a scientist doing science" in a classroom or an adult taking on a new role at work.

GAMES: Good games offer players identities that trigger a deep investment on the part of the player. They achieve this goal in one of two ways. Some games offer a character so intriguing that players want to inhabit the character and can readily project their own fantasies, desires, and pleasures onto the character. Other games offer a relatively empty character whose traits the player must determine, but in such a way that the player can create a deep and consequential life history in the game world for the character.

EXAMPLE: *Metal Gear Solid* offers a character (Solid Snake) that is so well developed that he is, though largely formed by the game's designers, a magnet for player projections. *Animal Crossing* and *Scrolls III: Morrowind* offer, in different ways, blank-slate characters for which the player can build a deeply involving life and history. On the other hand, an otherwise good game like *Freedom Fighters* offers us characters that are both too anonymous and not changeable enough by the player to trigger deep investment.

EDUCATION: School is often built around the "content fetish," the idea that an academic area like biology or social science is constituted by some definitive list of facts or body of information that can be tested in a standardized way. But academic areas are not first and foremost bodies of facts, they are, rather, first and foremost, the activities and ways of knowing through which such facts are generated, defended, and modified. Such activities and ways of knowing are carried out by people who adopt certain sorts of identities, that is, adopt certain ways with words, actions, and interactions, as well as certain values, attitudes, and beliefs.

Learners need to know what the "rules of the game" are and who plays it. They need to know how to take on the identity of a certain sort of scientist, if they are doing science, and operate by a certain set of values, attitudes, and actions. Otherwise they have no deep understanding of a domain and surely never know why anyone would want to learn, and even spend a lifetime learning in that domain in the first place.

Ironically, when learners adopt and practice such an identity and engage in the forms of talk and action connected to it, facts come free—they are learned as part and parcel of being a certain sort of person needing to do certain sorts of things for one's own purposes and goals (Shaffer 2004). Out of the context of identity and activity, facts are hard to learn and last in the learner's mind a very short time, indeed.

4. Manipulation and Distributed Knowledge

PRINCIPLE: As I suggested in the first part of this chapter, cognitive research suggests that for humans perception and action are deeply inter-connected (Barsalou 1999a, b; Clark 1997; Glenberg 1997; Glenberg & Robertson 1999). Thus, fine-grained action at a distance—for example, when a person is manipulating a robot at a distance or watering a garden via a web cam on the Internet— causes humans to feel as if their bodies and minds have stretched into a new space (Clark 2003). More generally, humans feel expanded and empowered when they can manipulate powerful tools in intricate ways that extend their area of effectiveness.

GAMES: Computer and video games inherently involve action at a (albeit virtual) distance. The more and better a player can manipulate a character, the more the player invests in the game world. Good games offer characters that the player can move intricately, effectively, and easily through the world. Beyond characters, good games offer the player intricate, effective, and easy manipulation of the world's objects, objects which become tools for carrying out the player's goals.

EXAMPLE: *Tomb Raider, Tom Clancy's Splinter Cell,* and *ICO* allow such fine-grained and interesting manipulation of one's character that they achieve a strong effect of pulling the player into their worlds. *Rise of Nations* allows such effective control of buildings, landscapes, and whole armies as tools that the player feels like "god." *Prince of Persia* excels both in terms of character manipulation and in terms of everything in its environment serving as effective tools for player action.

One key feature of the virtual characters and objects that game players manipulate is that they are "smart tools." The character the player controls— Lara Croft, for example—knows things the player doesn't, for instance, how to climb ropes, leap chasms, and scale walls. The player knows things the character doesn't, like when, where, and why to climb, leap, or scale. The player and the character each have knowledge that must be integrated together to play the game successfully. This is an example of distributed knowledge, knowledge split between two things (here a person and a virtual character) that must be integrated.

A game like *Full Spectrum Warrior* takes this principle much further. In this game, the player controls two squads of four soldiers each. The soldiers know lots and lots of things about professional military practice; for example, how to take various formations under fire and how to engage in various types of group movements in going safely from cover to cover. The player need not know these things. The player must learn other aspects of professional military practice, namely what formations and movements to order, when, where, and why. The real actor in this game is the player and the soldiers blended together through their shared, distributed, and integrated knowledge.

EDUCATION: What allows a learner to feel that his or her body and mind have extended into the world being studied or investigated, into the world of biology or physics, for example? Part of the answer here is "smart tools," that is, tools and technologies that allow the learner to manipulate that world in a fine-grained way. Such tools have their own in-built knowledge and skills that allow the learner much more power over the world being investigated than he or she has unaided by such tools.

Let me give one concrete example of what I am talking about. Galileo discovered the laws of the pendulum because he knew and applied geometry to the problem, not because he played around with pendulums or saw a church chandelier swinging (as myth has it). Yet is common for liberal educators to ask children innocent of geometry or any other such tool to play around with pendulums and discover for themselves the laws by which they work. This is actually a harder problem than the one Galileo confronted—geometry set possible solutions for him and led him to think about pendulums in certain ways and not others. Of course, today there are a great many technical tools available beyond geometry and algebra (though students usually don't even realize that geometry and algebra are smart tools, different from each other in the way they approach problems and the problems for which they are best suited).

Do students in the classroom share knowledge with smart tools? Do they become powerful actors by learning to integrate their own knowledge with the knowledge built into their tools? The real-world player and the virtual soldiers in *Full Spectrum Warrior* come to share a body of skills and knowledge that is constitutive of a certain type of professional practice. Do students engage in authentic professional practices in the classroom through such sharing? Professional practice is crucial here, because, remember, real learning in science, for example, is constituted by *being a type of scientist doing a type of science* not reciting a fact you don't understand. It is thinking, acting, and valuing like a scientist of a certain sort. It is "playing by the rules" of a certain sort of science.

II. Problem Solving

5. Well-Ordered Problems

PRINCIPLE: Given human creativity, if learners face problems early on that are too free-form or too complex, they often form creative hypotheses about how to solve these problems, but hypotheses that don't work well for later problems (even for simpler ones, let alone harder ones). They have been sent down a "garden path." The problems learners face early on are crucial and should be well-designed to lead them to hypotheses that work well, not just on these problems, but as aspects of the solutions of later, harder problems, as well.

GAMES: Problems in good games are well ordered. In particular, early problems are designed to lead players to form good guesses about how to proceed when they face harder problems later on in the game. In this sense, earlier parts of a good game are always looking forward to later parts.

EXAMPLE: *Return to Castle Wolfenstein* and *Fatal Frame2: Crimson Butterfly*. Although radically different games, each does a good job of offering players problems that send them down fruitful paths for what they will face later in the game. They each prepare the player to get better and better at the game and to face more difficult challenges later in the game.

EDUCATION: Work on connectionism and distributed parallel processing in cognitive science has shown that the order in which learners confront problems in a problem space is important (Clark 1989; Elman 1991a, b). Confronting complex problems too early can lead to creative solutions, but approaches that won't work well for even simpler later problems. "Anything goes"—"just turn learners loose in rich environments"—"no need for teachers"—these are bad theories of learning; they are, in fact, the progressive counterpart of the traditionalists' skill-and-drill.

Learners are novices. Leaving them to float amidst rich experiences with no guidance only triggers human beings' great penchant for finding creative but spurious patterns and generalizations that send learners down garden paths (Gee 1992, 2001). The fruitful patterns or generalizations in any domain are the ones that are best recognized by those who already know how to look at the domain, know how the complex variables at play in the domain relate and inter-relate to each other. And this is precisely what the learner does not yet know. Problem spaces can be designed to enhance the trajectory through which the learner traverses it. This does not mean leading the learner by the hand in a linear way. It means designing the problem space well.

6. Pleasantly Frustrating

PRINCIPLE: Learning works best when new challenges are pleasantly frustrating in the sense of being felt by learners to be at the outer edge of, but within, their "regime of competence." That is, these challenges feel hard, but doable. Furthermore, learners feel—and get evidence—that their effort is paying off in the sense that they can see, even when they fail, how and if they are making progress.

GAMES: Good games adjust challenges and give feedback in such a way that different players feel the game is challenging but doable and that their effort is paying off. Players get feedback that indicates whether they are on the right road for success later on and at the end of the game. When players lose to a boss, perhaps multiple times, they get feedback about the sort of progress they are making so that at least they know if and how they are moving in the right direction towards success.

EXAMPLE: *Ratchet and Clank: Going Commando, Halo,* and *Zone of the Enders: The Second Runner* (which has different difficulty levels) manage to stay at a "doable," but challenging level for many different sorts of players. They also give good feedback about where the player's edge of competence is and how it is developing, as does *Sonic Adventure 2 Battle. Rise of Nations* allows the player to customize many aspects of the difficulty level and gain feedback of whether things are getting too easy or too hard for the player.

EDUCATION: School is often too easy for some kids and too hard for others even when they are the same classroom. Motivation for humans lies in challenges that feel challenging, but doable, and in gaining continual feedback that lets them know what progress they are making. Learners should be able to adjust the difficulty level while being encouraged to stay at the outer edge of, but inside, their level of competence. They should gain insight into where this level is and how it is changing over time. Good games don't come in grade-levels that players must be "at." They realize that it doesn't matter when the player finishes or how he or she did in comparison to others—all that matters is that the player learns to play the game and comes to master it. Players who take longer and struggle longer at the beginning are sometimes the ones who, in the end, master the final boss most easily.

There are no "special" learners when it comes to video games. Even an old guy like me can wander the plains of Morrowind long enough to pick up the ropes and master the game. The world doesn't go away, I can enter any time, it gives me constant feedback, but never a final judgment that I am a failure, and the final exam—the final boss—is willing to wait until I am good enough to beat him.

7. Cycles of Expertise

PRINCIPLE: Expertise is formed in any area by repeated cycles of learners practicing skills until they are nearly automatic, then having those skills fail in ways that cause the learners to have to think again and learn anew (Bereiter & Scardamalia 1993). Then they practice this new skill set to an automatic level of mastery only to see it, too, eventually be challenged. In fact, this is the whole point of levels and bosses. Each level exposes the players to new challenges and allows them to get good at solving them. They are then confronted with a boss that makes them use these skills together with new ones they have to learn, and integrate with the old ones, to beat the boss. Then they move on to a new level and the process starts again.

GAMES: Good games create and support the cycle of expertise, with cycles of extended practice, tests of mastery of that practice, then a new challenge, and then new extended practice. This is, in fact, part of what constitutes good pacing in a game.

EXAMPLE: *Ratchet and Clank: Going Commando, Final Fantasy X, Halo, Viewtiful Joe,* and *Pikmin* do a good job of alternating fruitful practice and new challenges such that players sense their own growing sophistication, almost as an incremental curve, as the game progresses.

EDUCATION: The cycle of expertise has been argued to be the very basis of expertise in any area. Experts routinize their skills and then challenge themselves with the new problems. These problems force them to open up their routinized skills to reflection, to learn new things, and then to integrate old and new. In turn this new integrated package of skills, a higher level of mastery, will be routinized through much practice. Games let learners experience expertise, schools usually don't. The cycle of expertise allows learners to learn how to manage their own life-long learning and to become skilled at learning to learn. It also creates a rhythm and flow between practice and new learning and between mastery and challenge. It creates, as well, a feeling of accumulating knowledge and skills, rather than standing in the same place all the time or always starting over again at the beginning.

8. Information "On Demand" and "Just in Time"

PRINCIPLE: Human beings are quite poor at using verbal information (i.e., words) when given lots of it out of context and before they can see how it applies in actual situations. They use verbal information best when it is given "just in time" (when they can put it to use) and "on demand" (when they feel they need it).

GAMES: Good games give verbal information—for example, the sorts of information that is often in a manual—"just in time" and "on demand" in a game. Players don't need to read a manual to start, but can use the manual as a reference after they have played a while and the game has already made much of the verbal information in the manual concrete through the player's experiences in the game.

EXAMPLE: *System Shock 2* spreads its manual out over the first few levels in little green kiosks that give players—if they want it—brief pieces of information that will soon thereafter be visually instantiated or put to use by the player. *Enter the Matrix* introduces new information into its "on demand" glossary when and as it becomes relevant and useable and marks it clearly as new. The first few levels of *Goblin Commander: Unleash the Hoard* allows the player to enact the information that would be in the manual, step by step, and then the game seamlessly moves into more challenging game play.

EDUCATION: If there is one thing we know, it is that humans are not good at learning through hearing or reading lots of words out of contexts of application that give these words situated or experiential meanings. Game manuals, just like science textbooks, make little sense if one tries to read them before having played the game. All one gets is lots of words that are confusing, have only quite general or vague meanings, and are quickly forgotten. After playing the game, the manual is lucid and clear because every word in it now has a meaning related to an action-image, can be situated in different contexts of use for dialogue or action. The player even learns how to readjust (situate, customize) the meanings of game-related words for new game contexts. Now, of course, the player doesn't need to read the manual cover to cover but, rather, can use it as reference work to facilitate his or her own goals and needs.

Lectures and textbooks are fine "on demand," used when learners are ready for them, not otherwise. Learners need to play the game a bit before they get lots of verbal information, and they need to be able to get such information "just in time" when and where they need it, and can see how it actually applies in action and practice. Since schools rarely do this, we are all familiar with the well-known phenomenon of students gaining As because they can pass multiple choice tests, yet can't apply their knowledge in practice.

9. Fish tanks

PRINCIPLE: In the real world, a fish tank can be a little simplified eco-system that clearly displays some critical variables and their interactions that are otherwise obscured in the highly complex eco-system in the real world. Using the term metaphorically, fish tanks are good for learning: if we create simplified systems, stressing a few key variables and their interactions, learners who would otherwise be overwhelmed by a complex system (e.g., Newton's Laws of Motion operating in the real world) get to see some basic relationships at work and take the first steps towards their eventual mastery of the real system (e.g., they begin to know what to pay attention to).

GAMES: Fish tanks are stripped down versions of the game. Good games offer players fish tanks, either as tutorials or as their first level or two. Otherwise it can be difficult for newcomers to understand the game as a whole system, since they often can't see the forest because of the trees.

EXAMPLE: *Rise of Nations'* tutorial scenarios (like "Alfred the Great" or "The 100 Years War") are wonderful fish tanks, allowing the player to play scaled down versions of the game that render key elements and relationships salient.

EDUCATION: In traditional education, learners hear words and drill on skills out of any context of use. In progressive education, they are left to their own devices immersed in a sea of complex experience, for example studying pond ecology. When confronted with complex systems, letting the learner see some of the basic variables and how they interact can be a good way into confronting more complex versions of the system later on. This follows from the same ideas that give rise to the well-ordered problems principle above. It allows learners to form good strong fruitful hypotheses at the outset and not go down garden paths by confronting too much complexity at the outset.

The real world is a complex place. Real scientists do not go out unaided to study it. Galileo showed up with geometry, ecologists show up with theories, models, and smart tools. Models are all simplifications of reality and initial models are usually fish tanks, simple systems that display the workings of some major variables. With today's capacity to build simulations, there is no excuse for the lack of fish tanks in schools (there aren't even many real fish tanks in classrooms studying ponds!).

10. Sandboxes

PRINCIPLE: Sandboxes in the real world are safe havens for children that still look and feel like the real world. Using the term metaphorically, sandboxes are good for learning: if learners are put into a situation that feels like the real thing, but with risks and dangers greatly mitigated, they can learn well and still feel a sense of authenticity and accomplishment.

GAMES: Sandboxes are game play much like the real game, but where things cannot go too wrong too quickly or, perhaps, even at all. Good games offer players, either as tutorials or as their first level or two, sandboxes. You can't expect newcomers to learn if they feel too much pressure, understand too little, and feel like failures.

EXAMPLE: *Rise of Nations'* "Quick Start" tutorial is an excellent sandbox. You feel much more of the complexity of the whole game than you do in a fish tank, but risks and consequences are mitigated compared to the "real" game. The first level of *System Shock 2* is a great example of a sandbox—exciting play where, in this case, things can't go wrong at all. In many good games, the first level is a sandbox or close to it.

EDUCATION: Here we face one of the worst problems with school: it's too risky and punishing. There is nothing worse than a game that lets you save only after you have gone through a whole long arduous level. You fail at the end and have to repeat everything, rather than being able to return to a save part-way through the level. You end up playing the beginning of the level perfectly over and over again until you master the final bits. The cost of taking risks, trying out new hypotheses, is too high. The player sticks to the tried and true well-trodden road, because failing will mean boring repetition of what he or she already well knows.

Good games don't do this. They create sandboxes in the beginning that make the player feel competent when they are not ("performance before competence") and thereafter they put a moratorium on any failures that will kill joy, risk taking, hypothesizing, and learning. Players do fail, of course; they die and try again, but in a way that makes failure part of the fun and central to the learning.

In school, learners, especially so-called "at risk" learners need what Stan Goto (2003) has called "horizontal learning," that is, time to "play around," to explore the area they are about to learn, to see what is there and what the lay of the land is, before they are forced up the vertical learning ladder of ever new skills. They need always to see failure as informative and part of the game, not as a final judgment or a device to forestall creativity, risk taking, and hypothesizing.

11. Skills as Strategies

PRINCIPLE: There is a paradox involving skills: people don't like practicing skills out of context over and over again, since they find such skill practice meaningless, but, without lots of skill practice, they cannot really get any good at what they are trying to learn. People learn and practice skills best when they see a set of related skills as a strategy to accomplish goals they want to accomplish.

GAMES: In good games, players learn and practice skill packages as part and parcel of accomplishing things they need and want to accomplish. They see the skills first and foremost as a strategy for accomplishing a goal and only secondarily as a set of discrete skills.

EXAMPLE: Games like *Rise of Nations, Goblin Commander: Unleash the Hoard,* and *Pikmin* all do a good job at getting players to learn skills while paying attention to the strategies these skills are used to pull off. *Rise of Nations* even has skill tests that package certain skills that go together, show clearly how they enact a strategy, and allow the player to practice them as a functional set. The training exercises (which are games in themselves) that come with *Metal Gear Solid* and *Metal Gear Solid: Sons of Liberty* are excellent examples (and are great fish tanks, as well).

EDUCATION: We know very well that learning is a practice effect for human beings—the conservatives are right about that, we humans need practice and lots of it. But skills are best learned (often in sets) as strategies for carrying out meaningful functions that one wants and needs to carry out.

Sounding out letters, together with thinking of word families and looking for sub-patterns in words, work best when they are seen as functional devices to comprehend and use texts. It's not that one can't get reading tests passed by drilling isolated skills out of context—one certainly can. But what happens is that we then fuel the so-called "fourth-grade slump," the long known phenomenon in which children seem to do all right learning to read (decode) in the early grades (at least in terms of passing tests), but then cannot handle the complex oral and written language they confront later in the content areas of school, e.g., science, math, social studies, etc. (Chall, Jacobs, & Baldwin 1990; see the papers in the special issue of the *American Educator* 2003a devoted to what they call the "fourth-grade plunge").

These children aren't learning to "play the game"—and the game in school is ultimately using oral and written language to learn academic areas each of which uses language far more complicated than our everyday vernacular forms of language. Learners need to know how skills translate into strategies for playing the game.

III. Understanding

12. System Thinking

PRINCIPLE: People learn skills, strategies, and ideas best when they see how they fit into an overall larger system to which they give meaning. In fact, any experience is enhanced when we understand how it fits into a larger meaningful whole. Players can not view games as "eye candy," but must learn to see each game (actually each genre of game) as a distinctive semiotic system affording and discouraging certain sorts of actions and interactions.

GAMES: Good games help players see and understand how each of the elements in the game fit into the overall system of the game and its genre (type). Players get a feel for the "rules of the game"—that is, what works and what doesn't, how things go or don't go in this type of world.

EXAMPLE: Games like *Rise of Nations*, *Age of Mythology*, *Pikmin*, *Call of Duty*, and *Mafia* give players a good feel for the overall world and game system they are in. They allow players to develop good intuitions about what works and about how what they are doing at the present moment fits into the trajectory of the game as a whole. Players come to have a good feel for and understanding of the genre of the game they are playing (and in *Pikmin*'s case, this is a rather novel and hybrid genre). *Metal Gear Solid* and *Metal Gear Solid: Sons of Liberty* come with training exercises that strip away the pretty graphics to make clear how the player is meant to read the environment to enhance effective action and interaction in the game. If players stare at the pretty fish in island paradise of *Far Cry*, they'll die in a minute. Players have to think of the environment they are in as a complex system that must be properly understood to plan effective action and anticipate unintended consequences of one's actions.

EDUCATION: We live, in today's high-tech, global world, amidst a myriad of complex systems, systems which interact with each other (Kelly 1994). In such a world, unintended consequences spread far and wide. In such a world, being unable to see the forest for the trees is potentially disastrous. In school, when students fail to have a feeling for the whole system which they are studying, when they fail to see it as a set of complex interactions and relationships, each fact and isolated element they memorize for their tests is meaningless. Further, there is no way they can use these facts and elements as leverage for action—and we would hardly want them to, given that acting in complex systems with no understanding can lead to disasters. Citizens with such limited understandings are going to be dangers to themselves and others in the future.

13. Meaning as action image

PRINCIPLE: Humans do not usually think through general definitions and logical principles. Rather, they think through experiences they have had and imaginative reconstructions of experience. You don't think and reason about weddings on the basis of generalities, but in terms of the weddings you have been to and heard about and imaginative reconstructions of them. It's your experiences that give weddings and the word "wedding" meaning(s). Furthermore, for humans, words and concepts have their deepest meanings when they are clearly tied to perception and action in the world.

GAMES: This is, of course, the heart and soul of computer and video games (though it is amazing how many educational games violate this principle). Even barely adequate games make the meanings of words and concepts clear through experiences the player has and activities the player carries out, not through lectures, talking heads, or generalities. Good games can achieve marvelous effects here, making even philosophical points concretely realized in image and action.

EXAMPLE: Games like *Star Wars: Knights of the Old Republic*, *Freedom Fighters*, *Mafia*, *Medal of Honor: Allied Assault*, and *Operation Flashpoint: Cold War Crisis* do a very good job of making ideas (e.g., continuity with one's past self), ideologies (e.g., freedom fighters vs. terrorists), identities (e.g., being a soldier) or events (e.g., the Normandy Invasion) concrete and deeply embedded in experience and activity.

EDUCATION: This principle is clearly related to the Information "just in time" and "on demand" principle above. For human beings the comprehension of texts and the world is "grounded in perceptual simulations that prepare agents for situated action" (Barsalou 1999a: p. 77). If you can't run any models in your head—and you can't if all you have is verbal, dictionary-like information—you can't really understand what you are reading, hearing, or seeing. That's how humans are built. And, note, by the way, that this means there is a kinship between how the human mind works and how video games work, since video games are, indeed, perceptual simulations that the player must see as preparation for action, or else fail.

Conclusion

When we think of games, we think of fun. When we think of learning we think of work. Games show us this is wrong. They trigger deep learning that is itself part and parcel of the fun. It is what makes good games deep.

For those interested in spreading games and game technology into schools, workplaces, and other learning sites, it is striking to meditate on how few of the learning principles I have sketched out here can be found in so-called educational games. "Non-educational" games for young people, such as *Pajama Sam*, *Animal Crossing*, *Mario Sunshine*, and *Pikmin*, all use many of the principles fully and well. Not so for many a product used in school or for business or workplace learning. It is often said that what stops games from spreading to educational sites is their cost, where people usually have in mind the wonderful "eye candy" that games have become. But I would suggest that it is the cost to implement the above principles that is the real barrier. And the cost here is not just monetary. It is the cost, as well, of changing people's minds about learning—how and where it is done. It is the cost of changing one of our most change-resistant institutions: schools.

Let me end by making it clear that the above principles are not either "conservative" or "liberal," "traditional" or "progressive." The progressives are right in that situated embodied experience is crucial. The traditionalists are right that learners cannot be left to their own devices, they need smart tools and, most importantly, they need good designers who guide and scaffold their learning (Kelly 2003). For games, these designers are brilliant game designers like Warren Spector and Will Wright. For schools, these designers are teachers.

CHAPTER 5

Learning about Learning from a Video Game

Rise of Nations

Introduction

This chapter will further develop the argument that computer and video games have a great deal to teach us about how to facilitate learning, even in domains outside games. Good computer and video games are complex, challenging, and long; they can take 50 or more hours to finish. If a game cannot be learned well, then it will fail to sell well, and the company that makes it is in danger of going broke. Shortening and dumbing games down is not an option, since most avid players don't want short or easy games. Thus, if only to sell well, good games have to incorporate good learning principles in virtue of which they get themselves well learned. Game designers build on each other's successes and, in a sort of Darwinian process, good games come to reflect better and better learning principles.

The learning principles that good games incorporate are by no means unknown to researchers in the learning sciences. In fact, current research on learning supports the sorts of learning principles that good games use, though these principles are often exemplified in games in particularly striking ways (for a survey and citations to the literature, see Gee 2003). However, many of these principles are much better reflected in good games than they are in today's schools, where we also ask young people to learn complex and challenging things. With the current return in our schools to skill-and-drill and curricula driven by standardized tests, good learning principles have, more and more, been left on the cognitive scientist's laboratory bench and, I will argue, inside good computer and video games.

Game design involves modeling human interactions with and within complex virtual worlds, including learning processes as part and parcel of these interactions. This is, in fact, not unlike design research in educational psychology where researchers model new forms of interaction connected to learning in classrooms (complex worlds, indeed), study such interactions to better understand how and why they lead to deep learning, and then ultimately disseminate them across a great many classrooms (see, for example, the papers in Kelly 2003).

As we have seen, there are many different types of computer and video games, such as shooters (e.g., *Deus Ex, Return to Castle Wolfenstein, Unreal II: The Awakening*), squad-based shooters (e.g., *Tom Clancy's Ghost Recon, Operation Flashpoint: Cold War Crisis*), adventure games (e.g., *The Longest Journey, Siberia*), simulations (e.g., *The Sims, SimCity 4, Black and White*), role-playing games (e.g., *Baldur's Gate II: Shadows of Amn, The Elder Scrolls III: Morrowind, Star Wars: Knights of the Old Republic*), real-time strategy games (e.g., *Age of Empires, Age of Mythology, Rise of Nations*), action/arcade games (e.g., *Sonic Adventure 2 Battle, Super Smash Brothers, Sly Cooper and Thievius Raccoonus*), and a good number of other types.

This paper discusses one real-time strategy game, namely *Rise of Nations*. Hereafter I will refer to real-time strategy games as "RTS games" and to *Rise of Nations* as "*RoN.*" RTS games are among the most complex and demanding of computer and video games. In such games, players play a civilization of their choosing, a civilization for which they must make a myriad of decisions. They send their citizens out to gather resources (e.g., food, wood, minerals, gold, etc.) and use these resources to build domestic and military buildings and engage in various forms of research. In these buildings, they can train soldiers and other sorts of people (e.g., leaders, priests, scientists, and/or professors), as well as build military and other sorts of apparatus. As they gather and build, they can advance to different ages, allowing their civilization to achieve higher levels of complexity and sophistication. All the while they must go to war against or engage in diplomacy with other civilizations.

All of this is done in real time. While the player builds up his or civilization, other players (or the computer representing other players) are building up theirs as well. Players must decide when to attack or engage in diplomacy. Victory may come to the swift, that is, to those who attack early (a strategy called "rushing"), or to those who wait and patiently build up (a strategy called "turtling").

RoN is one of the best RTS games ever made (along with such excellent games as *Civilization III, StarCraft, WarCraft III: Reign of Chaos,* and *Age of Mythology*). *RoN* allows the player to play one of 18 civilizations (e.g., Aztecs, Bantu, British, Chinese, Egyptians, Mayan, Nubians, Russians, Spanish, etc.), each with different advantages and disadvantages. The player can play against one to seven opponents (other real people or the computer playing other civilizations). Players can move through eight ages from the Ancient Age to the Information Age through various intervening ages such as the Medieval Age, the Gunpowder Age, and the Enlightenment Age. Like all RTS games, *RoN* involves players learning well over a hundred different commands, each connected to decisions that need to be made, as they move through a myriad of different menus (there are 102 commands on the abridged list that comes printed on a small sheet enclosed with the game). Furthermore, players must operate at top speed if they are to keep up with skilled opponents who are building up as they are. *RoN* involves a great deal of micromanagement and decision making under time pressure.

This chapter is based on an analysis of my own learning and personal interactions with the game as a game player. Learning differs from individual to individual, so we need to base our discussions of learning around actual cases of actual people learning. This is not to say, however, that no generality exists here. How any one of us learns throws light, both by comparison and contrast, on how others learn. Learning is not infinitely variable and there are patterns and principles to be discovered, patterns and principles that ultimately constitute a theory of learning. Indeed, what I am offering here is a case study meant to offer suggestions for a theory of how deep learning works (see, also, Barsalou 1999a, b; diSessa 2000; Glenberg 1997; Glenberg & Robertson 1999). In the end, I hope to convince you that today's young people often see deeper and better forms of learning going on in the games they play than in the schools they attend.

Though some of the information below is personal, I intend and hope readers will think about the comparisons and contrasts of my learning experience with *RoN* to the sorts of learning that goes on in schools. Ironically, perhaps, a baby-boomer trying to learn a modern computer or video game is not, in some respects, unlike a child in school trying to learn science or math. Both parties are being asked to learn something new and, in some respects, alien to their taken-for-granted ways of thinking.

Preparation for learning: before *RoN*

By the time I started up *RoN* I had played lots of computer and video games. They had taught me new ways of learning and new things about myself as a learner (Gee 2003). However, I had not had good experiences with RTS games. I felt overwhelmed by their many details and by the pressure of competing in real time. I had watched my twin brother play RTS games at a high level and was amazed by the number of details he had mastered and the speed with which he had acted and thought in the games. I had watched my seven-year-old play the wonderful *Age of Mythology* and was stunned that he and his friends could play such a complicated game so well. Far from giving me confidence these experiences just made me think that I was not suited for the micromanagement and on-the-spot decision-making RTS games demanded. In regard to RTS games, I was an "at risk" learner, at risk for failing to be able to learn and enjoy these sorts of games.

Though timid about RTS games, when *WarCraft III* came out, I tried it, prodded by my brother who loved the game. I made some progress in the single-player campaign, but eventually found the game "too hard." We should pause a moment, though, at this phrase "too hard." *WarCraft III* is a superbly designed game. In fact, it is well designed to get itself learned. So when I say it was "too hard," what I really mean is that I failed to engage with it in a way that fully recruited its solid design and learning principles. Good games are never really "too hard." They fail, for some players, either because their designers did not use good learning principles or because players have, for one reason or another, failed to engage the good learning principles that are built into the games.

So something has to come even before good learning principles. What has to come before is *motivation for an extended engagement* with the game. Without a commitment to an extended engagement no deep learning of a complex domain can happen (diSessa 2000). So what made me motivated to offer such extended engagement to *RoN* and not earlier to *WarCraft III*? Well, as good as *WarCraft III* is, *RoN* is yet better at allowing newcomers to learn it. But, more importantly, and ironically, perhaps, my "failure" at *WarCraft III* motivated me to try *RoN*. I had liked *WarCraft III*. It had made me feel that RTS games were important and worth playing. Though I had had limited success with the game, I had had some small success that made me feel that at another time and place, perhaps, I would do better. It had led me to read about RTS games and reflect on them. *WarCraft III*, it turned out—though I realized this fully only when I started *RoN*—had *prepared me for future learning* (Bransford & Schwartz 1999) of RTS games. When I started *RoN*, I realized that I already knew something, somewhat more than I had thought. I felt I had a small foot up.

In a school setting, my experience with *WarCraft III* would simply have been seen as a failure as I received my low or failing grade. In reality, it was not a failure, but an important precursor for later learning. My experience with *WarCraft III* is what I will call, following the work of Stan Goto (2003), a "horizontal" learning experience. "Vertical" learning experiences are cases where a learner makes lots of incremental progress on a scale from low skills to high skills, as if moving up a ladder. "Horizontal" learning experiences are experiences where one does not make a lot of progress up the ladder of skills, but stays on the initial rungs awhile, exploring them and getting to know what some of the rungs are and what the ladder looks like. Horizontal experiences look like mucking around, but they are really ways of getting your feet wet, getting used to the water, and getting ready, eventually, to jump in and go swimming. They may, in one form or another, be essential to learning, or, at least, essential for learners who are "at risk."

So, is there a contradiction in saying that when I started *RoN* I was still an "at risk" learner, but that my experiences with *WarCraft III* were important preparation for future learning? No. All that my being "at risk" meant, in the end, was that if *RoN* had failed to reward my preparation for future learning (the future was here with *RoN*) or had been a bad learning experience—a real failure— then I may have given up on RTS games forever, assuming I was too "dumb" to learn them. This is all "at risk" needs to mean in schools, too, though there it often means giving "at risk" learners a special dumbed-down curriculum meant to catch them up on "basic skills," a curriculum that all too often is a bad learning experience for these students.

Computer and video games have a built in advantage in the creation of motivation for an extended engagement. Human beings feel that their bodies and minds extend, in a rather intimate way, to the area around them over which they have direct control, usually a fairly small area (Clark 2003). Thus, as I type, I feel that my keyboard and mouse seem almost like extensions of my fingers, just as blind people often feel that their cane is an extension of their hand. The space closely around my body seems to be connected to it in such a way that I can feel that it is being "invaded" by others.

When humans can manipulate something at a distance, for example controlling with a keyboard a far-away robot seen on a screen, they get an uncanny feeling that their minds and bodies have been vastly extended (Clark 2003; Goldberg 2001). When people are playing a computer or video game they are manipulating a character (or many different things in a RTS game) at a distance in a very fine-grained way—in this case a virtual distance. They feel that their minds and bodies have been extended into this virtual world. This process appears to allow players to identify powerfully with the virtual character or characters they are playing in a game and to become strongly motivated to commit themselves to the virtual world the game is creating with their help.

When students are learning a content area in school—such as some area of science—this domain could be seen as a special world of its own, the world of doing science in a certain way and acting with certain values. Students could be encouraged to take on identities as scientists of a certain sort, to see and think about themselves and their taken-for-granted everyday world in new ways. In this case, school would be functioning more like a good game than traditional schooling, which stresses knowledge apart from action and identity.

RoN's Tutorials: Fish tanks

Let's begin to explore what makes *RoN* a good learning engine. When a player starts *RoN*, the designers immediately have two problems. First, learners are all different and the designers don't know what each one already knows, nor what their favored style of learning will be. Second, learners don't necessarily themselves know how much they do or do not already know and what their best style of learning will be in a given situation. Schools tend to handle these problems by assessing the learner and then deciding for the learner how these problems ought to be dealt with. *RoN*, like many other good games, solves the problem by letting learners assess themselves and learn things about what they do and do not know and what style of learning suits them here and now. Learners then decide for themselves how they want to proceed. Of course, *RoN* is designed to assist learners in this task; they are not left solely to their own devices. By the time you have interacted with *RoN*'s tutorials and skill tests and played your first few real games, you know a good deal about yourself as a learner, in general, and a learner of RTS games, in particular [In this paper the games called "Quick Battles" in *RoN* are what I refer to as the "real" game; a game called "Conquer the World" is also part of *RoN* , but I do not discuss that game in this chapter. Conquer the World is composed of Quick Battles and other elements].

When *RoN* starts, you see a screen with the following choices (the numbers on the right are dates, ranging from 60 AD to 1940):

Tutorial

Learn to Play	Quick Start	
Boadicia	Beginning Player	60
Alfred the Great	Beginning Player	878

The 100 Years War	Experienced Real-Time Strategy Player	1337
Henry VIII	Experienced Real-Time Strategy Player	1513
Battle of Britain	Advanced Topics	1940

Right away the learner sees choices: jump right in (Quick Start), learn step-by-step (moving from beginning player to experienced player to advanced topics), start with the experienced or advanced topics (thereby testing one's own assumptions about one's previous knowledge), or skip the tutorials altogether. Choice is built in from the beginning. Notice, too, there is no "remedial" in this learning world. You begin where you begin and move to advanced when you move there. None of this is timed. There are no invidious judgments based on one's previous "failures."

When the learner places the mouse on each choice above, a box is displayed at the bottom of the screen detailing just what historical event each choice will deal with and what skills the learner will learn by making that choice. Table 1 below shows each choice and what is displayed in the box when the learner places the mouse over that choice:

Table 1: Tutorial Screens

Learn to Play   Quick Start

Quick Learn Learn-As-You-Play Introduction
- One-on-one battle
- Hints and suggestions as you play

Boadicia   Beginning Player   60

Boadicia—Tutorial 2
Help a queen fight off the Romans to reclaim her nation
- unit selection
- movement
- map scrolling
- help text
- basic combat

Alfred the Great   Beginning Player   878

Alfred the Great—Tutorial 3
Turn back the raging Viking hoard
- Constructing and using buildings
- Training units
- Minimap

The 100 Years War   Experienced Real-Time Strategy Player   1337

The 100 Years War—Tutorial 4

- Library research
- Food, timber, and metal gathering
- Capturing cities
- Repairing buildings
- Unit combat advantages and disadvantages
- Transporting units across water

Henry VIII   Experienced Real-Time Strategy Player   1513

Henry VIII—Tutorial 5

Defend against Scottish raids

- City construction
- National borders
- Knowledge and wealth gathering
- Merchants and rare resources

Battle of Britain   Advanced Topics   1940

Battle of Britain—Tutorial 6

Battle the Germans in Britain's finest hour

- Diplomacy
- Air combat
- Generals
- Oil
- Enhancement buildings
- Formations

All is not as it at first seems here, though. What you see in the boxes are by no means all or even the majority of the skills you need to play *RoN* well. They are the "basic skills" you need to play the game, but "basic" in a special sense: they are the skills that allow you to actually start playing and learning from playing. I will point out below that the designers of *RoN* don't just take it for granted that players will be able to move from the basic skills in the tutorials to learning by playing. Once the player actually starts the "real" game, they ensure that this transition—from basic skill learning to learning by playing—will happen. But before I tell you how they do this (it's all about players being able to customize the game to their own desires and goals), let me finish my discussion of the tutorials.

If we look back at the terms "experienced real-time strategy player" and "advanced topics" in Table 1 we see something interesting. "Experienced" and "advanced" mean something quite different here than they do in places like schools. The skills taught in the tutorials, as we have said, are "basic" (in the sense defined). They are not the deeper skills required to play *RoN* or any other RTS game well, skills like time management, speed, micro-managing many details at once, and strategic thinking. So it may seem odd that terms like "experienced" and "advanced" are used. But "experienced" and "advanced" here mean what players need to know to begin to take yet greater control over their own learning by discovery through playing. They don't mean "at the top of the vertical ladder of skills" (or "you get an A in this subject"). The player is experienced and advanced in the sense of being prepared for future learning "on site," not in the sense of necessarily being an expert.

Each tutorial places its basic skills in a scenario that is just a simplified version of the real game. This allows learners always to see how these basic skills fit into the game as a whole system and how different skills integrate with each other. In school, on the other hand, very often these days children are exposed to basic skills one-by-one, step-by-step. For example, in early reading instruction they are taught first awareness of the sounds that compose words, then the decoding of letters, then reading aloud to attain more fluent decoding, then comprehension skills (Coles 2003). Then and only then do they get to play the real "game" of reading, namely reading for meaning and to carry out their own purposes. In schools, too often, skills are decontextualized from the system (the "game") and from each other. This never happens in *RoN* or any other good game.

As an example of what I am trying to get at here, consider the tutorial labeled "Alfred the Great" (see Table 1 above). When you click on this tutorial, while the scenario is loading, you see the following in print, while listening to the same thing (my own remarks below are placed inside brackets):

> Eight hundred years after Boadicia rebelled against the Romans [this event was dealt with in the preceding tutorial labeled "Boadicia"], Britain was savaged by repeated Viking attacks. Alfred King of Wessex has been paying tribute to stave off the raiders, *but* in 878 the Vikings prepare for conquest. After a defeat, Alfred retreats to rebuild his forces and drive the Vikings away.

Once you press "Start" to start the scenario, you see the Vikings attacking the British town of Ethandum and hear the following:

> Alfred suffers a stinging defeat when the Vikings attack in battle. The Norsemen loot the town and Alfred is driven back to his stronghold in

Carlisle. Alfred must rebuild his forces and attempt to retake Ethandum.

Here we see that the scenario opens with a short context within which to understand and make sense of what one is going to do. After the Vikings' victory, the
scene changes to the British town of Carlisle, the place to which Alfred has
retreated. This is where we will play out our tutorial. We don't start from scratch,
though. We start in the Classical Age, the second of *RoN*'s eight ages, not in the
Ancient Age where real games start. We also start with a large city, granary,
lumber mill, market, and fort, as well as several citizens and their farms. While
the game always starts with a (small) city and some citizens, the rest of these things
players would normally build for themselves. Furthermore, while players in the
real game always start with a library where they can do lots of different types of
research, including research that leads to new ages, this scenario has no library,
because we are not going to use it.

The setting of the scenario has been designed to be a minimal game setting
with no more and no less than we need to learn at this point, but with enough
to see how things fit together as a system. I will call this a "fish tank tutorial,"
because a fish tank can be, when done right, a simplified environment that lets
one appreciate an ecosystem (e.g., a river, a pond, or reef in the ocean) by strip-
ping away a good deal of complexity, but keeping enough to bring out some
basic and important relationships.

As we stare at the town of Carlisle, we hear and see the following, which importantly gives us an overall purpose and goal within which to situate the actions
we are going to carry out and the skills we are going to learn:

> The Vikings now control Ethandum. Before we can rally the nation, we
> must retake that city. Our first goal is to scout the Viking position and find
> a route for our attack. We need to keep watch on the Viking preparations
> and defenses. A Lookout [a type of building] is needed as close to the
> Vikings as possible. This is a good spot for the look out [the camera moves
> to a spot at the edge of the town and we see a big red circle marking the
> spot], close enough to see what's happening, but not so close that they'll
> notice it and attack. Now we'll learn how to construct new buildings. The
> actions a selected citizen [the camera moves back to town and we see a
> big red circle marking a citizen] can perform are found in the lower left
> panel [we see a red arrow pointing to the panel]. Click the Build Military
> Button [we see a small yellow circle marking the button in the panel] to
> access a menu of building choices, one of which is the Lookout.

While you would normally have to click on the citizen to get the panel for types
of buildings you can build (e.g., domestic ones, military ones, public monuments,

etc.), in this case it is done for you when the game highlights the citizen. All you have to do is click on the Build Military Building button, which has a small flashing yellow circle around it. When you click on it, you see another panel appear, a panel for building different sorts of military buildings. This time there is a flashing yellow circle around the button for building a Lookout. We also hear "Select the highlighted Build Lookout button." Once we do this, we hear "Select the location for your Lookout by clicking near the target marker. Your citizen will begin construction there " and see a big red flashing circle at the spot that had been indicated earlier. When we click this spot, we hear: "Good, now your citizen will move to that site and begin construction."

We are having our hands held as we move through the fish tank (it's what we can call a "supervised fish tank"). But notice some crucial features of this hand-holding. Information is given multimodally (Kress & van Leeuwen 2001), that is, in print, orally, and visually (note, as well, that if you place your mouse cursor on any person, building, or environmental object on the screen, a box will appear that tells you what it is and what you can do with it). There is lots of redundancy. Information is always given "just in time" when it can be used and we can see its meaning in terms of effects and actions. Unlike in school, we don't get lots of verbal information up front and then have to remember it all when we can actually use it much later.

We see clearly how each piece of information we are given and each skill we are learning (and doing) is inter-connected to everything else we are learning and doing. We see the game as a system, not just a set of discrete skills. For example, we see how selecting a citizen, selecting a spot, and building a building are an integrated skill set. We see also how they relate to our overall purpose in this case, that is, to observe the enemy without getting too close. This lets us see that this skill set is both a general one (used for building and placing all sorts of buildings) and a *strategy* in the specific case when we are building Lookouts. In fact, we learn that all skills and skill sets are always ultimately strategies when they are concretely instantiated in practice.

This fish tank tutorial is also, of course, an example of what Vygotsky (1978) called learning within the learner's "Zone of Proximal Development." The "teacher" (in this case, the very design of the game) helps learners (players) pull off more than they could on their own and yet still feel a sense of personal accomplishment. Furthermore, the "teacher" (the design) tells the learner how to interpret things (what they mean), but these interpretations (meanings) become part and parcel of the learner's own mind as he or she carries out actions that embody those interpretations, e.g., building a Lookout as an initial plan in battle.

RoN'S Tutorials: Supervised sandboxes

All the tutorials below "Quick Start" in Table 1 function as fish tanks. So, then, what about the Quick Start tutorial? By its placement at the top of the list you are coaxed to take this choice first, though you need not (and if you don't like it, you can always quit, go back to the main menu, and make another choice). If you click on Quick Start what you get, in fact, is something a bit different from a fish tank. You get what I call a "sandbox tutorial." In the real world, a sandbox is a piece of the real world, but sealed off to be a protected and safe place where children can explore. You can throw anything you want in the sandbox for the kids to play with so long as it isn't dangerous (there may be spiders in there, but, presumably we don't let the family python in). It need not be as controlled and clean an environment as a fish tank.

So, too, the Quick Start tutorial is a space where the player is really playing the game, but is protected from quick defeat and is free to explore, try things, take risks, and make new discoveries. Nothing bad will happen. In other sorts of games, for example shooters, the first or first couple of levels of the game often function as sandbox tutorials (e.g., the excellent *System Shock 2*), though they are not labeled as tutorials, but as real levels of the actual game (in the first level of *System Shock 2*, though it looks as if you must escape a failing space ship rapidly and are in great danger, in actuality the level is not timed and the player cannot get hurt).

Quick Start begins by telling the player:

> This is a preformed scenario where you can play the game at your own
> pace. Try to capture the Barbarian capital or conquer 70% of the map.
> There'll be hints and reminders to help you as you play.

The Quick Start scenario is actually the "real" game set an easy level of difficulty with copious comments and hints. There is an opponent (in the real game you can have multiple opponents), but the opponent builds up slowly and does not make the smartest choices. The player gets a real sense of being in the game, even a sense of urgency, but can't really lose or, at least, lose at all early before having put up a very good stand.

Let me just show you the beginning of the Quick Start tutorial, so that you get the flavor of what is going on. The material below deals with how I operated in the Quick Learn tutorial. Here, once again, I print my own remarks in brackets:

[Voice:] The leadership of your fledging tribe has fallen on your shoulders. The first task is to unify a new nation under your rule. You're free to build your nation at your own pace. Occasionally you may receive advice to help keep things moving, but otherwise it's all up to you.

[If you wait, eventually you will read and hear hints about what to do. But there is "wait time" here to allow you to explore the screen and click on whatever you like. I clicked on the scout. When I did so I saw the box printed below and simultaneously heard the remarks listed below that:]

Scout: Currently selected (Hotkey)
Scouts, Ancient Age [picture with hotkey]—fast, but unarmed; good for exploring the map and finding enemies
- Can spot hidden enemy units, such as spies and commandos
- Can also destroy enemy spies
- Strong vs. spies; Weak vs. Archers, Gunpowder Infantry

[Voice:] This is your scout. Use him to discover rare resources or locate the enemy position. Scouts are very fast and can see farther than most units, but cannot attack. You can move your scout around the map manually or click the auto explore button to have him explore on his own.

[After a few moments, I saw the message printed below on the top left of the screen and simultaneously heard the words below that:]

[Top Left Corner:] Create citizens to gather more resources

[Voice:] Your first priority in the Ancient Age is to create citizens and gather resources. Click your capital city and click Create Citizen to add to your work force. Put as many of your people to work gathering food and timber as you can. If you're running low on resources, you can always build farms to gather food and fill up woodcutter's camps with citizens to gather timber.

[During another "wait time," I clicked on the library and then clicked on a red button that lets the player research military technologies. Once this research is finished, the player can build military buildings. After clicking on the red button, I hear the following]:

[Voice:] Now that you have studied the first red military technology, you can build a barracks and begin training troops to protect your nation.

[After a few moments, I hear the following:]

[Voice:] If you want to see more of the map, you can always zoom in and out by using the mousewheel or pressing Page Up and Page Down on the keyboard.

The Quick Start tutorial goes on in this way for a while. If the player explores and does things, the tutorial confirms these acts and explains them. If the player waits, the tutorial prints a hint about what to do on the top left of the screen and says the hint orally and explains what it means. There are also, from time to time, remarks about how the game works, for example, the remark above about how to see more of the map. The tutorial is a nice dance of the player's actions and designers' guidance and instructions.

Midway through the Quick Start scenario the following box pops up:

MID GAME

At this point you should be having fun exploring the game and following some of the prompts that appear in the top left of the screen. If you're not having fun, you may want to try one of the following options.

- I'm having fun I want to continue playing
- I need to know more basic information, take me back to the tutorial screen
- The game is too slow. Let me start a Quick Battle.

This box is an excellent example of alerting players to the fact that they need to assess their own progress, desires, and learning styles. They need to be proactive, make decisions, think about what they are doing and learning, and take control of their own learning.

When I started *RoN*, I started by doing the Quick Start tutorial. I did this for a rather perverse reason. I was so sure I would fail that I wanted to reconfirm my own view that actually playing the game would be too tedious and complex for me. What happened was that I got excited, feeling, "Wow, I'm actually playing a RTS game and winning, to boot!" (Of course, this may remind you of the great scene in the movie *What About Bob?* where the ever fearful Bob is lashed to the sail of a sail boat and yells to his friends, "Look, I'm sailing, I'm actually sailing!"). The Quick Start tutorial is a sandbox. The sandbox feels like the real world to a child, but is guaranteed not to destroy the child's trust and ego before the child is strong enough to face more significant challenges. But this tutorial is a specific type of particularly efficacious sandbox. It is a sandbox with a wise parent present to guide and confirm efficacious play in the sandbox, in this case proactive game designers. Let's call this a "supervised sandbox."

Once I had done the Quick Start tutorial, I was energized to learn more, but, of course, I could not remember all the details the tutorial had introduced—nor was I meant to. Now I could turn to the specific fish tank tutorials and make each of these details, through focused practice, a part of my embodied intelligence and not just the caprice of my risky verbal memory. But I also knew now how these details fit into the larger scheme of the whole game, remembering that even in the fish tank tutorials skills are also introduced in terms of how they relate to other skills and to a simplified game system. Of course, other learners might do the fish tank tutorials first and use the supervised sandbox of the Quick Start tutorial to assess their learning and readiness to jump into the "real" game.

There is one last important point to make about the Quick Start tutorial. What it does, in addition to what we have already surveyed, is introduce the *genre* of RTS games to players who may have not played such games before. "Genre" just means what *type* of thing a thing is, for example whether a novel is a mystery, romance, science fiction, etc., or a piece of writing is a story, report, essay, and so forth. RTS games are one type of computer/video game (there are many others, e.g., shooters, adventure games, role-playing games, etc.). They involve typical actions, rules, and strategies that are different from those involved in other types of games.

Schools often try to teach kids to read and write, rather than read or write specific types of things like stories, reports, field notes, essays, or expositions. But, just like games, these different types of reading and writing operate by different principles and are used to carry out different types of actions. Good learning always involves knowing early and well what *type* of thing we are being asked to learn and do (Christie 1990; Cope & Kalantzis, 1993; Martin 1990). Learners need to see this type of thing in action, not to be given static rules, if they are really to understand. In fact, for most types of things—like types of games, writing, movies, and so forth—there are no clear and static rules that define different types. Each type (e.g., a RTS game or an essay) is composed of many different instances that are variations around a theme. The only way to learn is to see some instances and live with them concretely.

Sure, there are some things you need to learn that help you to play most games, regardless of their type (e.g., moving and clicking a mouse), but these are the tip of an iceberg compared to what you need to know about how different specific

types of games work. Thinking a RTS game is a shooter will make you a particularly bad learner of the RTS game or, at the least, will make you disappointed
with it and not like it. The same thing is true of writing—there are some basic
all-purpose things to learn (e.g., where to put commas and periods), but they, too,
are but the tip of an iceberg, and writing an essay thinking it is supposed to be
a personal narrative won't work.

RoN: Unsupervised sandboxes

We are now ready—as the player is—to leave *RoN*'s tutorials and start the "real"
game. I said that the skills *RoN*'s fish tank tutorials taught were "basic skills" in
the sense that they are the skills that will allow you to actually start playing and
learning from playing the game. The designers of *RoN* have ensured that these
skills, once you learn them, will function just this way by building certain devices
into the game play itself. When you leave the tutorials and actually start playing, there is a pause key that will stop time. This allows you to explore what icons
on the screen mean and think about what you want to do. When time is paused,
your opponent(s) do not continue building and so you do not have to worry
about falling behind. Furthermore, you can set the game at one of two easy difficulty settings (easiest and easy) that greatly decreases the pressure of time. On
these settings, opponents move slowly and not always in the smartest fashion.
Finally, you can turn on (or off) hints that appear from time to time to remind
you of what you have learned in the tutorials and teach you new things.

What all this means is that the player learns in the tutorial just enough to
move on to learn more—and more subtle things—by actually playing the game,
but playing it in a protected way so that deeper learning can occur through playing. The player can customize the game play to be, in fact, another sort of sandbox, in this case what we might call an unsupervised sandbox. The player is
protected to explore and take risks, but, aside from the small hint notes that
can be turned off and on, there is much less guidance and direction from *RoN*'s
designers.

We see, then, that in *RoN* there is no clear division between the tutorials
as a learning space and the player's first "real" games with difficulty set on easiest or easy and use of the pause key. These first real games are actually "hidden
tutorials" which assist players in teaching themselves how to play *RoN*, not as
a set of discrete skills, but as strategic thinking using an integrated system of
skills. These unsupervised sandboxes make for a smooth transition between official tutorials and "really" playing the game (set on normal or a harder level).

Learning and playing

But there is a yet deeper principle at work here than the smooth transition between tutorials and playing. In a good game like *RoN* there is never a real distinction between learning and playing. The tutorials are simplified versions of playing the game. The game itself has a number of difficulty levels and at each level players must refine their skills and learn new ones. Players can also play other players in a multiplayer form of *RoN* on the Internet, getting into games with others whose skill levels are equivalent to their own. They can move up to play better and better players as their own skills progress and, in doing so, will constantly be learning new things. When learning stops, fun stops, and playing eventually stops. For humans, real learning is always associated with pleasure, is ultimately a form of play—a principle almost always dismissed by schools.

There is one crucial learning principle that all good games incorporate that recognizes that people draw deep pleasure from learning and that such learning keeps people playing. Good games allow players to operate within, but at the outer edge of their competence. At lots of moments, a good game feels highly challenging, but ultimately "doable." Perhaps the player fails a few times at a given task, but good games show how much progress the player has made on each try and the player sees that this progress is increasing each time he or she "fails." Eventually success comes. This feeling of being highly challenging, but ultimately doable, gives rise to a feeling I have called pleasurable frustration, one of the great joys of both deep learning and good gaming.

Good games, however, do not at all points operate at the outer and growing edge of the player's competence. This is because they also recognize another important learning principle, what I call the "principle of expertise," because it is the foundation of expertise in all significant domains (Bereiter & Scardamalia 1993). When learners learn a new skill set/strategy, they need to practice it over and over in varied contexts in order to make it operate at an almost unconscious routinized level. Then they are really good at it. But they are also in danger of resting on their laurels and learning nothing new. At this point, a good game throws a problem at the player where the routinized skill set/strategy won't work. This forces the player to think consciously again about skills that have become unconscious, taken-for-granted, and routine. The player must integrate his or her old skills with new ones, forming a new and higher skill set/strategy.

Now, in turn, the game will let this new skill set/strategy get practiced until it is routine. The player has moved to a new level of expertise and will then eventually face a yet harder problem that will start the process all over again. Thus, good games cycle through times when they operate at the outer edge of (but within) the player's competence and times when they allow players to solidify their skills. The times where players are solidifying their skills to the point of routine and taken-for-granted application give rise to another form of pleasure, the pleasure of mastery. Games cycle through periods of pleasurable frustration and routine mastery, a cycle of storm and calm.

These cycles are actually clearer in games like shooters (e.g., *Return to Castle Wolfenstein, Deus Ex, Unreal 2*, etc.) than they are in RTS games like *RoN*. In a game like *RoN* they are partially under the players' own control through the ways in which players can customize the game to their own skill level and interest. Players can themselves choose periods of skill solidification and high challenge, though the game gives them plenty of feedback as to when things are getting too easy or too hard.

But how do players know when they are prepared to move beyond the unsupervised sandboxes they can create by playing the game on easy difficulty levels? How do they know when they are ready to move on to the more rigorous challenges of the normal difficulty level and harder levels, as well as multiplayer play? As it happens—as happened with me, in fact—the player can certainly tell the game is becoming too easy by how fast and thoroughly he or she gains victory over the opponent(s). However, I found that when I moved on to the normal level, it was, at first, too hard, harder than I had thought it would be, given my swift victories on lower difficulty levels. The problem, of course, was that I had not properly evaluated my skills. I did not realize that my skill sets/strategies were not fast and efficient enough to take on harder challenges.

RoN does two things to speak directly to this problem. First, it offers players a whole set of "Skill Tests." I list the skill tests in Table 2 below. Note that some tests are defined in terms of skills (e.g., mouse clicking) and others in terms of strategies (e.g., getting to the Classical Age fast). As we have said, in games, skills are always seen as strategies.

Table 2: *RoN* Skill Tests

Aging Madness—Age 2

How fast can you get to Classical Age? Find out if your resource management skill is good enough.

Aging Madness—Age 4

How fast can you get to Gunpowder Age? Find out if your resource management skill is good enough.

Aging Madness—Age 8

How fast can you get to the Information Age? Find out if your resource management skill is good enough.

Raiding Party

Take your bloodthirsty Mongol horde and pay a visit to some enemy towns in an exercise of micromanagement.

Hotkey Handling

Do you know your hotkeys? This is a test of hotkey knowledge.

Protect the Wonder

Protect your Wonder from jealous enemies in a exercise of defense.

Tactics

Defeat the enemy troops to take control of a valuable resource without losing more than half your army in this test of generalship.

Whack the General

How fast can you click your mouse? This is a test of clicking ability.

These skill tests allow players to assess how well their skills fit into an efficient strategy set—how well integrated with each other and with the game as a system they are. The skill tests are, as they often are not in school, developmental for the learner and not evaluative (judgments carried out by authority figures). Furthermore, they are tests of what skills mean as strategies, not decontextualized tests of skills outside contexts of application where they mean quite specific things.

The second thing *RoN* does to solve the problem of letting players know where the cutting edge of their competence is is to render the whole matter *social*. Sadly, I failed my very first skill test several times. But I knew just how to increase my learning curve so I could pass the test. Every player knows there are an immense number of Internet sites and chat rooms from which loads of things can be learned and to which lot of questions can be directed.

One very effective thing—though there are a great many others—that players can do is download recordings of *RoN* games played by players at different levels of expertise. Players can watch these to learn new things at ever increasing levels of expertise. Players can also easily record their own games and review them. They can also pit the computer against itself—at whatever level of difficulty they choose—and watch how things are done. On line, there is a world-wide university of peers and experts available to any player all the time. *RoN* lists its own web site on its program file, a site with much information, chat rooms, and links to other sites. There are also published strategy guides and many game magazines that will discuss games like *RoN*, offering hints, guides, and other sorts of helpful information.

This social aspect of *RoN*, and games in general, makes *RoN* and other games the focus of what I have elsewhere called an "affinity group" (Gee 2004. See Chapter 8 below). An affinity group is a group of people who affiliate with others based primarily on shared activities, interests, and goals, not shared race, class, culture, ethnicity, or gender. The many sites and publications devoted to *RoN* create a social space in which people can, to any degree they wish, small or large, affiliate with others to share knowledge and gain knowledge that is distributed and dispersed across many different people, places, Internet sites, and modalities (e.g., magazines, chat rooms, guides, recordings, etc.). Distributed and dispersed knowledge that is available "just in time" and "on demand" is, then, yet another learning principle built into a game like *RoN*. Too often in schools knowledge is not shared across the students, is not distributed so that different students, adults, and technologies offer different bits and pieces of it as needed, and is not garnered from dispersed sites outside the classroom (for a case where it was, see Brown 1994). *RoN* has no such problems.

Conclusion

By way of summary, let me collect together here in a list some of the learning principles that are built into *RoN* and reflected in my interaction with the game. I believe that these principles would be efficacious in areas outside games, for example, in science instruction in schools, though I must leave that argument until later. However, it is clear that these principles resonate with what theorists in the learning sciences have said about learning in content areas in school.

1 Create motivation for an extended engagement
2 Create and honor preparation for future learning
3 Create and honor horizontal learning experiences, not just vertical ones
4 "At risk" doesn't need to mean any more than that you don't need another bad learning experience
5 Let learners themselves assess their previous knowledge and learning styles and make decisions for themselves (with help)
6 Build in choice from the beginning
7 Banish "remedial"—the word and the experience
8 "Basic skills" means what you need to learn in order to take more control over your own learning and learn by playing
9 "Experienced" doesn't need to mean "expert," it can mean being able to

take more control over your own learning and being able to learn by playing

10 Teach basic skills in the context of simplified versions of the real game so that learners can see how these skills fit into the game as a system and how they integrate with each other

11 Teach skills as sets and make it clear how they are instantiated in practice as strategies for accomplishing specific goals or carrying out specific activities

12 Offer supervised (i.e., guided) fish tank tutorials (simplified versions of the real system)

13 Offer supervised (i.e., guided) sandbox tutorials (safe versions of the real system)

14 Give information via several different modes (e.g., print, orally, visually). Create redundancy

15 Give information "just in time" and "on demand"

16 Learning should be a collaborative dance between the teacher's (designer's) guidance and the learner's actions and interpretations

17 Let learners create their own unsupervised sandboxes (i.e., let them be able to customize what you are offering)

18 Teach learners the genre they are involved with early and well (supervised sandboxes are good for this)

19 Ensure that there is a smooth transition between tutorials and actually playing (customized unsupervised sandboxes are good for this)

20 There should be no big distinction between learning and playing at any level

21 Allow learners to discover the outer edge of their competence and to be able to operate just inside that edge

22 Allow learners to practice enough so that they routinize their skills and then challenge them with new problems that force them to re-think these taken-for-granted skills and integrate them with new ones.

23 Offer learners developmental (not evaluative) skill tests that allow them to judge where the outer edge of their competence is and that let them make decisions about what new things they need to learn on their path to mastery

24 Ensure that learners at every level of expertise can readily use knowledge that is distributed and dispersed across a great many other people, places, sites, texts, tools, and technologies

25 Ensure that the learners become part of an affinity group composed of peers and masters near them and spread across the community and world

Young people exposed to these principles so powerfully in a game like *RoN* are engaged in a form of learning that, in my view, makes many schools look uninspired and out of touch with the realities of how human learning works at a deep level. Perhaps, too, this exposure causes in some of these young people a critique of schooling as it currently exists.

CHAPTER 6

Pleasure and "Being a Professional"

Learning and Video Games

Introduction

In this chapter I am going to connect pleasure, being a professional, learning, and video games—surely a list of things that don't seem to go together. While the word "professional" brings to mind doctors and lawyers and other sorts of people with high status who get paid well for specialist skills, this is not what I want to mean by the word here. What I want to mean by the word "professional" is what I will call an "authentic professional." Authentic professionals are people who have special knowledge and distinctive values tied to specific skills gained through a good deal of effort and experience. They do what they do because they are committed to an identity in which their skills and the knowledge that generates them are seen as valuable and significant. They don't operate just by well-practiced routines; they can think for themselves and innovate in their domains when they have to (Bereiter & Scardamalia 1993). Finally, authentic professionals welcome challenges at the cutting edge of their expertise. Being a professional is a commitment to being in the world in a certain way with a certain style and operating by certain values. I will argue here that some good video games recruit this sense of being a professional for deep learning and that we can learn a good deal from such games about how learning can work better in and out of schools, even when we are not using a game or game-like technologies.

As I have emphasized throughout this book, I believe that good commercial video games are by no means trivial phenomena. They are deep technologies for recruiting learning as a form of profound pleasure (Gee 2004). I also believe that good video games are extensions of life in a quite strict sense, since they recruit and externalize some of the most fundamental features of how human beings orient themselves in and to the real world, especially when they are operating at their best. Good video games create what I call a "projective stance"—a double-sided stance towards the world (virtual or real) in terms of which we humans see the world simultaneously as a project imposed on us and as a site onto which we can actively project our desires, values, and goals (Gee 2003). A special category of video games allows players to enact the projective stance of an "authentic professional" and thereby experience deep expertise of the sort that so often eludes learners in schools.

The projective stance

In video games, players *inhabit* the goals of a virtual character in a virtual world and the virtual world is designed to be *attuned* to those goals. In a game the real-world player gains a *surrogate*: i.e., the virtual character the player is playing, e.g., Garrett in *Thief: Deadly Shadows*. By "inhabit" I mean that you, the player, act in the game as if the goals of your surrogate are *your* goals.

Virtual characters have virtual minds and virtual bodies. They become the player's surrogate mind and body. You may wonder what I mean by the "mind" of a virtual character. What I mean is this: as a player, you must—on the basis of what you learn about the game's story and the game's virtual world—attribute certain mental states (beliefs, values, goals, feelings, attitudes, and so forth) to the virtual character. You must take these to be the character's mental states; you must take them as a basis for explaining the character's actions in the world.

By "attuned" I mean that the virtual character, that character's goals, and the virtual world of the game are designed to *mesh* or fit together in certain ways. The virtual character (in terms of the character's skills and attributes) and the virtual world are built to go together such that the character's goals are easier to reach in certain ways than they are in others.

Let's consider an example. Take the game *Thief: Deadly Shadows*. In this game, the player plays the master thief Garrett. In inhabiting Garrett's body (whether playing the game in first person or third person mode), the player inherits specific powers and limitations. In inhabiting Garrett's body, with its powers and limitations, the player also inhabits Garrett's specific goals, goals having to do with stealing, infiltrating, and stealthily removing or sneaking past guards to accomplish specific story-related ends in the game. Given Garrett's powers and limitations, these goals are easier to reach in some ways than others within the specific virtual world of this game.

The virtual world in *Thief*—the world through which you as Garrett move— is a world designed to interact with Garrett's powers and limitations in terms of specific affordances and disaffordances. These affordances and disaffordances do not reside in the world alone, but in the combination of the specific mind/body Garrett brings to the that world and the way in which that world encourages or discourages that specific mind/body in terms of possible actions.

It is a world of shadows and hiding places, a world well fit for Garrett's superb (mental and physical) skills at hiding, waiting, watching, and sneaking. It affords hiding and sneaking of all sorts. It is not a world well made for outright confrontations and frontal fights: in this world, Garrett can find no guns or weapons much beyond a small dagger and the spaces that would allow outright fights with multiple guards are pretty cramped, allowing guards easily to surround Garrett. The way the world is made, the way that Garrett's mind/body is made, and how they mesh, has major consequences for the sorts of effective plans and goals (you as) Garrett can make and carry out.

So, we see, that a video game creates a three-way interaction among the virtual character's mind/body, the character's goals, and the design features of the virtual world in terms of affordances for effective action: virtual character ←→ goals ←→ virtual world.

In a game, the virtual character's powers and limitations mesh with the way in which the game's virtual world is designed in quite specific ways so that the virtual character's goals can be accomplished better in some ways than others. Finding this mesh or fit—"sweet spots" for effective action—is, of course, one of the key skills required in playing a video game. You CAN play *Thief* as an out and out fighting game, eschewing stealth, but you will be fighting the mesh (that discourages such actions) between Garrett's mind/body (your surrogate mind/body) and the virtual world of the game all the way.

So I have argued so far that players *inhabit* the goals of a virtual character in a virtual world and the virtual world is designed to be *attuned* to those goals. But in video games the virtual character—e.g., Garrett—also *instantiates* the goals of a real-world player. The virtual world of the game is designed to *invite* the real-world player to form certain goals of his or her own.

According to the first claim, in a game like *Thief: Deadly Shadows*, you, the player, see the world from Garrett's perspective and need to find ways to use the mesh ("fit") in the world among Garrett's mind/body, his goals, and the design of the virtual world to carry out *his* goals effectively. But things work the other way round, as well. Garrett becomes a reservoir that can be filled with *your own* desires, intentions, and goals. By placing your goals within Garrett—by seeing them as Garrett's goals—you can enact your desires in Garrett's virtual world. But note that this is a process that works well only if you carefully consider the mesh ("fit") that exists in the game among Garrett's mind/body, his goals, and the design of the virtual world. This is the only way in which your own goals will be effectively added to Garrett's and accomplished, since the game will resist goals that fall outside this mesh. In this sense, your own personal goals must become Garrett-like goals, goals that flow from his (virtual) mind and body as they are placed in this specific game world.

Let me give an example. At one point in *Thief*, Garrett needs to break into a museum to get an important object. This is Garrett's goal and you need to inhabit him and see the game world from the perspective of his affordances in this particular virtual world if you are to play this part of the game successfully.

But let's say that you as a player decide that you want to get through the museum by sneaking up on and knocking out every guard or, alternatively, by sneaking by them all and leaving them all unharmed, never knowing you were there. This is not a goal that Garrett has in the game. There is no in-game way to decide what his goal would be in this respect. To realize this goal, you have to make it Garrett's in-game goal, treat it just the way you would his own goals, the goals that you are inhabiting. You must do this, because the world in which Garrett moves allows this goal to be reached in some ways and not others, and it allows it to be reached more easily and effectively (even more elegantly) in some ways than others.

So, we can revise our three-way interaction a bit: we can say now that a video game creates a three-way interaction among the virtual character's mind/body (the player's surrogate), the character's goals *and* the player's goals, and the design features of the virtual world in terms of affordances for effective action: virtual character (player's surrogate) ←→ character's goals + player's goals ←→ virtual world.

So, in playing a game, we players are both imposed upon by the character we play (i.e., we must take on the character's goals) and impose ourselves on the character (i.e., we make the character take on our goals). It is interesting to note that this is a theme Bakhtin (1981, 1986) focuses on for language. He uses the term "centripetal force" for my term "being imposed upon" and the term "centrifugal force" for my term "impose upon." I think there is good reason for this—this symmetry between games and language—but this is a topic for another place (Gee 2003, 2004).

Garrett is a *project* I inherit from the game's designers, and, thus, in that sense an imposition. But Garrett is also a being into whom I *project* my own desires, intentions, and goals, but with careful thought about Garrett as a project. To both carry out the Garrett project and to project my desires, intentions, and goals into Garrett, I have to *think like a game designer*. I have to reflect on and "psych out" the design of the game. This dual nature of game characters— that they are projects the player has been handed and beings into which the players project their desires, intentions, and goals—is why I refer to them as *projective beings*, a phrase meant to capture their double-sided nature (Gee 2003).

In the real world we humans receive our deepest pleasure—our most profound feelings of mastery and control—when we can successfully take a *projective stance* to and in the real world. This is when things really "work" for us. This is, indeed, one of the deep sources of pleasure in gaming—that we regularly enact a stance that is rarer, but just as powerful, in our real lives.

I will describe what I mean by the projective stance in a series of steps. But the first two steps can be taken in either order or carried out simultaneously. So, here is what I mean by "taking a projective stance" to and in the real world: First, we look at the real world, at a given time and place, and see it (i.e., other people and objects in the world) in terms of features or properties that would allow and enhance certain patterns of actions in word or deed. Second, we see that these actions would, in turn, realize the desires, intentions, and goals of a human actor who took on a certain sort of identity or played a certain sort of role (and not others). These two steps amount to seeing, imagining, or construing a fit or mesh among the world (construed in a certain way), a particular type of actor, and specific goals that actor wants to carry out. Third, we then try to become that actor—become that sort of person, but also attempt, within that framework, simultaneously to realize goals and values that are part of the core self (our own personal history) we bring to any social identity we enact. We act in word or deed in terms of that identity.

Of course, we humans often form goals first and then turn to the world to realize them, though there are times when the world suggests goals to us that we have not preformulated. If we take step 1 first, we are letting the world suggest vectors of effective action to us. If we take step 2 first, we come to the world with goals and an identity we want to render effective in the world and seek to find the mesh in the world that will make things work out right. In reality, we very often iterate the process—bringing goals to the world, looking for an effective mesh, reconstruing our goals, reconstruing the world, and eventually acting and, if not effective, repairing and acting again. This sort of iterative process is not untypical of video game play, either.

Let me be yet more blunt. What I am suggesting is that when we humans act in the world (in word or deed) we are "virtual characters" (i.e., taking on specific identities such as "tough cop," "sensitive male," "hip young adult," "caring teacher," "savvy consumer," "needy friend," "nationalist African-American," and so on and so forth through an indefinite list) acting in a "virtual world" (i.e., construing the world in certain ways, and not others). Of course, the consequences are usually more costly in the real world than in a game world, but in both cases we seek to see how the situation is "designed" or can be viewed as "designed" to enhance a fit or mesh among ourselves, our goals, and the world.

The argument, then, is that video games build on and play with a stance that is the norm for effective physical and social human action in the world. They externalize in images much of what remains "mental" (usually unconsciously imaginative) in the real world when we are operating powerfully and effectively. In video games we play with life as if life were a toy.

The professional projective stance and ways of seeing

Video games differ in an important way in terms of how they handle the projective stance. In this respect I want to talk about two different types of games (Gee 2005). The first type of game I will consider is a game like *Castlevania: Symphony of the Night,* one of the classic games in the *Castlevania* series. In this game the player plays Alucard ("Dracula" spelled backwards), the half-human son of Dracula, who enters Dracula's castle to defeat his father.

The skills that Alucard and the player need and use to get through this game are generic action-game skills. Alucard walks, runs, jumps, blocks, and attacks in ways that are typical of a great many video game characters. When I play *Castlevania* I, like Alucard, call on my rather generic action-gaming skills, skills that I use in one form or another in many other games. I push buttons to make Alucard walk, run, block, or attack. Timing and combining the buttons in certain ways can be important.

However, we need to note that Alucard has different game skills than I do. He knows how to move and fight in the game world, while I know how and when to order him to do so. I also control Alucard's timing, though he controls his own execution of his attacks, which he varies depending on the weapon with which I have equipped him. So Alucard and I have different action game skills—different game relevant action abilities—but we need to combine and coordinate these to play the game well and to succeed at it.

Let's call these game skills, parts of which Alucard has and parts of which I (the player) have and which become a coherent system only when they are combined, "action gaming expertise." Thus, in a game like *Castlevania*, we get something like this: Alucard ← action gaming expertise → me. I place an arrow pointing to both sides to notate that the gaming expertise is parceled out between Alucard and myself, neither of whom has the whole set of abilities needed to play the game.

We can now see how we can get to a very different sort of game than *Castlevania*, if we consider one of Alucard's and my (the player's) limitations in a game like *Castlevania*. Alucard—like all the heroes in *Castlevania* games—is a vampire hunter. When I play him, I am playing as a vampire hunter. However, even though Alucard is a vampire hunter, he has no distinctive skills associated with this profession. As I have said, he has pretty much the same skills as any character—e.g. Mario—in action video games, i.e., running, breaking things, and fighting with enemies.

As a player of *Castlevania*, I need not develop or use any skills distinctive of a vampire hunter, either. To win *Castlevania*, I have to think like a gamer, not like a professional vampire hunter. Now I must admit that I personally have no idea what the professional values, knowledge, and practices of vampire hunters are. And *Castlevania* makes no attempt to emulate these, nor to teach them to players.

Things, however, are different in a game like *Full Spectrum Warrior*, the second type of game I want to discuss and one we have met already [**NOTE**: I am well aware that this game is ideologically laden. I am well aware that it carries messages, beliefs, and values about war, warfare, terrorism, cultural differences, the U.S. military, and the role of the U.S. and its army in the modern, global world. I myself don't agree with many of these messages, beliefs, and values. But all that needs to be left to the side for now. It is not that these issues are not important. However, right now, our only mission is to understand the game *Full Spectrum Warrior* as an example of a particular type of game—and a game like *S.W.A.T 4* would have done just as well. Without such understanding, critique would be superficial at best, in any case].

This game teaches the player how to be, albeit not a professional vampire hunter, but a professional soldier. It demands that the player thinks, values, and acts like one to "win" the game. You cannot bring just your game playing skills— the skills you use in *Castlevania*, *Super Mario*, or *Sonic Adventure 2 Battle*—to this game. You do need these, but you need another set of skills, as well. And these additional skills are, in fact, a version of the professional practice of modern soldiers, specifically, in this game, the professional skills of a soldier commanding a dismounted light infantry squad composed of two teams.

In *Full Spectrum Warrior*, the player controls two (sometimes three) squads of four soldiers each. The player uses the buttons on the controller to give orders to the soldiers, as well as to consult a GPS device, radio for support, and communicate with command. The Instruction Manual that comes with the game makes it clear from the outset that players must think, act, and value like a professional soldier to play the game successfully:

> You command a dismounted light infantry squad, a highly trained group of soldiers who understand how to operate in a hostile, highly populated environment. Everything about your squad—from the soldiers to its equipment to its tactics— is the result of careful planning and years of experience on the battlefield. Respect that experience, soldier, since it's what will keep your soldiers alive. (p. 2)

We have seen that in *Castlevania*, neither Alucard nor the player incorporates any depth of professional knowledge about vampire hunting into his skill set. However, in *Full Spectrum Warrior* **both** the characters the player manipulates (the soldiers on the squads) and the player him or herself knows (or comes to know) professional military practice. As the manual says, the soldiers "understand how to operate in a hostile, highly populated environment" and the player learns this or fails at the game.

Full Spectrum Warrior is designed in such a way that certain sorts of professional knowledge and certain types of professional skill are built right into the virtual characters, the soldiers (and into the enemies, as well). The game is also designed to teach players some of the attitudes, values, practices, strategies, and skills of a professional officer commanding a squad. For instance, consider what the manual has to say about "Moving Your Soldiers":

> Moving safely in the environment is the most important element of successful command. The soldiers on your teams have been trained in movement formations, so your role is to select the best position for them on the field. They will automatically move to the formation selected and take up their scanning sectors, each man covering an arc of view. (p 15)

Note, again, the value statement here: "Moving safely in the environment is the most important element of successful command." I guarantee you that, in this game, if you do not live and play by this value, you will not get far in the game. You'll just spend all your time carrying wounded soldiers back to CASEVACs, because of another value the game demands: "The U.S. Army has zero tolerance for causalities!" This value is enforced by the very design of the game, since if even one of your soldiers dies, the game is over and you have lost.

But note also that your soldiers, the virtual characters in the game, actually have professional knowledge built into them: "The soldiers on your teams have been trained in movement formations, so your role is to select the best position for them on the field. They will automatically move to the formation selected and take up their scanning sectors, each man covering an arc of view." In turn, the game demands that you, the player, attain such knowledge, as well: "your role is to select the best position for them on the field."

There are lots of things your soldiers know and lots of things you, the player, need to come to know. However, these are not always the same things. That is, your soldiers know different things than you know, they have mastered different bits of professional military practice than the bits you need to master to play the game. For example, they know how to take a variety of different formations and you need to know when and where to order them into each such formation. You yourself, however, do not need to know how to get into such formations (e.g., in the game you don't place each soldier in position—on the order, they assume the formation as a group).

As another example of the way in which knowledge is parceled out between you and your troops in this game, consider ways of moving your soldiers from one position to the next in hostile territory. There two ways to do this, one is called "rushing" and the other is called "bounding":

> The standard press version [single push of the A button, JPG] of a move order is the Rush. It is the fastest way to move since all four soldiers move toward the destination simultaneously. Well trained U.S. soldiers never fire a weapon without stopping their movement and going sighted (raising the gun to a firing position). In other words, Rushing soldiers never fire while moving, so they will not engage targets until they finish the move and you issue a fire order.

> The hold version [hold the A button down] of a move order is the Bounding Overwatch or Bound. Bounding is the safest way to move when your team is going into unknown territory or moving against one or more enemies that are close together because your soldiers are sighted and return fire as they move.

> Issuing a bound order has two steps. First you press and hold the A button while the movement cursor is out to order the bound. This automatically opens the fire sector cursor so you can set the area for your soldiers to cover. Pressing the A button again completes the Bound order.

> Once they receive a Bound order, the soldiers will move into position. The first two soldiers will start toward the destination while the rear two soldiers provide cover fire. Once the first two soldiers finish their movement, they cover the rear soldiers' move. When soldiers fire while Bounding, they automatically suppress to keep the target's head down.
>
> Note that Bounding is very unsafe if there are enemies who are too far apart to be in the same fire sector. If you Bound under these circumstances, you are very likely to lose one of your soldiers. (p. 16).

Note, once again, the values: "Well trained U.S. soldiers never fire a weapon without stopping their movement and going sighted (raising the gun to a firing position)." Note, again, as well, the parceled out knowledge. Your soldiers know how to rush and bound (and they will abide by the value of not firing without stopping and going sighted). You need to know when to rush and when to bound and what area to have your bounding soldiers cover (i.e., to be prepared to stop and fire at if they see any enemies in the area). Note, too, the strategic knowledge that is needed: "Note that Bounding is very unsafe if there are enemies who are too far apart to be in the same fire sector. If you Bound under these circumstances, you are very likely to lose one of your soldiers."

Of course, most of the knowledge, values, strategies, and skills the player picks up in this game, he or she picks up, not from reading the manual, which is, after all, only a small booklet, but from playing the game. The game has a tutorial, hints, and much in its design that helps players learn the knowledge, values, practices, strategies, and skills necessary to be enact professional military knowledge and play the game well.

So, a game like *Full Spectrum Warrior* requires more than generic gamer knowledge and skills, it requires professional knowledge and skills, as well. But this professional military knowledge is parceled out, shared between, the virtual characters and the player, each of whom knows some things in common, but different things as well. The technical term for a situation like this, where parts of a coherent knowledge domain (like military knowledge) are parceled out in this way, is to say that the knowledge is *distributed* (Hutchins 1995).

What a game like *Full Spectrum Warrior* adds to the gaming space, something that is not in games like *Castlevania*, is a shared professional role and distributed professional knowledge between the virtual character (or characters) and the real-world player. *Full Spectrum Warrior* allows players to experience *expertise*, to feel like an expert.

We argued above that in a game like *Castlevania* the formula Alucard ← action gaming expertise → player is at work. In such a game, the virtual character and the real-world player share knowledge and skills in respect to gaming. In a game like *Full Spectrum Warrior*, this formula, while still required, is overlaid with an additional one: Soldiers ← military expertise → player. In *Full Spectrum Warrior*, the virtual character(s) and the real-world player share both gaming expertise (as in *Castlevania*) and military expertise, which are, of course, combined and integrated.

Many video games involve the formula virtual character(s) ← authentic professional expertise → real-world player. For example, *Thief: Deadly Shadows* involves the professional identity of a master thief. Thieving expertise is distributed among the virtual character (Garrett) and the real-world player. There need be no name for the profession that the virtual character and the player share. In the game *The Chronicles of Riddick: Escape from Butcher Bay*, you play Riddick. Riddick has special sight that allows him to see clearly even in the darkest corridor. He is so tough in words and demeanor that he inspires fear in the toughest characters. He can engage in great feats of athleticism in quickly moving around the vents and corridors of the prison. And, like Garrett, he can hide in shadows and attack from the dark. He exemplifies and exudes "attitude." But, you, the player, must supply the specialist tactics and strategies to instantiate Riddick's skills and values, you and Riddick must combine your skills to pull off being a professional hard-ass prison escapee of a quite distinctive sort.

To be Garrett or Riddick requires thought, strategy, decisions, and values. *Thief* requires these precisely because the game demands that the player share an authentic professional identity and skills with a master thief. It demands more: the player must make Garrett an authentic professional thief *of his or her own sort*. My Garrett, for example, would not kill anyone, except in extreme cases, and loved, at times, to taunt guards by showing himself only to disappear before they could find him. Your Garrett might be different.

By creating a joint authentic professional identity (in terms of knowledge, values, attitudes, practices, strategies, and skills) games like *Full Spectrum Warrior*, *Thief*, and *Riddick* demand that the player *learn to see the world* in a certain way, different for each game. Though set in quite different locales and time periods, the physical worlds of these games are at a general level pretty much the same. Like the real world they are composed of buildings and spaces. But each game, to be played successfully, demands that each of these worlds be looked at in very different ways.

Full Spectrum Warrior requires that you (the Soldiers-you) see the world as routes between cover (e.g., corners, cars, objects, walls, etc.) that will keep you protected from enemy fire. *Thief* requires that you (Garrett-you) see the world in terms of light and dark, in terms of places where you are exposed to view and places where you are hidden from view. *Riddick* requires that you (Riddick-you) see the world also in terms of light and dark (where you can hide and where you can't), though much less so than *Thief*, but also in terms of spaces where you have room for maneuver in all out physical attacks on your enemies (e.g., you don't want to get backed into a corner).

It is important—and this is something we know from recent research on the mind—that seeing, knowing, and action are deeply inter-connected for human beings (Barsalou 1999a, b; Glenberg 1997; Glenberg & Robertson 1999). Humans, when they are thinking and operating at their best, see the world in terms of affordances for actions they want to take. Thus, we see the world differently as we change our needs and desires for action.

You see the world in *Full Spectrum Warrior* as routes between cover because this prepares you for the actions you need to take, namely attacking without being vulnerable to attack yourself. You see the world of *Thief* in terms of light and dark, illumination and shadows, because this prepares you for the different actions you need to take in this world, namely hiding, sneaking, appearing at just the right moment for a surprise attack, and moving unseen to your goal. So, too, with *Riddick*. And, when you see the world in the right way you have effective knowledge of and for that world—it's the difference between knowing Galileo's Laws of Motion as a set of symbols you can repeat and actually being able to see how they apply to specific situations in the world to accomplish something.

What I am saying here is that games like *Full Spectrum Warrior*, *Thief*, and *Riddick* allow players to take a projective stance to the (virtual) world, but a stance that is rooted in the knowledge, values, and ways of seeing and being in the world of an authentic professional, an "expert." In the real world, if you want, for example, to be a successful physicist, to know as a physicist in ways that are effective for action (problem solving), you must learn to see as a physicist. And this involves seeing the right "meshs" in the world in terms of who you, as an individual, are; who a physicist is; your goals and desires both as an individual and as a physicist; and the properties of the world at a time and place that will effectively allow your actions to enhance those goals and desires. But this is the heart and soul, too, of our second category of games, games like *Full Spectrum Warrior*.

Learning

If we took *Full Spectrum Warrior* as a model for learning, it would violate what both conservatives and liberals think about learning, especially learning in school. It forces the player (learner) to accept (for this time and place) a strong set of values connected to a very specific identity. Indeed, the player must follow military "doctrine" as formulated by the U. S. Army or find some other game to play. This is too constraining for the liberals.

On the other hand, *Full Spectrum Warrior* isn't about facts. There's no textbook on army doctrine. It doesn't teach by skill-and-drill. After the tutorial, which is pretty didactic, there is little explicit instruction. Rather, the player (learner) is immersed in a world of action and learns through experience, though this experience is guided or scaffolded by information the player is given and the very design of the game itself. Too much freedom here for conservative educators.

As a model of learning, *Full Spectrum Warrior* suggests that freedom requires constraints and that deep thinking requires a framework. Once the player adopts the strong values and identity the game requires, these serve as a perspective and resource from which to make decisions about actions and with which to think and resolve problems. If there is no such perspective, then there is really no basis for making any decision; no decision is really any better than any other. If there is no such perspective, then nothing I think counts as knowledge, because there is no framework within which any thought counts as any better than any other.

It is clear that if someone built a war game incorporating quite different doctrine—that is, requiring quite different values and identity—than *Full Spectrum Warrior*, then decisions and ideas that were right in that game might well be wrong in the other. For example, a doctrine that allowed soldiers to run and shoot at the same time, would lead to different sorts of decisions and different ways of solving problems in some contexts. Of course, the test of which doctrine was better in a given situation would be which one works best in that particular war setting. It is also clear that the absence of any doctrine would leave the player with no basis on which to make decisions, no basis on which to construct knowledge.

It is clear, then, too, that in *Full Spectrum Warrior*, its doctrine—its values and the identity it enforces on the player—is the foundation of the set of actions, decisions, and problem solutions from which the player can choose. Actions, decisions, or problem solutions outside this set are either not allowed by the game or are very unlikely to work. Of course, if there is no such set to choose from— if anything goes—then the learner has no basis on which to choose, is simply left to an infinity of choices with no good way to tell them apart.

Some liberal education does just this to children. They are immersed in rich activities—for example doing or talking about science—but with no guidance as to what are good choices, decisions, or problem solutions. The idea is, perhaps, that they will learn by making mistakes, but with so many choices available and so little basis for telling them apart, it is more likely they will go down (however creative) garden paths, wasting their time.

On the other hand, unlike conservative educators, *Full Spectrum Warrior* knows that knowledge—when one is going to engage in something like warfare— is not constituted by how many facts one can recite or how many multiple choice questions one can answer on a standardized test. No, *Full Spectrum Warrior* real- izes that true knowledge in a domain (like warfare) is based on one's ability to build simulations ("models") in one's head, based on previous experiences and thought- ful conjecture, that prepare one for future action. It is also based on being able to apply values to determine whether the simulation is a good one and to evalu- ate its outcome when one has acted on it—values given by the values and iden- tity with which the learner started.

One can have a purely verbal definition of a concept like "work" in physics or "bounding" in military practice. These verbal definitions are pretty useless (other than for passing tests), since they don't help facilitate future action in these domains (Gee 2004). On the other hand, if you can run a simulation in your head of how the word "work" applies to an actual type of situation in such a way that the simulation helps you prepare for action and dialogue in physics, then you really know what the concept means. The same goes for "bounding" in the mil- itary domain. Of course, you will run somewhat different simulations for "work" in different contexts and when preparing for different sorts of actions in physics. And, of course, the simulations you build will be partly determined by the wealth of experience you have had in doing and talking about physics.

If liberals often leave children too much to their own devices, conservatives often forestall their opportunities for learning to build good simulations to pre- pare themselves for fruitful action in a domain (like physics) by immersing them in facts, information, and tests detached from any meaningful contexts of action. Ironically, facts come free if we start from carefully guided experience (as in *Full Spectrum Warrior*) that helps learners build fruitful simulations to prepare for action. Anyone who plays *Full Spectrum Warrior* will end up knowing lots of mil- itary facts because these facts become necessary tools for building simulations and carrying out actions that the player wants and needs to carry out. The same facts become much harder to learn when detached from such simulations and actions.

Since fruitful thinking involves building simulations in our heads that pre- pare us for action, thinking is itself somewhat like a video game, given that video games are external simulations. *Full Spectrum Warrior* allows players to experience in a visual and embodied way military situations. They can then learn to build simulations of these in their heads and think about possible actions and out- comes before rushing into action. They can then act in the game, judge the con- sequences (partly based on the values and identity that military doctrine has given them), and build new, perhaps better, simulations to prepare for better actions. Without doubt the same process would work for learning in other domains, domains, say, such as biology, physics, or social science, the sorts of things we learn in school.

The recipe is simple: Give people well designed visual and embodied experiences of a domain, through simulations or in reality (or both). Help them use these experiences to build simulations in their heads through which they can think about and imaginatively test out future actions and hypotheses. Let them act and experience consequences, but in a protected way when they are learners. Then help them to evaluate their actions and the consequences of their actions (based on the values and identities they have adopted as participants in the domain) in ways that lead them to build better simulations for better future action. Though this could be a recipe for teaching science in a deep way, it is, in *Full Spectrum Warrior*, a recipe for an engaging and fun game. It should be the same in school, in learning science, for example, by being a scientist of a certain sort in the way in which I am a soldier of a certain sort in *Full Spectrum Warrior*.

Full Spectrum Warrior also realizes, as we have already seen, that deep learning—real learning—is too hard to do all by oneself. The learner needs powerful tools. We have seen that soldiers in *Full Spectrum Warrior* are smart, they know things. They know different things than the player, things the player doesn't have to know. This lowers the player's learning load. Furthermore, as the player gains knowledge, this knowledge can be integrated with the soldiers' knowledge to create a bigger and more powerful type of knowledge. This allows the player (learner) to do and be much more than he or she could if left all alone to his or her own devices. The actor in *Full Spectrum Warrior* is an integration of the soldiers' knowledge and the player's knowledge. The soldiers are smart tools and knowledge is distributed between them and the player.

Full Spectrum Warrior allows players to integrate their emerging professional military knowledge with the professional knowledge of the soldiers. The player, in this way, is guided into thinking, acting, valuing, and deciding like a professional of a certain sort. The player experiences the feel of expertise even before the player is a real expert or even really expert at the game. This is a beautiful example of an important learning principle virtually ignored in school: performance before competence.

Schools usually insist that learners study hard, become competent (the test shows it!), and then perform (and, yet, research shows they usually can't actually do anything beyond answer test questions). Of course, there is little motivation to study and become competent, when the learner has no real idea what it feels like to act effectively in a domain or why anyone would want to become competent in the area. Further, all the facts and information the learner is studying would make a lot more sense if the learner had had any opportunities to see how they applied to the world of action and experience. Without that, they are "just words" for the learner.

Learning school things, things like biology, say, could work in just the same way. Strong doctrine, values and identity, smart tools, distributed knowledge, well designed experience, guidance on how to build useful mental models or simulations and on how to evaluate their outcomes, performance before competence, competence that goes beyond verbal definitions and test taking (Shaffer 2004). But, in reality, this is all very rare, indeed, in school, though common in good video games.

Of course, I know that some readers are put off by my military example and are still quite disturbed by that strong term "doctrine." Strong doctrine, leading to values and identity, engagement and commitment, real choices from within a reasonable and fruitful set of choices, and ways to evaluate what one has done are necessary for real learning, however much they comport badly with the beliefs of liberal educators. It is a pity, indeed, that we have such good examples of such good learning in the military domain, both in the case of commercial games like *Full Spectrum Warrior* and non-commercial simulations used by the military for training, and *not* in domains like biology, physics, history, social science, urban planning, ecology, and many other more academic-like domains. It is equally a pity that the military does not have simulations as good as the ones they have for warfare for understanding culture and building peace (or running prisons).

But, of course, strong doctrine, values, and identity can lead to intolerant ideologues, as well, whether these be soldiers, scientists, or religious fanatics. There is a paradox here, of course: no deep learning without doctrine, and yet doctrine can be dangerous. But this paradox is easy to resolve at the educational level: be sure that learners have lived and acted in multiple worlds based on different doctrines. Be sure they can compare and contrast and think about the relationships among doctrines. They'll make smart choices, then, I believe, about what ultimately to believe and how ultimately to act.

Some doctrines work better than others for given situations and learners will learn this. Here, again, the video game industry is out ahead: the store shelves are full of different worlds based on different doctrines. *Full Spectrum Warrior* sits alongside *Thief* and *Riddick*. Maybe someday it will sit beside Galileo's world and doctrines, as well.

CHAPTER 7

Why Game Studies Now?

Video Games: A New Art Form

Video games are a new art form. That is one reason why now is the right time for Game Studies (for other reasons, see Gee 2003). The importance of this claim is this: As a new art form, one largely immune to traditional tools developed for the analysis of literature and film, video games will challenge us to develop new analytical tools and will become a new type of "equipment for living," to use Kenneth Burke's (1973) phrase for the role of literature. The claim that video games are art is highly controversial, so let me explain what I mean.

In *Tetris*, one of the most popular video games ever, players rotate simple shapes as they fall down the screen, attempting to lock them together with other shapes at the bottom of the screen. The shapes and movements in *Tetris* have no particular meaning. In a sense, all video games are like *Tetris*. They are composed of rules that specify the allowable shapes, movements, and combinations of shapes and movements in the game (Koster 2004).

In a game like *Castlevania: Symphony of the Night*, however, each of the shapes, movements, and combinations that constitute the game is assigned a meaning. A given shape is assigned to represent an actor like Alucard (Dracula's half-human son) or a Sword Lord; another shape is assigned to represent an object like a treasure chest or a pool of water, and so forth. A certain combination of shapes and movements is assigned to represent an action like "Alucard kills a Sword Lord with an axe." Long-time players are aware that the shapes and movements in a game don't have to look much like what they mean. The original *Metroid* is made up of pixels so crude that one can barely tell what they stand for, but players still know they are helping Samus Aran infiltrate the space pirates' home planet Zebes.

What *Castlevania* and *Metroid* do, and *Tetris* doesn't, is marry an abstract rule system about shapes, movements, and combinations with *story* elements. By "story elements" I mean actors (e.g., hunters and vampires), objects (e.g., chests and pools), actions (e.g., opening chests, killing monsters), states (e.g., being damaged) and events (e.g., dying). I call these "story elements" because, after all, stories are composed of such things. By manipulating theses shapes, movements, and combinations, the player produces and manipulates story elements. Thus, games like *Castlevania* and *Metroid* are story-element generators.

Of course, one could do the same with *Tetris* and people have done just that, in particular making versions of the game where the pieces look like humans in different poses and locking them together represents sex. *Tetris* becomes—sadly in this case—a story element generator about sex. I use the term "story elements" and not "story," because in no sense does such story-element generation, either in *Castlevania* or in sex *Tetris*, generate, by itself, whole stories of any depth—just elements of stories.

So what? So what that *Castlevania* allows players to freely generate story elements? There are three answer to this question.

The first answer is this: The assignment of meaning to each shape, movement, and combination in *Castlevania* helps determine what they should look like and sound like, either in the game or in the player's mind. Just as saying that a given shape in *Tetris* represents a human suggests we might draw the shape to look like a contorted person, the meaning assignments in *Castlevania* suggest—help generate—the very visual design of the game. The Sword Lord looks the way he does because this object has been assigned the meaning "Sword Lord" in a Dracula universe. There is, of course, still lots of room for what the Sword Lord can look like in detail, but he's not likely to look like an ice-cream cone. This creates an *ambiance* or *sensory metaphor* for the game. It quite literally gives what is, after all, just an abstract rule system a certain mood, feeling, sound, and look.

Ambiance, mood, feeling, sound, look: these all sound like mere window dressing. But they are a large part of the pleasure the game gives. The original *Castlevania* game for the *Sony PSone* is subtitled "Symphony of the Night." And, indeed, moving through this game is like moving through a symphony where every "tone" (image) and combination of "tones" (images) creates moods, feelings, and ambiance, not primarily information (as in movies and books). The experience of playing the game is closer to living inside a symphony than to living inside a book. And the symphony is not just visual, but it is composed, as well, of sounds, music, actions, decisions, and bodily feelings that flow along as the player and virtual character (Alucard) act together in the game world.

The second answer to our "So what?" question is this: Humans find story-elements profoundly meaningful and are at a loss when they cannot see the world in terms of such elements. We try to interpret everything that happens as if it were part of some story, even if we don't know the whole story—and, in fact, in life we rarely know the whole story (Bruner 1986). *Castlevania* allows players to flow through the game always producing obvious narrative sense, even in the absence of some whole and finished narrative.

This generation of story elements is also part of the symphony I discussed above. Since all the objects and movements in the game have been assigned meanings and these meanings have helped generate the visual and auditory design of the game, the actions we players carry out produce more and more of that design. We produce more and more "notes" that help create the symphony. *Castlevania* is an instrument on which the player plays a visual, motoric, auditory, kinesthetic, and decision-making symphony. For example, for me, the look, feel, and flow of Alucard's movements as he jumps across underground springs of water at the bottom of the castle while simultaneously breaking Frozen Shades into ice crystals is one particularly beautiful movement (and moment) in the overall symphony that the playing of *Castlevania* constitutes. And it is one I produce.

The third answer to our "So What?" question is this: The marriage of rules and story-element meanings in *Castlevania* allows for two quite different stories to exist in the game. The first story is the one told in the *Castlevania* games. This is the designer's story (which, of course, gets elaborated and transformed on fan fiction sites).

But there is a second story. Every player of *Castlevania* who does everything you can do in the game will, in the end, have done all the same things. A player who does less will have done some sub-set of this. However, each player of *Castlevania* will have done and found things in different orders and in different ways from each other. Players will have ventured into the parts of the castle in different orders, they will have revisited them a different number of times. They will have faced the bosses at different times and will have defeated them in different ways. They will have found key items in different orders. They will have made different choices of what strategies to use and what equipment to wear and use. This is to say that each player will have enacted a different *trajectory* through the game.

What allows us to feel and recognize a different trajectory in a game like *Castlevania* is the story-elements. We can recognize that one distinctive event (e.g., Alucard killed his first Sword Lord) happened before or after another distinctive event (Alucard found the gold ring). Story-elements give the player a way to mark time and against this marking each player comes to see that they have enacted a unique trajectory through the game space.

This trajectory has an important consequence. Your Alucard is different from mine. Yours had a different trajectory from mine. The hero is, thus, not Alucard from the designer's story, nor you the real-world player. It is "Alucard-you," a melding of the virtual character, Alucard, and you, the real-world player who has steered Alucard on a unique trajectory through the game.

This trajectory is the second story. Since it is a story produced jointly by the real-world player and the virtual-world character, I call it the real-virtual story (Gee 2005). This is the important story in *Castlevania*. It is to this story that players attach their fantasies and desires. This trajectory is personal and individual in a game like *Castlevania*; it is personal and social in a multiplayer game like *World of WarCraft*.

This proactive production by players of story elements, a visual-motoric-auditory-decision-making symphony, and a unique real-virtual story produces a new form of performance art co-produced by players and game-designers. We have as yet no useful tools for analyzing the elements that make up this art form. But it is a form that has the potential to integrate pleasure, learning, reflection, and expanded living in ways that we expect from art.

CHAPTER 8

Affinity Spaces

From *Age of Mythology* to Today's Schools

Introduction: From groups to spaces

A wide body of research, applied to schools and workplaces, has used the notion of a "community of practice" (Lave 1996; Lave and Wenger 1991; Rogoff 1990; Wenger 1998). In this paper I consider an alternative notion. This alternative focuses on the idea of a space in which people interact, rather than on membership in a community. I want to consider this alternative because I believe that what I will call "affinity spaces" are particularly important contemporary social configurations with implications for the future of schools and schooling.

The notion of a "community of practice" has been a fruitful one and there are certainly many cases where the term is apt (see Wenger, McDermott, and Snyder 2002 for a clear demarcation of what is and what is not a community of practice). However, it has given rise to several problems, some of which are:

a The idea of "community" can carry connotations of "belongingness" and close-knit personal ties among people which do not necessarily always fit classrooms, workplaces, or other sites where the notion of a community of practice has been used. As an anonymous reviewer of an earlier version of this chapter pointed out, the notion of "community" tends to project a warm sense of peaceful relations among members, which we know is often not the case in schools or workplaces, and "does not only miss the reality of schools and schooling but also misleads research and practices in that it may direct people to the wrong places looking for solutions and improvements."

b The idea of "community" seems to bring with it the notion of people being "members." However, "membership" means such different things across different sorts of communities of practice and there are so many different ways and degrees of being a member in some communities of practice that it is not clear that membership is a truly helpful notion. Again, an anonymous reviewer of an earlier version of this work pointed out that while "community" assumes a sense of collective purpose or group goals, this is often not the case in school, where "individuals actually have different views of why they are in school or in a class and consequently their goals are different."

c While Wenger (see Wenger, McDermott, & Snyder 2002) has tried to be careful in delineating just what is and what is not a community of practice, distinguishing it from other sorts of affiliations, the notion has been used by others to cover such a wide array of social forms that we may be missing the forest for the trees.

In my view, the key problem with notions like "community of practice" is that that they make it look like we are attempting to label a group of people. Once this is done, we face vexing issues over which people are in and which are out of the group, how far they are in or out, and when they are in or out. The answers to these questions vary (even their very answerability varies) greatly across different social groupings. If we start with the notion of a "community" we can't go any further until we have defined who is in and who is not, since otherwise we can't identify the community. Yet it is often issues of participation, membership, and boundaries that are problematic in the first place.

Take a high-school science class. Johnny and Janie are both in the class. Janie is proactively attempting to engage with the science in the class, but Johnny is "playing the game" for a passing grade. Are they in the same community of practice or is Janie in a school-science community of practice and Johnny in a "doing school" community of practice. What sense does it make to say all the students in this class are in some (one?) community of practice just because they are all contained by the same four walls? Or if we think beyond those four walls, if some parents are helping their children in science, are they in the community of practice too? What about the principal, the other science teachers, the reading specialist who comes into the class once a week, the author of the textbook, or for that matter the curriculum specialists and policy makers who help shape the classroom's practices in regard to science and schooling more generally?

I suggest that the problem here is trying to start with a label (like community of practice) which looks like a label for a group of people, a group which must then be identified in terms of its "members." What I want to suggest, instead, is that (at least, sometimes) we start with "spaces" and not groups.

Let me start with an analogy. It is hard to say who is and who is not an "American" (I mean by this not who is officially a "citizen" or not, but who is in "American culture," whatever that may mean. There are people who are not citizens who impress me as very "American" and there are citizens who impress me as not very "American"). For some purposes, it may be easier to draw the boundaries of the United States as a geographical space on a map and then look at how different sorts of people use that space, i.e., what they do there and what they get from that space (e.g., import or export from it). In the case of Johnny and Janie in the science class, the two students are taking quite different things from the space.

If we start by talking about spaces, rather than "communities," we can then go on and ask to what extent the people interacting within a space, or some sub-group of them, do or do not actually form a community. That is, rather than assume a community at the outset, we can ask of given spaces whether or not the people interacting within them are communities and in what sense. The answer will be different in different cases. Even if the people interacting within a space do not constitute a community in any real sense, they still may get a good deal from their interactions with others and share a good deal with them. Indeed, some people interacting within a space may see themselves as sharing a "community" with others in that space, while other people view their interactions in the space differently. In any case, creating spaces wherein diverse sorts of people can interact is a leitmotif of the modern world (Gee 2000–2001; Gee 2003; Rifkin 2000).

I don't want to talk just about physical or geographical spaces. Just as people can enter a physical space like the United States, they can enter a virtual space like a web site or a chat room. People interacting with each other about a specific disease on a patient empowerment web site are in a virtual space together. There are spaces that are mixtures of the real and the virtual, such as a meeting in which some people are physically together in a room and others are interacting with the group via the Internet or over a video conferencing system. People who play chess with each other by sending moves via email or letters are interacting, at a distance, in a space created by email or the postal service. Modern technologies allow the creation of more and more spaces where people can enter and interact with others (and with objects and tools) at a distance. So when I talk about "spaces" I don't mean just physical spaces.

My goal, however, is not just or primarily to introduce this idea of spaces. Rather, it is to discuss a particular type of space that I will call an "affinity space." I will first define what I mean by a space generally and then define what I mean by an affinity space in particular. When I get to affinity spaces, I will argue that they capture one characteristically modern and important form of social affiliation, one that can fruitfully be compared and contrasted with other forms (Gee 2000–2001). I will define what I mean by a space through one concrete example, an example that also happens to be an affinity space. This will allow me to characterize what makes this example a space and then turn to what makes it an affinity space.

Before we start in earnest, let me take up two methodological questions. First, is the "So What?" question: How does my analysis matter for people interested in schooling and learning? I want to offer a new analytic lens with which to look at classrooms and other learning sites. Affinity spaces are an important form of social affiliation today, places where effective learning occurs (Gee 2003). They are a form with which young people today are particularly familiar. These young people are in a position to compare and contrast how learning works in such spaces and how it works in schools, not always to the credit of schools. I believe that educators ought to do the same.

I also believe that each of the features that I offer as definitive of an affinity space can be present in a school curriculum or not. Thus, these features can be used as a sort of checklist of how much a given classroom verges on being an affinity space or not. While not every reader will accept my value system in terms of which affinity spaces are a good, effective, and modern way to organize learning, nonetheless, the features of affinity spaces are similar to the core features that some educational reformers, on wholly other grounds, have argued are crucial for deep learning (e.g., Brown 1994; Brown, Collins, and Duguid 1989; diSessa 2000).

Finally, I believe that the notion of affinity spaces can do lots of the sorts of work we have asked the notion of a "community of practice" to do, but without some of the baggage that "community" carries. The notion of affinity spaces can lead us to ask some new questions about classroom learning or ask some old ones in new ways.

The second question concerns the empirical status of my analysis. I am not offering an empirical study of today's classrooms, many of which are returning to "skill-and-drill" and decontextualized content, as compared to affinity spaces. There are lots of empirical descriptions of different sorts of classrooms already available and readers can and should compare and contrast these to what I say about the particular affinity space I use as my key example below. My account offers a close analysis of the semiotic features of one particular affinity space so as to generate a general description of affinity spaces. In this sense, it is akin to a discourse analysis (see, e.g., Gee 1999, especially the material on validity in Chapter 5). Readers can check on the "trustworthiness" of my analysis by looking at and interacting with the materials I use as my data.

Of course, a next step from here would be to engage in research that compares affinity spaces and classrooms of different sorts at a micro-analytic level. But we cannot engage in such research until we have developed the analytical apparatus necessary for carrying out such research. This chapter is meant to contribute to that purpose.

Social spaces: *AoM*

To define what I mean by a space, I will use "real-time strategy" computer games as the basis for an illustrative example, using the game *Age of Mythology* ("AoM" for short) as a paradigmatic instance of such a game (see http://www.microsoft.com/games/ageofmythology/greek_home.asp). Computer and video games come in many different types (genres). They are usually long—they can take up to 50 or more hours in play in some cases—complex, and difficult. There are games where players roam around a virtual world solving problems and shooting or sneaking past enemies (e.g., *Return to Castle Wolfenstein*, *Metal Gear Solid*), games where they build simulated worlds or businesses and run them (e.g., *The Sims*, *RollerCoaster Tycoon*), games where they build, organize, and develop civilizations through historical time (e.g., *Civilization III*, *Rise of Nations*), games where they role-play a fantasy character making decisions that shape that character's life, skills, and personality (e.g., *The Elder Scrolls III: Morrowind*, *Baldur's Gate*), games that involve fast action, jumping, running, and shooting through a wealth of obstacles (e.g., *Mario Sunshine*, *Sonic Adventure*) and many more.

Players can play alone against the computer or with and against other human players. Whether they play alone or together, the enterprise is social since almost all players need to get and share information about the games in order to become adept at playing them. Furthermore, since many games involve building, interacting with, and progressively shaping a simulated world, they are not unlike some forms of cutting-edge science where scientists build simulations of complex systems like cells, ecological systems, weather systems, or the universe so that they can test various hypotheses about relationships and emergent properties within the system.

In a real-time strategy game of the sort we will look at here (i.e., *Age of Mythology*), the player builds buildings, settlements, towns, and/or cities for a given "civilization," using workers to collect gold, farm land, cut wood, and hunt animals to gain the necessary resources for building and sustaining his or her civilization. As the player builds various types of buildings, he or she can use the buildings to construct or train different types of warriors and military apparatus, as well as other types of actors such as priests or scientists (e.g., in *AoM* one can a use a Temple to gain mythological figures, an Academy to train Hoplites, an Archery Range to train archers, a Stable to train cavalry, a Fortress to train heroes, a Dock to build various types of boats, a Town Center to get more villagers, etc., through many other choices).

Eventually, the player goes off with his or her "army" to fight one or more other players (real people or the computer) who have also been building up their civilizations during the same time. If the player waits too long, the opponent may be too strong, if the player does not take enough time to build up properly, he or she may be too weak to fight well. Timing is important and so are the decisions about what and where to build (and there are always a great many options).

In *AoM* the "civilizations" one can play are ancient Greeks, Romans, or Norse, building buildings from these ancient civilizations and eventually gaining, for example, various types of Greek soldiers, heroes, military apparatus, and mythological figures to fight other civilizations. On the other hand, in *Galactic Battlegrounds* (a *Star Wars* game), the "civilizations" one can play are the Trade Federation, Gungans, Royal Naboo, Rebel Alliance, Galactic Empire, or Wookies— all groups from the *Star Wars* universe. In *Galactic Battlegrounds*, the buildings, soldiers, heroes and apparatus are all specific to one of these groups. For each "civilization" in this game there are over 160 choices about what to build or train— each choice having consequences for the other choices one makes. This is typical of the level of complexity in real-time strategy games.

Now I will define a space step-by-step. To define any space, we need first to start with some *content*, something for the space to be "about." Whatever gives the space some content, I will call a *generator*. In the case of real-time strategy games, one of the generators of the content is, of course, an actual game like *AoM*.

Such games offer up a characteristic set of multi-modal signs (words, images, graphs, etc.) to which people can give specific sorts of meanings and with which they can interact in various ways. We have seen some of these above: "civilizations," warriors and heroes, buildings, and real-time competition. In a cooking club, the cookbooks and shared recipes are generators.

Once we have one or more generators, we have some content, something for the space to be "about." Given this content, we can look at the space in two different ways. First, we can look at it directly in terms of *content,* i.e., what signs does it have and how are they organized. Second, we can look at it in terms of how people *interact* with that content or with each other over that content.

The same distinction can be made for a painting. We can view a painting as content, that is, as a work of art designed in a certain way. Notice that content always brings up the issue of design, since someone has to design the content. Or we can view the painting in terms of how people react to, use, or interact with the painting and with each other over the painting. To say of a Monet painting that "It is made up of a myriad of pastel dabs" or "It depicts a hayfield in the early morning light" is to comment on its content (and the design of that content). To say that the painting "Makes people feel they are present in the field" or that "Most people appreciate the painting best when they stand at a fair distance from it" or that "People strongly disagree in terms of how realistic they think the painting is" is to comment on how people interact with the painting or with each other over the painting.

We have already seen above some of the content in *AoM* and other real-time strategy games. If we point out that in such games there are trees, farms, and gold that can be collected and used as resources with which to build buildings, we are talking about the content of the space. Indeed, this is just part of the basic content of all real-time strategy games.

On the other hand, people actually play real-time strategy games in the world. Different players use different strategies. People sometimes play such games alone and sometimes with other people on the Internet. They may also talk to other players about such games and read magazines and Internet sites devoted to them. When we talk about how people play such games and how they organize their own behaviors and their interactions with other people in regard to real-time strategy games, we are talking about the space in interactional terms.

To take a content view of the space of real-time strategy games is to ask about the design of such games. To take an interactional view of the space of real-time strategy games is to ask about the ways in which people organize their thoughts, beliefs, values, actions, and social interactions in relation to the signs made available in such games.

What is wonderful about computer and video games is that people can inter-act so directly with the content of the game. In a real-time strategy game, a vir-tual "citizen" goes out and farms or collects wood. But the human player manipulates the virtual citizen—i.e., moves him or her to the farm or the for-est. Here content and interaction come directly together, because the virtual char-acter is part of the content of the game, but the manipulation of the character is an interaction made by the human player. Of course, interaction goes much further than this, however, since people can interact with the game and each other in regard to the game in a myriad of different ways.

Let us say, then, that every space has a "content organization" (that is, how its content is designed or organized) and an "interactional organization" (namely, how people organize their thoughts, beliefs, values, actions, and social interac-tions in regard to those signs and their relationships). The content organiza-tion of a game emerges from the work of designers. The interactional organization emerges from people's actions and interactions with and over the space (in this case, AoM) as these begin to take on some (however loose) regularity or patterning.

And, of course, the acts of people helping to form the interactional organ-ization of the space as a set of social practices and typical identities can rebound on the acts of those helping to design the content of the space, since the design-ers must react to the pleasures and displeasures of the people interacting with the content they have designed. At the same time, the acts of those designing the content rebound on the acts of those helping to organize the interaction organ-ization as a set of social practices and identities, since that content shapes and transforms (though by no means fully determines) those practices and identities.

But one more thing is needed to define a space, namely one or more *portals* that people can use to enter the space (remember, it's a type of space, not a group of people). A portal is anything that gives access to the content and to ways of interacting with that content, by oneself or with other people.

For AoM, there are a number of different portals. The disk on which the game comes, slipped into a computer so that one can play the game by oneself, is one such portal. An Internet site on which a player can play the game against other players is another portal. An Internet site in which players discuss the game or download content about the game is another portal. The strategy guide for AoM, which one can purchase (a book replete with information about the game, rec-ommended strategies, and a complete walkthrough of the single-player cam-paign), is also a portal. Each of these portals gives one access to the signs (content) used in AoM. There are many others.

Portals are places where people get access to interact with the content gen-erators generate. But portals can also be or become generators themselves (though this is not always the case), if they allow people to add to content or change the content other generators have generated. So, for example, it is common on game sites on the Internet for fans to offer others new maps on which to play the game or to allow others to access recordings of games they have played to learn how to play better. In this case, the portal is also a generator, since people (who are not the game's designers) are making new content for others.

Likewise, a generator can also be a portal, though this need not always be the case (think of a teacher's manual that students never see; it is a generator, but not a portal, for the students, though it is a portal for the teacher). As we have said, the game disk is both a generator (it offers up the signs or content) and a portal, since one can use it to play the game and thereby interact with the signs.

Let us pause a moment to ask how these terms would apply to a science classroom and what sorts of questions they would lead us to ask. We first have to ask what is the generator that is the (or a) source of the sign system (content) that the classroom is interacting with. In the classroom, this might be the text-book, the teacher, lab materials, and/or other things. For analytical purposes, we could restrict ourselves to one generator or consider several at a time. We also might (or might not) find that the textbook functions as the core or original generator.

We can then ask questions about how the signs generated by the generator are designed to communicate a certain content. This is to ask about the content organization of the space. In turn, we can ask questions about what sorts of thoughts, values, deeds, interactions, and identities people take up in regard to these signs. This is to ask about the interactional organization of the space.

We can also ask questions about how the content and interactional organ-izations reflexively shape each other, if indeed they do, i.e., how does the content (and its design) shape thought, deed, and practice and how do thought, deed, and practice shape and re-shape (re-design) content (e.g., Does the teacher rethink the content based on student beliefs, actions, and interactions? Do new editions of the textbook change, based on changing beliefs, values, and practices? Do new generators or revisions of old ones change people's thoughts, deeds, and interactions?).

We can also ask about portals, that is, what gives students access to inter-actions with the signs, either by themselves or with others. The generator is often a portal (e.g., the textbook), but there are other portals, as well. For exam-ple, one portal may be small group discussions, another might be question and answer sessions between the teacher and the class, another might be lab work. Of course, we would want to know who uses each portal and how, as well as the ways in which the portal shapes thought and interaction.

Finally, we can ask whether a generator is also a portal. Of course, if the students have a textbook and use it, this generator is also a portal. However, as mentioned earlier, if the teacher is following a teacher's manual that the students never see, this is a generator that is not, in fact, a portal for the students (though it is for the teacher). And, we can ask, as well, if portals ever become themselves also generators. For example, can students through, say, their group work on a project change the sign system (content) with which the class is interacting in any serious way? Can they add new signs, subtract signs, or change the relationship among the signs that the class is interacting with? If so, the portal of the group project is also a generator; otherwise it is not.

Let me hasten to add that it is degrees that are often of most importance here, not simply binary distinctions. We really want to know, for instance, how strong a generator a given portal is, not just whether it is one or not (perhaps, it is a very weak one). We want to know whether content organization and interactional organization reflexively shape each other in strong or weak ways, not just whether they do or not.

Affinity spaces

I want now to turn to a particular type of space that I will call an "affinity space." Affinity spaces are a particularly common and important form today in our high-tech new-capitalist world. It is instructive to compare affinity spaces to the sorts of spaces that are typical in schools, which usually do not have the features of affinity spaces. As previously noted, this comparison is particularly important because many young people today have lots of experience with affinity spaces and, thus, have the opportunity to compare and contrast their experiences with these to their experiences in classrooms.

Let's return to *Age of Mythology*. The core generator for *AoM* as a space (remember this is a sub-space of the larger real-time strategy game space) is, of course, the game itself. Its content organization is typical of real-time strategy games, a form that has been shaped quite strongly by the demands, pleasures, and displeasures of players. This is true not only over time, as real-time strategy games change in response to player reactions, but also in the present. Games like *AoM* offer players (sometimes repeated) "patches" over the Internet to correct problems of many sorts players have discovered. Thus, this core generator is continually updated; the content organization is continually transformed by the interactional organization of the space.

The portals to *AoM* as a space are, of course, the game (single-player and multi-player), but also strategy guides, official web sites and fan web sites. These portals, as we will see below, are also all fairly strong generators, too, adding to and changing the relationships among the signs generated by the *AoM* core generator (i.e., the game).

To define *AoM* as not just a space, but also an affinity space, I want to look at just one of its portals, namely the web site *AoM* Heaven (http://AoM.heavengames.com), a fan produced web site. It would take several hundred pages to print this site out (not counting its many links to other sites) and it is updated every day. Some of the many things one can access from this site are:

- **The latest news** about *AoM*, the company that made the game, what players are doing, and when and where they can play games against each other;
- **Polls** that take votes on various questions and issues (e.g., "Have you played any custom scenarios for *AoM*?," "What do you think is the most useful classical age myth unit?," or "What aspect of the Norse culture impresses you most?");
- **Previews and reviews** of *AoM* and other real-time strategy games;
- **Interviews** with people about *AoM* and related matters;
- **Forums** (discussion groups) to which one can contribute, each devoted to a different topic germane to *AoM*, including general discussions, strategy, the new expansion pack, technical issues, scenario design, mythology, clan discussions (a clan is a group that plays together), and other topics;
- **Links** to other sites of interest to people interested in *AoM* or other real-time strategy games;
- **Ladder forums** that give the rankings and scores of players who play against others on the Internet;
- **FAQs** (frequently asked questions) that explain various aspects of the game and give players help with the game;
- **Strategy guides and walkthroughs** for "newbies" (new players);
- **General information about and pictures of** a new expansion of *AoM* that will appear soon (*Titans X-Pack*);
- **Game information** which gives technical details and statistics about all aspects of the game (e.g., how long it takes to build each type of building);
- **Images** from the game and artwork, including art by fans, inspired by the game;
- **Downloads** of many different sorts, including new maps and scenarios made by players, recorded instances of multi-player games, and even improvements players have made to different parts of the game's "AI" (artificial intelligence), for example, improvements to the "AI" used

on maps with a lot of water or even programs players can use to adjust the AI in different ways each time they play the game.

This portal to the *AoM* space has a set of features that are definitive of what I will call an "affinity space." I describe each of these features below. Together they constitute a definition of an affinity space. Let me make it clear here, though, that what people have an affinity with (or for) in an affinity space is not first and foremost the other people using the space, but the endeavor or interest around which the space is organized, in this case the real-time strategy game *AoM*. This is why the sorts of romantic notions of people bonding to each other that are carried by the term "community" do not apply here. In affinity spaces people "bond" first and foremost to an endeavor or interest and secondarily, if at all, to each other. We do not have to see an affinity space as an all or nothing thing. Rather, we can say that any space that has more of these features than another is more of an affinity space than the other or is closer to being a paradigmatic affinity space. The features defining an affinity space (eleven in all)— as these are exemplified by *AoM*—are as follows:

1 **Common endeavor, not race, class, gender, or disability, is primary.** In an affinity space, people relate to each other primarily in terms of common interests, endeavors, goals, or practices, not primarily in terms of race, gender, age, disability, or social class. These latter variables are backgrounded, though they can be used (or not) strategically by people if and when they choose to use them for their own purposes. This feature is particularly enabled and enhanced in *AoM* Heaven because people enter this and other *AoM* portals with an identity (and name) of their own choosing. They can make up any name they like and give any information (fictional or not) about themselves they wish to. This identity need not—and usually does not—foreground the person's race, gender, age, disability, or social class.

2 **Newbies and masters and everyone else share common space.** This portal does not segregate newcomers ("newbies") from masters. The whole continua of people from new to experienced, from unskilled to highly skilled, from minorly interested to addicted, and everything in-between, is accommodated in the same space. They each can get different things out of the space—based on their own choices, purposes, and identities— and still mingle with others as they wish, learning from them when and where they choose (even "lurking" on advanced forums where they may be too unskilled to do anything but listen in on the experts). Affinity

spaces may have portals where people with more expertise are segregated from people with less (e.g., players usually choose who they will play against on multi-player game sites in terms of their level of expertise), but they also have ones where such segregation does not occur.

3 **Some portals are strong generators.** The portal allows people to generate new signs and relationships among signs for the AoM space. That is, the portal is also a major generator. Fans create new maps, new scenarios for the single-player and multi-player games, adjust or redesign the technical aspects of the game, create new artwork, and even give tutorials on mythology as it exists in the game or outside the game world.

4 **Content organization is transformed by interactional organization.** Based on what the players do and say on sites like AoM Heaven, the core original generator (the game) is changed via patches, new content, and new expansions offered by the company that makes the game. That is, the content of AoM as a space is transformed by the actions and interactions of players acting and interacting on sites like AoM Heaven.

5 **Encourages intensive and extensive knowledge.** The portal encourages and enables people who use it to gain and spread both intensive knowledge and extensive knowledge. They can readily develop and display specialized knowledge (intensive knowledge), in one or more areas, for example, learning how to tweak the game's AI and advising others in this area. At the same time, the portal encourages and enables people to gain a good deal of broader, less specialized, knowledge about many aspects of the space (extensive knowledge), which they share with a great many others who use the portal or otherwise use the AoM space. Intensive knowledge is specialized, extensive knowledge is less specialized, broader, and more widely shared. This creates people who share lots of knowledge, but each has something special to offer.

6 **Encourages individual and distributed knowledge.** The portal also encourages and enables people to gain both individual knowledge (stored in their heads) and to learn to use and contribute to distributed knowledge. Distributed knowledge is knowledge that exists in other people, material on the site (or links to other sites), or in mediating devices (various tools, artifacts, and technologies) and to which people can connect or "network" their own individual knowledge. Such knowledge allows people to know and do more than they could on their own. People are encouraged and enabled to act with others and with various mediating devices (e.g., level editors, routines for tweaking the AI of the

game, strategy guides, etc.) in such a way that their partial knowledge and skills become part of a bigger and smarter network of people, information, and mediating devices.

7   **Encourages dispersed knowledge.** The portal also encourages and enables people to use dispersed knowledge, that is knowledge that is not actually at the site itself, but at other sites or in other spaces. For example, the portal enables and encourages people to learn about mythology in general, including mythological facts and systems that go well beyond AoM as a game. Much of this information is not directly in the AoM Heaven site, but on other sites it links to or in books or movies the site will mention or review. When a space utilizes dispersed knowledge it means that its distributed knowledge exists in a quite wide and extensive network. When knowledge is dispersed in a space, the space does not set strict boundaries around the areas from which people will draw knowledge and skills.

8   **Uses and honors tacit knowledge.** The portal encourages, enables, and honors tacit knowledge—that is, knowledge players have built up in practice, but may not be able to explicate fully in words. This knowledge may be about how to play the game, how to design new maps and scenarios for the game, how to form a forum party, or a great many other things. Players pass on this tacit knowledge via joint action when they interact with others via playing the game with them or interacting with them in other spaces. At the same time, the portal offers ample opportunities for people, if they wish, to try to (learn to) articulate their tacit knowledge in words, for example, when they contribute to a forum on technical matters like how to design good maps.

9   **Many different forms and routes to participation.** People can participate in AoM Heaven or other portals to the AoM space in many different ways and at many different levels. People can participate peripherally in some respects, centrally in others; patterns can change from day to day or across larger stretches of time.

10 **Lots of different routes to status.** A portal like AoM Heaven, and the AoM space as a whole, allows people to achieve status, if they want it (and they may not), in many different ways. Different people can be good at different things or gain repute in a number of different ways. Of course, playing the game well can gain one status, but so can organizing forum parties, putting out guides, working to stop hackers from cheating in the multi-player game, posting to any of a number of differ-

ent forums, or a great many other things.

11 **Leadership is porous and leaders are resources.** A space like AoM and a portal to it like AoM Heaven do not have "bosses." They do have various sorts of leaders—people who design the game or the website—though we have seen that the boundary between leader and follower is vague and porous, since players can generate content for the game or site. Leadership in an affinity space like AoM comprises designers, resourcers (i.e., they resource other people), and enablers (teachers). They don't and can't order people around or create rigid, unchanging, and impregnable hierarchies.

Affinity spaces are common today in our global high-tech new capitalist world (Gee 2000–2001; Rifkin 2000). Many businesses organize such spaces for their customers. For example, the company that makes the Saturn car creates web sites and activities (e.g., social gatherings, newsletters, Internet chat rooms) around which its customers can identify as Saturn owners. Businesses in the new capitalist era (Gee, Hull, & Lankshear 1996) of cross-functional, dispersed, networked teams and project-based work often seek to create affinity spaces to motivate, organize, and resource their "partners" (they seek to avoid the term "worker" which implies a traditional boss-worker relationship in which one party "bosses" the other).

Social activists, whether their cause be ecology, anti-globalization, or school vouchers, also often organize themselves and others in terms of affinity spaces (Beck 1999). In such spaces, people who may share little else, and even differ dramatically on other issues, affiliate around their common cause and the practices associated with espousing it via affinity spaces that have most or all of the above eleven features. Fans of everything (e.g., movies, comic books, television shows, video games, various life-style choices, etc) create and sustain affinity spaces of which AoM is, of course, just one of a great many. Scientists in many different disciplines network with colleagues, funders, policy makers, and the public across the globe via networks of activities, newsletters and other sorts of texts, web sites, computer bulletin boards, e-mail chains, and conferences in ways that have progressively taken on more and more of the features of an affinity space.

There have, of course, been educators who have sought to create in classrooms something akin to an affinity space. The best known efforts here, perhaps, are Ann Brown and Joseph Campione's classroom "learning communities" (see Brown 1994 for an overview). In my view, these "communities"—at least as they were described in idealized ways—could better be viewed as affinity spaces than as communities in any traditional sense. They involved the use of multiple sorts of mediating devices (computers and email to outside experts), distributed knowledge as students worked in teams with those mediating devices, dispersed knowledge as students drew on expertise outside the classroom, and intensive knowledge as individual students chose to "major" in some aspect of the curriculum and help other students in that respect, and extensive shared knowledge as the students taught each other different parts of a common curriculum (via the jigsaw method, Aronson 1978).

Since at times the students taught each other, they took over some of the teacher's traditional leadership role. These classrooms incorporated a number of the remaining eleven features above, as well, and one could imagine this process (largely stopped today by our return to "the basics" and skill-and-drill under the new accountability and testing agenda) going much further (to the point where not all students would actually be in the classroom together face-to-face each day).

However, if we compare the eleven features of an affinity group to most classrooms today, we usually find that the classroom either does not have a given feature or has it much more weakly than a prototypical affinity space. In classrooms, the common endeavor (that which they are supposed to have affinity with) is often unclear (e.g., "science," "doing school," "school-science," etc.) to the students, and race, class, gender, and disability are often much more foregrounded than they are in an affinity space. Furthermore, race, class, gender, and disability are often much less flexible in classrooms and serve much less as resources students can use strategically for their own purposes.

In classrooms, students are segregated by things like grade level, ability, and skills more often than they are mixed together across the whole continuum of these. Even in heterogeneous grouping the differences are small compared to the differences one can find and access in an affinity space. For example, I myself am light years away from being able to understand how to program anything that would modify the AI of a computer game, yet I can access such information and the people connected to it at AoM Heaven (and did so and actually learned a lot).

In classrooms, portals are rarely strong generators where students both interact with the signs that constitute the content of the classroom instruction and are able to modify, transform, and add to them, as well. Furthermore, rarely is the core generator (e.g., the text book or the curriculum guide) modified ("patched") in an ongoing way based on student desires, pleasures, displeasures, actions, and interactions.

In classrooms, students are encouraged to gain pretty much the same knowledge across the board, knowledge which is often extensive and not intensive, or some students are encouraged and enabled to gain intensive knowledge, but others are not. Furthermore, when some students do gain intensive knowledge, they are rarely allowed to teach the teacher and the other students. In an affinity space, no one is stopped from gaining intensive knowledge because someone else thinks they are "my low students" or "struggling." Classrooms are rarely spaces where everyone shares lots of interests and knowledge (extensive knowledge), while each person has his or her own intensive knowledge to add as a potential resource for others.

Classrooms tend to encourage and reward individual knowledge stored in the head, not distributed knowledge. They don't often allow students to network with each other and with various tools and technologies and be rewarded for doing so, rather than to be rewarded for individual achievement. Further, classrooms tend to narrowly constrain where students can gain knowledge, rather than utilize widely dispersed knowledge. Furthermore, they rarely honor, or even acknowledge, for that matter, tacit knowledge that cannot (at least for now) be verbally articulated. In turn, they usually do a poor job in giving students help and practice with learning how to articulate such tacit knowledge, when and where it can be articulated (and it cannot always be articulated).

Classrooms usually do not have multiple routes to participation, engaging their students in different ways, to different levels, in different contexts. They usually do not have multiple routes to status, rather, students get A grades for narrow reasons, the same for all. Finally, in classrooms, leadership is not usually porous where it is, at times, hard to tell who is leading and who is following, where students sometimes lead and teachers follow, and where leadership is constituted by resourcing others and designing environments where they can learn on their own terms, rather than dictating what people "need" to do, believe, say, and write.

But, one may ask: "So what? What does it matter that schools don't use affinity spaces? Why should they?" At this point I can only state a hypothesis in answer to these questions. Young people today are confronted with and enter more and more affinity spaces. They see a different and arguably more powerful vision of learning, affiliation, and identity when they do so. Learning becomes both a personal and unique trajectory through a complex space of opportunities (i.e., a person's own unique movement through various affinity spaces over time) and a social journey as one shares aspects of that trajectory with others (who may be very different from oneself and inhabit otherwise quite different spaces) for a shorter or longer time before moving on. What these young people see in school may pale by comparison. It may seem to lack the imagination that infuses the non-school aspects of their lives (Gee 2003). At the very least, they may demand an argument for "Why school?"

CHAPTER 9

Reading, Specialist Language Development, and Video Games

Reading: A Trajectory Approach

Consider the situation of a child learning to read. What should our goal for this child be? On the face of it, the goal would seem to be that the child learn to decode print and assign basic or literal meanings to that print. But the situation is not that simple. We know from the now well-studied phenomenon of the "fourth-grade slump" (the phenomenon whereby many children, especially poorer children, pass early reading tests, but cannot read well to learn academic content later on in school) that the goal of early reading instruction has to be more forward looking than simple decoding and literal comprehension (American Educator 2003b; Chall, Jacobs, & Baldwin 1990; Snow, Burns, & Griffin 1998). The goal has to be that children learn to read early on in such a way that this learning creates a successful trajectory throughout the school years and beyond. Such a trajectory is based, more than anything else, on the child's being able to handle ever increasingly complex language, especially in the content areas (e.g., science and math), as school progresses. Children need to get ready for these increasing language demands as early as possible. It is as if school were more and more conducted in Greek as the grades increased: surely it would be better to be exposed to Greek as early as possible and not wait until school becomes the equivalent of advanced Greek.

Let's call this a "trajectory approach" to early reading. Such an approach has to look not only forwards, but backwards, as well. Early phonemic awareness and early home-based practice with literacy are the most important correlates with success in first grade, especially success in learning to read in the "decode and literally comprehend" sense (Dickinson and Neuman 2006). However, the child's early home-based oral vocabulary and early skills with complex oral language are the most important correlates for school success—not just in reading, but in the content areas—past the first grade, essentially for the rest of schooling (Dickinson and Neuman 2006; Senechal, Ouellette, and Rodney 2006). Thus, a child's oral language development is key to a successful trajectory approach to reading, that is, an approach that seeks to make a long-term school-based reader of academic content (and that's what's in the high school biology textbook, for example). It is the key to avoiding, even eradicating, the fourth-grade slump.

However, we must pause here, for two reasons. First, I am aware that some people consider the sort of academic language that is in a biology textbook simply to be exclusionary jargon attempting to colonize people's everyday cultural identities in the name of a rationalist positivism. I am as interested as anyone in the politics of schooling and science (Gee 1990, 1996), but in this chapter my concern is with the fate of children who get to high school and cannot cope with that textbook and related language practices. In my view, it does no good to rail against the language of the textbook, but, nonetheless, leave the textbook and other instances of academic language behind as the litmus test of school success— the "revolution" had better be total or children will suffer for adults' politics. For the record, while I fully concede that aspects of academic language have been used historically for little more than exclusion and the creation of status—and that textbooks should be replaced with texts more specially tied to activities and practices—by and large I believe that specialist varieties of language, when used appropriately, are critically and integrally tied to the functioning (workings) of specialist domains (whether this be an academic area or real-time-strategy video games) and access to these domains is severely limited without such language and related representational systems.

Second, I must pause because we are on the brink of what could be a major misunderstanding. Decades of research in linguistics has shown that every normal child's early language and language development are just fine (Chomsky 1986; Labov 1979; Pinker 1994). Every child, under normal conditions, develops a perfectly complex and adequate oral language, the child's "native language" (and, of course, sometimes children develop more than one native language). It never happens, under normal conditions—and normal here covers a very wide array of variation—that, in acquiring English, say, little Janie develops relative clauses, but little Johnnie just can't master them. That, is, of course, in a way, a surprising fact, showing that the acquisition of one's native language is not particularly a matter of ability or skill.

But, when I say, that children's early oral language—vocabulary and skills with complex language—are crucial correlates of success in school, correlates that show up especially after the child has learned to decode in first grade (one hopes)—I am not talking about children's everyday language, the sort of language that is equal for everyone. I am talking about their early preparation for language that is not "everyday," for language that is "technical" or "specialist" or "academic" (Gee 2004; Schleppegrell 2004). I will refer to people's "everyday" language—the way they speak when they are not speaking technically or as specialists of some sort—as their "vernacular style." I will refer to their language when they are speaking technically or as a specialist as a "specialist style" (people eventually can have a number of different specialist styles, connected to different technical, specialist, or academic concerns).

An Example

Let me give an example of what I am talking about, both in terms of specialist language and in terms of getting ready for later complex specialist language demands early on in life. Kevin Crowley has talked insightfully about quite young children developing what he calls "islands of expertise." Crowley and Jacobs (2002, p. 333) define an island of expertise as "any topic in which children happen to become interested and in which they develop relatively deep and rich knowledge." They provide several examples of such islands, including a boy who develops relatively deep content knowledge and a "sophisticated conversational space" (p. 335) about trains and related topics after he is given a Thomas the Tank Engine book.

Now consider a mother talking to her four-year-old son, who has an island of expertise around dinosaurs (the transcript below is adapted from Crowley and Jacobs 2002, pp. 343–344). The mother and child are looking at a replica fossil dinosaur and a replica fossil dinosaur egg. The mother has a little card in front of her that says:

- Replica of a Dinosaur **Egg**
- From the Oviraptor
- Cretaceous Period
- Approximately 65 to 135 million years ago
- The actual fossil, of which this is a replica, was found in the Gobi desert of Mongolia

In the transcript below, "M" stands for the mother's turns and "C" for the child's:

C: This looks like this is a **egg**.

M: Ok well this . . . That's exactly what it is! How did you know?

C: Because it looks like it.

M: That's what it says, see look *egg, egg* . . . . . . Replica of a dinosaur *egg*. From the oviraptor.

M: Do you have a . . . You have an oviraptor on your game! You know the **egg** game on your computer? That's what it is, an oviraptor.

M: And that's from the Cretaceous period. And that was a really, really long time ago. . . .

M: And this is . . . the hind claw. What's a hind claw? (pause) A claw from the back leg from a velociraptor. And you know what . . .

C: Hey! Hey! A velociraptor!! I had that one my [inaudible] dinosaur.

M: I know, I know and that was the little one. And remember they have those, remember in your book, it said something about the claws . . .

C: No, I know, they, they . . .

M: Your dinosaur book, what they use them . . .

C: Have so great claws so they can eat and kill . . .

M: They use their claws to cut open their prey, right.

C: Yeah.

This is a language lesson, but not primarily a lesson on vernacular language, though, of course, it thoroughly mixes vernacular and specialist language. It is a lesson on specialist language. It is early preparation for the sorts of academic (school-based) language children see ever increasingly, in talk and in texts, as they move on in school. It is also replete with "moves" that are successful language teaching strategies, though the mother is no expert on language development.

Let's look at some of the features this interaction has as an informal language lesson. First, it contains elements of non-vernacular, specialist language, for example: "**replica** of a dinosaur egg"; "from the **oviraptor**"; "from the **Cretaceous period**"; "the **hind claw**"; "their **prey**." The specialist elements here are largely vocabulary, though such interactions soon come to involve elements of syntax and discourse associated with specialist ways with words as well.

Second, the mother asks the child the basis of his knowledge: Mother: "How did you know? Child: Because it looks like it." Specialist domains are almost always "expert" domains that involve claims to know and evidence for such claims. They are in Shaffer's (2005) sense "epistemic games."

Third, the mother publicly displays reading of the technical text, even though the child cannot yet read: "That's what it says, see look *egg, egg* . . . . . . Replica of a dinosaur *egg*. From the oviraptor." This reading also uses print to confirm the child's claim to know, showing one way this type of print (descriptive information on the card) can be used in an epistemic game of confirmation.

Fourth, the mother relates the current talk and text to other texts the child is familiar with: "You have an oviraptor on your game! You know the **egg** game on your computer? That's what it is, an oviraptor"; "And remember they have those, remember in your book, it said something about the claws." This sort of intertextuality creates a network of texts and modalities (books, games, and computers), situating the child's new knowledge not just in a known background, but in a system the child is building in his head.

Fifth, the mother offers a technical-like definition: "And this is . . . the hind claw. What's a hind claw? (pause) A claw from the back leg from a velociraptor." This demonstrates a common language move in specialist domains, that is, giving relatively formal and explicit definitions (not just examples of use).

Sixth, the mother points to and explicates hard concepts: "And that's from the Cretaceous period. And that was a really, really long time ago." This signals to the child that "Cretaceous period" is a technical term and displays how to explicate such terms in the vernacular (this is a different move than offering a more formal definition).

Seventh, she offers technical vocabulary for a slot the child has left open: Child: "Have so great claws so they can eat and kill . . . Mother: They use their claws to cut open their **prey**, right." This slot and filler move co-constructs language with the child, allowing the child to use language "above his head" in ways in line with Vygotsky's concept of a "zone of proximal development" (Vygotsky 1978).

Informal Specialist-Language Lessons

So, let's be clear about two things. This is an informal language lesson. And such lessons involve more than language and language learning. They involve teaching and learning cognitive (knowledge) and interactional moves in specialist domains. Finally, they involve teaching and learning identities, the identity of being the sort of person who is comfortable with specialist, technical knowing, learning, and language. Of course, even formal language lessons—in learning a second language, for instance, in school—should involve language, knowledge, interaction, and identity. But this is not formal teaching, it is informal teaching, the teaching equivalent of informal learning. Let's call such informal language lessons, with the sorts of features I have just discussed, "informal specialist-language lessons" (ironically, they are informal formal-language lessons!).

Along with all we know about "emergent literacy" at home (Dickinson and Neuman 2006; Emergent Literacy Project, n.d.; Gee 2004), informal specialist language lessons are crucial if one wants to take a trajectory view of reading development. They are pre-school pre-reading activities that lead to early reading instruction that avoids the fourth-grade slump. Of course, the reading instruction the child receives at school must continue these language lessons, informally and formally. It must place reading from the get go in the context of learning specialist styles of language, just as this mother has done. This, however, raises the issue of what happens for children who come to school without such informal specialist language teaching, and, often, too, without other important aspects of emergent literacy. My view is that this cannot be ignored. We cannot just move on to reading instruction of the "decode and literally comprehend" sort as if it just doesn't matter that these children have missed out on early specialist language learning. For these children language teaching needs to start, start with a vengeance, and sustain itself throughout the course of reading instruction. And, again, remember, this claim has nothing to do with teaching "standard" English or ESL, *per se:* it is a claim that even native speakers of vernacular standard English need language learning to prepare for specialist varieties of language.

Specialist Language in Popular Culture

There are other things, beyond such informal specialist-language lessons, which can prepare children for the increasing language demands of school in the content areas. And we can see one of these if we look, oddly enough, at young people's popular culture today. Something very interesting has happened in children's popular culture. It has gotten very complex and it contains a great many practices that involve highly specialist styles of language (Gee 2004). Young children often engage with these practices socially with each other in informal peer learning groups. And, some parents recruit these practices to accelerate their children's specialist language skills (with their concomitant thinking and interactional skills).

For example, consider the text below, which appears on a *Yu-Gi-Oh* card. *Yu-Gi-Oh* is a card game involving quite complex rules. It is often played face-to-face with one or more other players, sometimes in formal competitions, more often informally, though it can be played as a video game, as well.

Armed Ninja
Card-Type: Effect Monster
Attribute: Earth | **Level:** 1
Type: Warrior
ATK: 300 | **DEF:** 300
Description: FLIP: Destroys 1 Magic Card on the field. If this card's target is face-down, flip it face-up. If the card is a Magic Card, it is destroyed. If not, it is returned to its face-down position. The flipped card is not activated.
Rarity: Rare

The "description" is really a rule. It states what moves in the game the card allows. This text has little specialist vocabulary (though it has some, e.g., "activated"), unlike the interaction we saw between mother and child above, but it contains complex specialist syntax. It contains, for instance, three straight conditional clauses (the "if" clauses). Note how complex this meaning is: First, if the target is face down, flip it over. Now check to see if it is a magic card. If it is, destroy it. If it isn't, return it to its face-down position. Finally, you are told that even though you flipped over your opponent's card, which in some circumstances would activate its powers, in this case, the card's powers are not activated. This is "logic talk," a matter, really, of multiple related "either-or," "if-then" propositions.

Note, too, that the card contains a bunch of classificatory information (e.g., type, attack power, defense power, rarity). All of these linguistic indicators lead the child to place the card in the whole network or system of *Yu-Gi-Oh* cards—and there are over 10, 000 of them—and the rule system of the game itself. This is complex system thinking with a vengeance.

I have watched seven year old children play *Yu-Gi-Oh* with great expertise. They must read each of the cards. They endlessly debate the powers of each card by constant contrast and comparison with other cards when they are trading them. They discuss and argue over the rules and, in doing so, use lots of specialist vocabulary, syntactic structures, and discourse features. They can go to web sites to learn more or to settle their disputes. If and when they do so, here is the sort of thing they will see:

> *8-CLAWS SCORPION* Even if "8-Claws Scorpion" is equipped with an Equip Spell Card, its ATK is 2400 when it attacks a face-down Defense Position monster.
>
> The effect of "8-Claws Scorpion" is a Trigger Effect that is applied if the condition is correct on activation ("8-Claws Scorpion" declared an attack against a face-down Defense Position monster.) The target monster does not have to be in face-down Defense Position when the effect of "8-Claws Scorpion" is resolved. So if "Final Attack Orders" is active, or "Ceasefire" flips the monster face-up, "8-Claws Scorpion" still gets its 2400 ATK.
>
> The ATK of "8-Claws Scorpion" becomes 2400 during damage calculation. You cannot chain "Rush Recklessly" or "Blast with Chain" to this effect. If these cards were activated before damage calculation, then the ATK of "8-Claws Scorpion" becomes 2400 during damage calculation so those cards have no effect on its ATK. (Accessed at http://www.upperdeckentertainment.com/yugioh/en/default.aspx)

I don't really think I have to say much about this text. It is, in every way, a specialist text. In fact, in complexity, it is far above the language many young children will see in their school books, until they get to middle school at best and, perhaps, even high school. But, seven year old children deal and deal well with this language (though *Yu-Gi-Oh* cards—and, thus, their language—are often banned at school).

Let's consider a moment what *Yu-Gi-Oh* involves. First and foremost it involves what I will call "lucidly functional language." What do I mean by this? The language on *Yu-Gi-Oh* cards, web sites, and in children's discussions and debates is quite complex, as we have seen, but it relates piece by piece to the rules of the game, to the specific moves or actions one takes in the domain. Here language—complex specialist language—is married closely to specific and connected actions. The relationship between language and meaning (where meaning here is the rules and the actions connected to them) is clear and lucid. The *Yu-Gi-Oh* company has designed such lucid functionality because it allows them to sell 10, 000 cards connected to a fully esoteric language and practice. It directly banks on children's love of mastery and expertise. Would that schools did the same. Would that the language of science in the early years of school was taught in this lucidly functional way. It rarely is.

So we can add "lucidly functional language" to our informal specialist-language lessons as another foundation for specialist language learning, one currently better represented in popular culture than in school. And, note, too, here that such lucidly functional language is practiced socially in groups of kids as they discuss, debate, and trade, with more advanced peers often playing a major educative role. They learn to relate oral and written language of a specialist sort, a key skill for specialist domains, including academic ones at school. At the same time, many parents (usually, but not always, more privileged parents) have come to know how to use such lucidly functional language practices—like *Yu-Gi-Oh* or *Pokémon*, and, as well as we will see below, digital technologies like video games— to engage their children in informal specialist-language lessons.

My son Sam (aged 10 at the time) told me during 2006 that he felt he had learned to read by playing *Pokémon*, another card and video game. He was referring to the games he had on the Nintendo Game Boy, games he played *before* he could read, when he was five. His mother or I sat with him and read for him— the game requires much reading. In a real sense, Sam did learn to read by playing *Pokémon*. But he learned to read, then, in a context that was also early preparation for dealing with complex specialist language, a type of language he would see later in school, though, for the most part, only after the first couple of grades. Of course, he learned other sorts of reading in other activities, as well. I am not arguing for early literacy that is focused on only specialist languages.

Of course, the sorts of lucidly functional language practices and informal specialist-language lessons that exist around *Yu-Gi-Oh* or *Pokémon* could exist in school—even as early as first grade—to teach school valued content. But they don't. Here the creativity of capitalists has far outrun that of educators.

Situated Meaning and Video Games

So far we have talked about two underpinnings of a trajectory view of reading: informal (and later formal) specialized-language lessons and practices built around lucidly functional language. Why are these underpinnings for reading, in a trajectory sense? Because they place reading development in the context of specialized language development, which is the basis for being able to keep up with the ever increasing demands for learning content in school via complex technical and academic varieties of language (and, indeed, other sorts of technical representations used in areas like science and math).

Now we move to a third underpinning of a trajectory view of reading development. Lots of research has shown, for years now, that, in areas like science, a good many students with good grades and passing test scores cannot actually use their knowledge to solve problems (Gardner 1991). For example, many students who can write down for a test Newton's Laws of Motion cannot correctly say how many forces are acting on a coin when it is tossed into the air and at the top of its trajectory—and, ironically, this is something that can be deduced from Newton's Laws (Chi, Feltovich, & Glaser 1981). They cannot apply their knowledge, because they don't see how it applies—they don't see the physical world and the language of physics (which includes mathematics) in such a way that it is clear to them how that language applies to that world.

There are two ways to understand words. I will call one way "verbal" and the other way "situated" (Gee 2004). A situated understanding of a concept or word implies the ability to use the word or understand the concept in ways that are customizable to different specific situations of use (Brown, Collins, & Duguid 1989; Clark 1997; Gee 2004). A general or verbal understanding implies an ability to explicate one's understanding in terms of other words or general principles, but not necessarily an ability to apply this knowledge to actual situations. Thus, while verbal or general understandings may facilitate passing certain sorts of information-focused tests, they do not necessarily facilitate actual problem solving.

Let me quickly point out that, in fact, all human understandings are, in reality, situated. What I am calling verbal understandings are, of course, situated in terms of other words and, in a larger sense, the total linguistic, cultural, and domain knowledge a person has. But they are not necessarily situated in terms of ways of applying these words to actual situations of use and varying their applications across different contexts of use. Thus, I will continue to contrast verbal understandings to situated ones, where the latter implies the ability to do and not just say.

Situated understandings are, of course, the norm in everyday life and in vernacular language. Even the most mundane words take on different meanings in different contexts of use. Indeed, people must be able to build these meanings on the spot in real time as they construe the contexts around them. For instance, people construct different meanings for a word like "coffee" when they hear something like "The coffee spilled, get the mop" versus "The coffee spilled, get a broom" versus "The coffee spilled, stack it again." Indeed, such examples have been a staple of connectionist work on human understanding (Clark 1993).

Verbal and general understandings are top-down. They start with the general, that is with a definition-like understanding of a word or a general principle associated with a concept. Less abstract meanings follow as special cases of the definition or principle. Situated understandings generally work in the other direction, understanding starts with a relatively concrete case and gradually rises to higher levels of abstraction through the consideration of additional cases.

The perspective I am developing here, one that stresses knowledge as tied to activity and experiences in the world before knowledge as facts and informa-tion and knowledge as situated as opposed to verbal understandings, has many implications for the nature of learning and teaching, as well as for the assessment of learning and teaching (Gee 2003a). Recently, researchers in several different areas have raised the possibility that what we might call "game-like" learning through digital technologies can facilitate situated understandings in the context of activity and experience grounded in perception (Games-to-Teach 2003; Gee 2003b, 2005; McFarlane, Sparrowhawk & Heald 2002; Squire 2003).

Before I discuss game-like learning in some depth, let me point out a phe-nomenon that all gamers are well aware of. This phenomenon gets to the heart and soul of what situated meanings are and why they are important: Written texts associated with video games are not very meaningful, certainly not very lucid, unless and until one has played the game. Let me take the small booklet that comes with the innovative shooter game *Deus Ex* to use as an example of what I mean by saying this. In the twenty pages of this booklet, there are 199 bolded refer-ences that represent headings and sub-headings (to take one small randomly chosen stretch of headings and subheadings that appears at the end of page 5 and the beginning of page 6: **Passive Readouts, Damage Monitor, Active Augmentation & Device Icons, Items-at-Hand, Information Screens, Note, Inventory, Inventory Management, Stacks, Nanokey ring, Ammunition**). Each of these 199 headings and subheadings is followed by text that gives information relevant to the topic and relates it to other information throughout the booklet. In addi-tion, the booklet gives 53 keys on the computer keyboard an assignment to some function in the game, and these 53 keys are mentioned 82 times in the booklet in relation to the information contained in the 199 headings and subheadings. So, though the booklet is small, it is just packed with concise and relatively technical information.

Here is a typical piece of language from this booklet:

> Your internal nano-processors keep a very detailed record of your condition, equipment and recent history. You can access this data at any time during play by hitting F1 to get to the Inventory screen or F2 to get to the Goals/Notes screen. Once you have accessed your information screens, you can move between the screens by clicking on the tabs at the top of the screen. You can map other information screens to hotkeys using Settings, Keyboard/Mouse (p. 5).

This makes perfect sense at a literal level, but that just goes to show how worth-less the literal level is. When you understand this sort of passage at only a lit-eral level, you have only an illusion of understanding, one that quickly disappears as you try to relate the information in this passage to the hundreds of other important details in the booklet. Such literal understandings are precisely what children who fuel the fourth-grade slump have. First of all, this passage means nothing real to you if you have no situated idea about what "nano-processors," "condition," "equipment," "history," "F1," "Inventory screen," "F2," "Goals/Notes screen" (and, of course, "Goals" and "Notes"), "information screens," "clicking," "tabs," "map," "hotkeys," and "Settings, Keyboard/Mouse" mean in and for playing games like *Deus Ex.*

Second, though you know literally what each sentence means, they raise a plethora of questions if you have no situated understandings of this game or games like it. For instance: Is the same data (condition, equipment, and history) on both the Inventory screen and the Goals/Notes screen? If so, why is it on two different screens? If not, which type of information is on which screen and why? The fact that I can move between the screens by clicking on the tabs (but what do these tabs look like, will I recognize them?) suggests that some of this information is on one screen and some on the other. But, then, is my "condition" part of my Inventory or my Goals/Notes—doesn't seem to be either, but, then, what is my "condition" anyway? If I can map other information screens (and what are these?) to hotkeys using "Setting, Keyboard/Mouse," does this mean there is no other way to access them? How will I access them in the first place to assign them to my own chosen hotkeys? Can I click between them and the Inventory screen and the Goals/Notes screens by pressing on "tabs"? And so on and so forth—20 pages is beginning to seem like a lot—remember there are 199 different headings under which information like this is given at a brisk pace through the booklet.

Of course, all these terms and questions can be defined and answered if you closely check and cross-check information over and over again through the little booklet. You can constantly turn the pages backwards and forwards. But once you have one set of links relating various items and actions in mind, another drops out just as you need it and you're back to turning pages. Is the booklet poorly written? Not at all. It is written just as well or poorly, in fact, like a myriad of school-based texts in the content areas. It is, outside the practices in the domain from which it comes, just as meaningless, however much one could garner literal meanings from it with which to verbally repeat things or pass tests.

And, of course, too, you can utter something like "Oh, yea, you click on F1 (function key 1) to get to the Inventory screen and F2 to get to the Goals/Notes screen" and sound like you know something. The trouble is this: in the actual game, you can click on F2 and meditate on the screen you see at your leisure. Nothing bad will happen to you. However, you very often have to click on F1 and do something quickly in the midst of a heated battle. There's no "at your leisure" here. The two commands really don't function the same way in the game—they actually mean different things in terms of embodied and situated action—and they never really *just* mean "click F1, get screen." That's their general meaning, the one with which you can't really do anything useful until you know how to spell it out further in situation-specific terms in the game.

When you can spell out such information in situation-specific terms in the game, then the relationships of this information to the other hundreds of pieces of information in the booklet become clear and meaningful. And, of course, it is these relationships that are what really count if you are to understand the game as a system and, thus, play it at all well. *Now* you can read the book if you need to piece in missing bits of information, check on your understandings, or solve a particular problem or answer a particular question you have.

When I first read this booklet before playing *Deus Ex* (and at that time I had played only one other shooter game before, a very different one)—yes, I, an overly academic baby-boomer, made the mistake of trying to read the book first, despite my own theories about reading—I was sorely tempted to put the game on a shelf and forget about it. I was simply overwhelmed with details, questions, and confusions. When I started the game I kept trying to look up stuff in the booklet. But none of it was well-enough understood to be found easily without continually re-searching for the same information. In the end, you have to just actively play the game and explore and try everything. Then, at last, the booklet makes good sense, but, then too, you don't need it all that much any more.

So now I would make just the same claim about any school content domain as I have just said about the video game *Deus Ex*: specialist language in any domain—games or science—has no situated meaning—thus no lucid or applicable meaning—unless and until one has "played the game," in this case the game of science, or, better put, a specific game connected to a specific science. Such "games"("science games") involve seeing the language and representations associated with some part of science in terms of activities I have done, experiences I have had, images I have formed from these, and interactional dialogue I have heard from and had with peers and mentors outside and inside the science activities. School is too often about reading the manual before you get to play the game, if you ever do. This is not harmful for kids who have already played the game at home, but is disastrous for those who have not.

Good video games don't just support situated meanings for the written materials associated with them in manuals and on fan web sites—and these are copious—but also for all language within the game. The meaning of such language is always associated with actions, experiences, images, and dialogue. Furthermore, players get verbal information "just in time," when they can apply it or see it applied, or "on demand," when they feel the need for it and are ready for it—and then, in some cases, games will give the player walls of print (e.g., in *Civilization IV*).

So my claim: what I will call "game-like learning" leads to situated and not just verbal meanings. In turn, situated meanings make specialist language lucid, easy, and useful. In order to demonstrate what I am talking about—and what I mean by "game-like learning"—I will turn first to an application of what I consider game-like learning that uses no real game, then to a game made explicitly to enhance school-based learning, then to a game-like simulation, built into an overall learning system.

Game-Like Learning: Andy diSessa

Andy diSessa's (2000) work is a good example, in science education, of building on and from specific cases to teach situated understandings. diSessa has successfully taught children in sixth grade and beyond the algebra behind Galileo's principles of motion by teaching them a specific computer programming language called Boxer.

The students write into the computer a set of discrete steps in the programming language. For example, the first command in a little program meant to represent uniform motion might tell the computer to set the speed of a moving object at one meter per second. The second step might tell the computer to move the object. And a third step might tell the computer to repeat the second step over and over again. Once the program starts running, the student will see a graphical object move one meter each second repeatedly, a form of uniform motion.

Now the student can elaborate the model in various ways. For example, the student might add a fourth step that tells the computer to add a value a to the speed of the moving object after each movement the object has taken (let us just say, for convenience, that a adds one more meter per second at each step). So now, after the first movement on the screen (when the object has moved at the speed of one meter per second), the computer will set the speed of the object at two meters per second (adding one meter), and, then, on the next movement, the object will move at the speed of two meters per second. After this, the computer will add another meter per second to the speed and on the next movement the object will move at the speed of three meters per second. And so forth forever, unless the student has added a step that tells the computer when to stop repeating the movements. This process is obviously modeling the concept of acceleration. And, of course, you can set a to be a negative number instead of a positive one, and watch what happens to the moving object over time instead.

The student can keep elaborating the program and watch what happens at every stage. In this process, the student, with the guidance of a good teacher, can discover a good deal about Galileo's principles of motion through his or her actions in writing the program, watching what happens, and changing the program. What the student is doing here is seeing in an embodied way, tied to action, how a representational system that is less abstract than algebra or calculus (namely, the computer programming language, which is actually composed of a set of boxes) "cashes out" in terms of motion in a virtual world on the computer screen.

An algebraic representation of Galileo's principles is more general than what diSessa's students have been exposed to, basically it is a set of numbers and variables that do not directly tie to actions or movements as material things. As diSessa points out, algebra doesn't distinguish effectively "among motion ($d = rt$), converting meters to inches ($i = 39.37 \times m$), defining coordinates of a straight line ($y = mx$) or a host of other conceptually varied situations." They all just look alike. He goes on to point out that "[d]istinguishing these contexts is critical in learning, although it is probably nearly irrelevant in fluid, routine work for experts," who, of course, have already had many embodied experiences in using algebra for a variety of different purposes of their own.

Once learners have experienced the meanings of Galileo's principles about motion in a situated and embodied way, they have understood one of the situated meanings for the algebraic equations that capture these principles at a more abstract level. Now these equations are beginning to take on a real meaning in terms of embodied understandings. As learners see algebra spelled out in more such specific material situations, they will come to master it in an active and critical way, not just as a set of symbols to be repeated in a passive and rote manner on tests.

diSessa does not actually refer to his work with Boxer as game-like learning, though some people pushing the design of actual games for learning have been inspired, in part, by his approach to learning and science education (Gee 2003b). And, indeed, Boxer produces simulations that are, in many respects, game like and certainly can entice from learners the sort of flexible consideration of possibilities that play can inspire. However, I turn now to an actual game designed to enhance situated learning that goes beyond verbal understandings.

Supercharged!

Kurt Squire and his colleagues (Squire, Barnett, Grant, & Higginbotham 2004; see also Jenkins, Squire, & Tan, in press; Squire 2003) have worked on a computer game called "*Supercharged!*" to help students learn physics. Players use the game to explore electromagnetic mazes, placing charged particles and controlling a ship which navigates by altering its charge. The game play consists of two phases: planning and playing. Each time players encounter a new level, they are given a limited set of charges that they can place throughout the environment, enabling them to shape the trajectory of their ship.

Each level contains obstacles common to electromagnetism texts. These include points of charge, planes of charge, magnetic planes, solid magnets, and electric currents. Each of these obstacles affects the player's movement according to laws of electromagnetism. The goal of the game is to help learners build stronger *intuitions* for electromagnetic concepts based on perceptual and embodied experiences in a virtual world where these concepts are instantiated in a fairly concrete way.

Squire, Barnett, Grant, and Higginbotham (2004) report some results that are part of a larger design experiment examining the pedagogical potential of *Supercharged!* in three urban middle school science classrooms with a good deal of cultural diversity. In this study, the experimental group outperformed the control group on conceptual exam questions. Post-interviews revealed that both experimental and control students had improved their understanding of basic electrostatics. However, there were some qualitative differences between the two groups. The most striking differences were in students' descriptions of electric fields and the influence of distance on the forces that charges experience. For example, one girl during her post interview described an electric field as:

> The electric[ity] goes from the positive charge to the negative charge like this [drawing a curved line from a positive charge to a negative charge]. I know this because this is what it looked like in the game and it was hard to move away or toward it because the two charges are close together so they sort of cancel each other out (p. 510).

It appears that students in the experimental group were recalling experiences and challenges that were a part of the game play of *Supercharged!*, whereas students in the control group relied more on their ability to memorize information. Playing *Supercharged!* enabled some students to confront their everyday (mis)conceptions of electrostatics, as they played through levels that contradicted these conceptions.

But Squire and his colleagues also acknowledge that the teachers came to realize that students were initially playing *Supercharged!* without a good deal of critical reflection on their play. The teachers then created log sheets for their students to record their actions and make predictions, which reinforced the purpose of the activity and encouraged students to detect patterns in their play. Later the teachers provided even more structure, using the projector to display game levels, encouraging the class to interpret the events happening on screen and make predictions about how they thought the simulation would behave. This added structure lent more focus to students' play and allowed the teacher to prompt deeper reflection on game play.

So we see, here, then a good example of what I would call a "post-progressive pedagogy" (Gee 2004), a well-integrated combination of embodied immersion in rich experience (the game wherein the learner virtually enters an electromagnetic field) and scaffolding and guidance, both through the design of the game itself as a learning resource and through teachers making the game part of a larger coherent learning activity system. The argument is not for games in and of themselves, but as part and parcel of a well-designed learning activity system.

Augmented by Reality: Madison 2020

In their Madison 2020 project, David Shaffer and Kelly Beckett at the University of Wisconsin have developed, implemented, and assessed a game-like simulation that simulates some of the activities of professional urban planners (Beckett & Shaffer 2004; see also Shaffer, Squire, Halverson, & Gee 2005). I call this a "game" because learners are using a simulation and role-playing new identities, but, of course, it is not a "game" in any traditional sense.

Shaffer and Beckett's game is not a stand-alone entity, but is used as part of a larger learning system. Shaffer and Beckett call their approach to game-like learning "augmented by reality," since a virtual reality—i.e., the game simulation—is augmented or supplemented by real-world activities, in this case further activities of the sort in which urban planners engage. Minority high-school students in a summer enrichment program engaged with Shaffer and Beckett's urban planning simulation game and, as they did so, their problem solving work in the game was guided by real-world tools and practices taken from the domain of professional urban planners.

As in the game *SimCity*, in Shaffer and Beckett's game students make land use decisions and consider the complex results of their decisions. However, unlike in *SimCity*, they use real-world data and authentic planning practices to inform those decisions. The game and the learning environment in which it is embedded is based on David Shaffer's theory of *pedagogical praxis*, a theory that argues that modeling learning environments on authentic professional practices—in this case, the practices of urban planners—enables young people to develop deeper understandings of important domains of inquiry (Shaffer 2004).

Shaffer and Beckett argue that the environmental dependencies in urban areas have the potential to become a fruitful context for innovative learning in ecological education. While ecology is, of course, a broader domain than the study of interdependent urban relationships, cities are examples of complex systems that students can view and with which they are familiar. Thus, concepts in ecology can be made tangible and relevant.

Cities are composed of simple components, but the interactions among those components are complex. Altering one variable affects all the others, reflecting the interdependent, ecological relationships present in any modern city. For example, consider the relationships among industrial sites, air pollution, and land property values: increasing industrial sites can lead to pollution that, in turn, lowers property values, changing the dynamics of the city's neighborhoods in the process.

Shaffer and Beckett's Madison 2020 project situated student experience at a micro level by focusing on a single street in their own city (Madison, Wisconsin):

> Instead of the fast-paced action required to plan and maintain virtual urban environments such as *SimCity*, this project focused only on an initial planning stage, which involved the development of a land use plan for this one street. And instead of using only a technological simulation [i.e., the game, JPG], the learning environment here was orchestrated by authentic urban planning practices. These professional practices situated the planning tool in a realistic context and provided a framework within which students constructed solutions to the problem. (pp. 11–12).

The high school students Shaffer and Beckett worked with had volunteered for a ten hour workshop (run over two weekend days) focused on city planning and community service. At the beginning of the workshop, the students were given an urban planning challenge: They were asked to create a detailed re-design plan for State Street, a major pedestrian thoroughfare in Madison, a street quite familiar to all the students in the workshop. Professional urban planners must formulate plans that meet the social, economic, and physical needs of their communities. To align with this practice, students received an informational packet addressed to them as city planners. The packet contained a project directive from the mayor, a city budget plan, and letters from concerned citizens providing input about how they wished to see the city redesigned. The directive asked the student city planners to develop a plan that, in the end, would have to be presented to a representative from the planning department at the end of the workshop.

Students then watched a video about State Street, featuring interviews with people who expressed concerns about the street's redevelopment aligned with the issues in the informational packet (e.g., affordable housing). During the planning phase, students walked to State Street and conducted a site assessment. Following the walk, they worked in teams to develop a land use plan using a custom-designed interactive geographic information system (GIS) called MadMod.

MadMod is a model built using Excel and ArcMap (ESRL 2003) that lets students assess the ramification of proposed land use changes.

MadMod—which is the "game" in the learning system—allows students to see a virtual representation of State Street. It has two components, a decision space and a constraint table. The decision space displays address and zoning information about State Street using official 2- or 3-letter zoning codes to designate changes in land use for property parcels on the street. As students made decisions about changes they wished to make, they received immediate feedback about the consequences of changes in the constraint table. The constraint table showed the effects of changes on six planning issues raised in the original information packet and the video: crime, revenue, jobs, waste, car trips, and housing. Following the professional practices of urban planners, in the final phrase of the workshop, students presented their plans to a representative from the city planning office.

MadMod functions in Shaffer and Beckett's curriculum like a game in much the same way *SimCity* does. In my view, video games are simulations that have "win states" in terms of goals players have set for themselves. In this case, the students have certain goals and the game lets them see how close or far they are from attaining those goals. At the same time, the game is embedded in a learning system that ensures that those goals and the procedures used to reach them are instantiations of the professional practices and ways of knowing of urban planners.

Shaffer and Beckett show, through a pre-interview/post-interview design, that students in the workshop were able to provide more extensive and explicit definitions of the term "ecology" after the workshop than before it. The students' explanations of ecological issues in the post-interview were more specific about how ecological issues are interdependent or interconnected than in the pre-interview. Concept maps the students drew showed an increased awareness of the complexities present in an urban ecosystem. Thus, students appear to have developed a richer understanding of urban ecology through their work in the project.

One hundred percent of the students said the workshop changed the way they thought about cities and most said the experience changed the things they paid attention to when walking down a city street in their neighborhood. Better yet, perhaps, Shaffer and Beckett were able to show transfer: Students' responses to novel, hypothetical urban planning problems showed increased awareness of the interconnections among urban ecological issues. All these effects suggest, as Shaffer and Beckett argue, "that students were able to mobilize understanding developed in the context of the redesign of one local street to think more deeply about novel urban ecological issues" (p. 21).

Video Games and Situated Learning

Just as children today often see complex specialist language in their popular culture activities like *Yu-Gi-Oh*, they also encounter complex and deep learning in their commercial video games. Modern video games set up a learning situation that is situated in the sense that meanings are situated, as we have just seen, and in the sense that skills and concepts are learned in an embodied way that leads to real understanding. There is a reason for this: games place language and learning in a setting that fits very well with how the human mind is built to learn and think. Schools sometimes do not. This is why I have stressed game-like learning above in my discussions of diSessa's work, *Supercharged!*, and *Madison 2020*. Let me explicate what I mean, by reference to a sequence of ideas raised in Chapter 4 above. [The remaining paragraphs in this section repeat ideas advanced at the outset of Chapter 4 about the ways in which video games illuminate how the human mind works. In the present context this argument is embedded within a particular set of problems, however, and needs to be read with these problems in mind.]

As I noted in Chapter 4, video games are a relatively new technology, whose implications are many but so far by no means fully understood (Gee 2003b). Throughout modern history many scholars have viewed the human mind through lenses of technologies they thought worked like the mind. For Locke and Hume the mind was like a blank slate on which experience wrote ideas—invoking the technology of literacy. Much later, modern cognitive scientists argued that the mind worked like a digital computer, calculating generalizations and deductions via a logic-like rule system (Newell & Simon 1972). More recently, some cognitive scientists, inspired by distributed parallel-processing computers and complex adaptive networks, have argued that the mind works by storing records of actual experiences and constructing intricate patterns of connections among them (Clark 1989; Gee 1992). Whence, different pictures of the mind: mind as a slate waiting to be written on, mind as software, mind as a network of connections.

Human societies get better through history at building technologies that more closely capture some of what the human mind can do and getting these technologies to do mental work publicly. Writing, digital computers, and networks each allow us to externalize some functions of the mind. Video games are a new technology in much the same vein, even though it is not common to think of them this way. They are a new tool with which to think about the mind and through which we can externalize some of its functions. Video games of the kinds sampled throughout this book are what I referred to as "action-and-goal-directed preparations for, and simulations of, embodied experience."

To clarify the claim that games act like the human mind and are a good place to study and produce human thinking and learning, it is helpful to begin by briefly summarizing some recent research in cognitive science, (Bransford, Brown, & Cocking 2000). Consider, for instance, the remarks below [in the quotes below, the word "comprehension" means "understanding words, actions, events, or things"]:

> . . . comprehension is grounded in perceptual simulations that prepare agents for situated action (Barsalou, 1999a: p. 77)

> . . . to a particular person, the meaning of an object, event, or sentence is what that person can do with the object, event, or sentence (Glenberg, 1997: p. 3)

These remarks mean that human understanding is not primarily a matter of storing general concepts in the head or applying abstract rules to experience. Rather, humans think and understand best when they can imagine (simulate) an experience in such a way that the simulation prepares them for actions they need and want to take in order to accomplish their goals (Barsalou 1999b; Clark 1997; Glenberg & Robertson 1999).

Video games turn out to be the perfect metaphor for what this view of the mind amounts to, just as slates and computers were good metaphors for earlier views of the mind. To see this, let me now turn to a characterization of video games and then I will put my remarks about the mind and games together.

Video games usually involve a visual and auditory world in which the player manipulates a virtual character (or characters). They often come with editors or other sorts of software with which the player can make changes to the game world or even build a new game world. The player can make a new landscape, a new set of buildings, or new characters. The player can set up the world so that certain sorts of actions are allowed or disallowed. The player is building a new world, but is doing so by using and modifying the original visual images (really the code for them) that came with the game. One simple example of this is the way in which players can build new skateboard parks in a game like *Tony Hawk Pro Skater*. The player must place ramps, trees, grass, poles, and other things in space in such a way that players can manipulate their virtual characters to skate the park in a fun and challenging way.

Even when players are not modifying games, they play them with goals in mind, the achievement of which counts as their "win state" (and it's the existence of such win states that, in part, distinguishes games from simulations) These goals are set by the player, but, of course, in collaboration with the world the game designers have created (and, at least in more open-ended games, players don't just accept developers' goals, they make real choices of their own). Players must carefully consider the design of the world and consider how it will or will not facilitate specific actions they want to take to accomplish their goals.

One technical way that psychologists have talked about this sort of situation is through the notion of "affordances" (Gibson 1979). An "affordance" is a feature of the world (real or virtual) that will allow for a certain action to be taken, but only if it is matched by an ability in an actor who has the wherewithal to carry out such an action. For example, in the massive multiplayer game *World of WarCraft* stags can be killed and skinned (for making leather), but only by characters that have learned the Skinning skill. So a stag is an affordance for skinning for such a player, but not for one who has no such skill. The large spiders in the game are not an affordance for skinning for any players, since they cannot be skinned at all. Affordances are relationships between the world and actors.

Playing *World of WarCraft*, or any other video game, is all about such affordances. The player must learn to see the game world—designed by the developers, but set in motion in particular directions by the players, and, thus, co-designed by them—in terms of such affordances (Gee 2005). Broadly speaking, players must think in terms of "What are the features of this world that can enable the actions I am capable of carrying out and that I want to carry out in order to achieve my goals?"

So now, after our brief bit about the mind and about games, let's put the two together. The view of the mind I have sketched, in fact, argues, as far as I am concerned, that the mind works rather like a video game. For humans, effective thinking is more like running a simulation than it is about forming abstract generalizations cut off from experiential realities. Effective thinking is about perceiving the world such that the human actor sees how the world, at a specific time and place (as it is given, but also modifiable), can afford the opportunity for actions that will lead to a successful accomplishment of the actor's goals. Generalizations are formed, when they are, bottom up from experience and imagination of experience. Video games externalize the search for affordances, for a match between character (actor) and world, but this is just the heart and soul of effective human thinking and learning in any situation.

As a game player you learn to see the world of each different game you play in a quite different way. But in each case you see the world in terms of how it will afford the sorts of embodied actions you (and your virtual character, your surrogate body in the game) need to take to accomplish your goals (to win in the short and long run). For example, you see the world in *Full Spectrum Warrior* as routes (for your squad) between cover (e.g., corner to corner, house to house) because this prepares you for the actions you need to take, namely attacking without being vulnerable to attack yourself. You see the world of *Thief* in terms of light and dark, illumination and shadows, because this prepares you for the different actions you need to take in this world, namely hiding, disappearing into the shadows, sneaking, and otherwise moving unseen to your goal.

When we sense such a match, in a virtual world or the real world, between our way of seeing the world, at a particular time and place, and our action goals—and we have the skills to carry these actions out—then we feel great power and satisfaction. Things click, the world looks as if it were made for us. While commercial games often stress a match between worlds and characters like soldiers or thieves, there is no reason why other games could not let players experience such a match between the world and the way a particular type of scientist, for instance, sees and acts on the world (Gee 2004). Such games would involve facing the sorts of problems and challenges that type of scientist does and living and playing by the rules that type of scientist uses. Winning would mean just what it does to a scientist: feeling a sense of accomplishment through the production of knowledge to solve deep problems.

I have argued for the importance of video games as "action-and-goal-directed preparations for, and simulations of, embodied experience." They are the new technological arena—just as were literacy and computers earlier—around which we can study the mind and externalize some of its most important features to improve human thinking and learning. But games have two other features that suit them to be good models for human thinking and learning externalized out in the world. These two additional features are: a) they distribute intelligence via the creation of smart tools, and b) they allow for the creation of "cross functional affiliation," a particularly important form of collaboration in the modern world.

Consider first how good games distribute intelligence (Brown, Collins, & Duguid 1989). In *Full Spectrum Warrior*, the player uses the buttons on the controller to give orders to two squads of soldiers. The instruction manual that comes with the game makes it clear from the outset that players, in order to play the game successfully, must take on the values, identities, and ways of thinking of a professional soldier: "Everything about your squad," the manual explains, "is the result of careful planning and years of experience on the battlefield. Respect that experience, soldier, since it's what will keep your soldiers alive" (p. 2). In the game, that experience—the skills and knowledge of professional military expertise—is distributed between the virtual soldiers and the real-world player. The soldiers in the player's squads have been trained in movement formations; the role of the player is to select the best position for them on the field. The virtual characters (the soldiers) know part of the task (various movement formations) and the player must come to know another part (when and where to engage in such formations). This kind of distribution holds for every aspect of military knowledge in the game.

By distributing knowledge and skills this way—between the virtual characters (smart tools) and the real-world player—the player is guided and supported by the knowledge built into the virtual soldiers. This offloads some of the cognitive burden from the learner, placing it in smart tools that can do more than the learner is currently capable of doing by him or herself. It allows the player to begin to act, with some degree of effectiveness, before being really competent— "performance before competence." The player thereby eventually comes to gain competence through trial, error, and feedback, not by wading through a lot of text before being able to engage in activity. Such distribution also allows players to internalize not only the knowledge and skills of a professional (a professional soldier in this case), but also the concomitant values ("doctrine" as the military says) that shape and explain how and why that knowledge is developed and applied in the world. There is no reason why other professions—scientists, doctors, government officials, urban planners (Shaffer 2004)—could not be modeled and distributed in this fashion as a deep form of value-laden learning (and, in turn, learners could compare and contrast different value systems as they play different games).

Finally, let me turn to the creation of "cross-functional affiliation." Consider a small group partying (hunting and questing) together in a massive multiplayer game like *World of WarCraft*. The group might well be composed of a Hunter, Warrior, Druid, and Priest. Each of these types of characters has quite different skills and plays the game in a different way. Each group member (player) must learn to be good at his or her special skills and also learn to integrate these skills as a team member within the group as a whole. Each team member must also share some common knowledge about the game and game play with all the other members of the group—including some understanding of the specialist skills of other player types—in order to achieve a successful integration. So each member of the group must have specialist knowledge (intensive knowledge) and general common knowledge (extensive knowledge), including knowledge of the other member's functions.

Players—who are interacting with each other, in the game and via a chat system—orient to each other not in terms of their real-world race, class, culture, or gender (these may very well be unknown or if communicated made up as fictions). They must orient to each other, first and foremost, through their identities as game players and players of *World of WarCraft* in particular. They can, in turn, use their real-world race, class, culture, and gender as strategic resources if and when they please, and the group can draw on the differential real-world resources of each player, but in ways that do not force anyone into pre-set racial, gender, cultural, or class categories.

This form of affiliation—what I will call cross-functional affiliation—has been argued to be crucial for the workplace teams in modern "new capitalist" workplaces, as well as in modern forms of social activism (Beck 1999; Gee 2004; Gee, Hull, & Lankshear 1996). People specialize, but integrate and share, organized around a primary affiliation to their common goals and using their cultural and social differences as strategic resources, not as barriers.

So video games, though a part of popular culture, are, like literacy and computers, sites where we can study and exercise the human mind in ways that may give us deeper insights into human thinking and learning, as well as new ways to engage learners in deep and engaged learning. What we see here—and it's the same message we saw with *Yu-Gi-Oh* and *Pokémon* before—is that areas of popular culture are beginning to organize thinking and learning in efficacious ways. The practices they recruit—lucidly functional language, situated meanings, and embodied understandings leveraging experiences to build simulations (in the mind and outside it), distributed intelligence, and cross-functional collaboration—are all ones that don't need to be restricted to military games. They are key to deep understanding in any specialist domain, whether in school or at work.

Conclusions

I have argued that learning to read, if a child is not to be a victim of the fourth-grade slump, must involve early preparation for specialist, technical, and academic forms of language, forms that will be seen more and more both in speech and, most characteristically, in writing as school progresses. I have discussed some of the underpinnings of effective early preparation for such styles of language. These underpinnings have included "informal specialist-language lessons," "lucidly functional language" practices, and practices which facilitate "situated meanings." These practices are common in certain homes and in some of the popular cultural practices of children. They are, perhaps, less common in the early years of schooling. More generally, I have argued that a game-like approach to learning—by which I mean, not "having fun," but thinking inside of and with simulations in a situated and embodied way, an approach well represented even in commercial video games—holds out a good deal of potential as a foundation for learning that leads to problem solving and not just paper and pencil test passing.

CHAPTER 10

Games and Learning

Issues, Perils, and Potentials

Overview

This chapter is based on a report to the Spencer Foundation, which had funded a set of meetings on games and learning that brought together members of the University of Wisconsin Games and Professional Practice Simulations Group (GAPPS) [James Paul Gee, Rich Halverson, Elisabeth Hayes, David Shaffer, Constance Steinkuehler, Kurt Squire] and people from a variety of other institutions [Doug Church, Robin Hunicke, Henry Jenkins, Barry Joseph, Cory Ondrejka, Katie Salen, John Seely Brown, T. L. Taylor, Lauren Young, Eric Zimmerman].

In the context of this collection of essays, the chapter serves as a lengthy summation that brings together in one place the key themes, ideas, and issues addressed throughout. In so doing it revisits and repeats earlier parts of the book, putting them together in a "big picture." The chapter brings together much of what I have done during the past five years in a way that plots some new directions. Readers who fear repetition can skip the piece if they choose. Others who will appreciate a review of what has been covered in the chapters so far plus new material are invited to read it.

The chapter is organized in 14 sections and begins with a brief overview of these sections in sequence.

Section 1. *Video Games and Learning: A New Field:* Over the last few years a new field has emerged around video games and learning. This field is built around the premise that video games can engage players with deep and fruitful forms of learning in a highly motivating context.

Section 2. *Video Gaming as a New Literacy:* Video Gaming is a new "literacy." In gaming literacy consumption ("reading") inherently involves certain forms of production ("writing") on the part of the player.

Section 3. *Equity and Access Issues:* It is possible that gaming literacy—together with related digital literacies—will create yet another equity gap as richer children attain productive stances toward design and tech-savvy identities to a greater degree than poorer ones.

Section 4. *The Traditional Literacy Gap:* For schooling after the earliest grades, the traditional literacy gap is due to children's early preparation for language that is "technical" or "specialist" or "academic;" the sort of language that is tied to learning content (e.g., science) in school.

Section 5. *Complex Language in Popular Culture:* If complex, specialist ("hard") language is the problem in terms of the traditional literacy gap, it is an irony, perhaps, that popular culture today has gotten very complex and contains a great many practices that involve highly specialist styles of language.

Section 6. *Real Understanding: Another Gap:* Beyond the traditional literacy gap—the literacy divide between rich and poor—there is another gap in education. This is the gap between passing tests and really understanding. Lots of research has shown, for years now, that, in areas like science, a good many students, even those getting good grades and passing test scores, cannot actually use their knowledge to solve problems.

Section 7. Video Games and the Human Mind: Video games place language and learning in a setting that fits very well with how the human mind is built to learn and think according to contemporary research in the Learning Sciences.

Section 8. Distributed Intelligence and Cross-Functional Teams: Good video games have two other features that suit them to be good models for human thinking and learning externalized out in the world: A) they distribute intelligence via the creation of smart tools, and B) they allow for the creation of "cross functional affiliation," a particularly important form of collaboration in the modern world.

Section 9. Games as Games: So far much of what we have said about good video games and learning doesn't have much to do with the fact that they are games *per se*. However, it is a leading question for research whether these features will work for learning well, or as well, if they are not embedded in video games that have these features and, moreover, are good games. What are the features that make a video game a game and a good game?

A. Interactivity: In a video game, players make things happen; they don't just consume what the "author" (game designer) has placed before them.

B. Customization: In some games, players are able to customize the game play to fit their learning and playing styles, for example through different difficulty levels or the choice of playing different characters with different skills

C. Strong Identities: Good games offer players identities that trigger a deep investment on the part of the player.

D. Well-ordered problems: Problems in good games are well ordered. In particular, early problems are designed to lead players to form good guesses about how to proceed when they face harder problems later on in the game.

E. Games are pleasantly frustrating: Good games adjust challenges and give feedback in such a way that different sorts of players feel the game is challenging but doable and that their effort is paying off.

F. Games are built around the cycle of expertise: Good games create and support what has been called in the Learning Sciences the "cycle of expertise."

G. "Deep" and "Fair": These terms of art in the gaming community should become evaluative terms of learning in and out of schools.

Section 10. Mentoring: The traditional dichotomy between overt instruction/guidance, on the one hand, and agentful immersion in experience is a false one. Good video games offer lots of guidance without taking away immersion or ownership.

Section 11. Models and Modeling: If games are to be used in educational settings, there is another element beyond the role of mentors that needs to be stressed, namely the role of models and modeling in thinking, learning, and building knowledge. Models are basic to human play and science, as well as a great many other human activities.

Section 12. A New Crisis?: If we want to move games or game-like learning to school, will the structure of schooling have to change significantly or not? Can game-based learning speak to the looming crisis in American education that we are not producing enough innovation and creativity in school learning?

Section 13. Game Design and Education as a Design Science: Game design has another contribution to make to education: Game design as an enterprise is, at a deep level, similar to education seen as a "design science."

Section 14. Learning to Be: Deep learning—learning that can lead to real understanding, the ability to apply one's knowledge, and even to transform that knowledge for innovation—requires that we move beyond "learning about" and move to "learning to be." It requires that learning be not just about "belief" (what the facts are, where they came from, and who believes them) but also strongly about "design" (how, where, and why knowledge, including facts, are useful and adequate for specific purposes and goals).

1. Video Games and Learning: A New Field

Over the last few years a new field has emerged around video games and learning. This field is built around the premise that video games can engage players with deep and fruitful forms of learning in a highly motivating context. Good video games, it is argued, incorporate powerful learning principles—that is, they incorporate fruitful learning methods—into their designs.[1] These principles are, by and large, strongly supported by current research in the Learning Sciences, even though such research rarely focuses on their implementation via games.[2]

This claim is more about the process of learning than the content of what is learned. But, questions do need to be asked about content: What is the content being learned in commercial video games? What sorts of additional content should commercial games engage with? Can we build engaging games that deal with content typically connected to school (e.g., science) or workplaces (e.g., collaboration)?

Before thinking about content more narrowly (e.g., science or math), we should realize that learning in and around games involves content in a broad sense. As we have seen, video gaming has turned out—despite early predictions to the contrary—to be a deeply social enterprise. Even single-player gaming often involves young people in joint play, collaboration, competition, sharing, and a myriad of websites, chat rooms, and game guides, many of them produced by players themselves. But the social nature of gaming goes much further. Multiplayer gaming—games where small teams play against each other—is very popular among many young people. And massively-multiplayer games—games where thousands or millions of people play the same game—have recently (thanks, in part, to the tremendous success of *World of WarCraft*) become mainstream forms of social interaction across the globe. Such games are introducing new "states" or "communities" into the world. They are pioneering new forms of social capital, new forms of communities of practice, and new forms of social experimentation. In such games, people are learning new identities, new forms of social interaction, and even new values: a broad form of "content," indeed.[3]

There are, of course, different types of video games. And there are a number of different parameters along which games can be categorized. One such parameter is the distinction between so-called "casual games" like *Tetris* or *Bejeweled* and larger-scale games like *Half-Life* or *Rise of Nations*.[4] A better distinction here, perhaps, is between what we can call "problem games" and "world games," though the distinction is not air tight. Problem games focus on solving a given problem or class of problems (e.g. *Tetris*, *Diner Dash*), while world games simulate a wider world within which, of course, the player may solve many different sorts of problems (e.g., *Half-Life*, *Rise of Nations*). Classic early arcade games like *Super Mario* sit right at the border of this division. In either case, problem solving is crucial to gaming. In addition, in educational terms, we can think about chaining a series of problem games together to establish a larger curriculum.

Right at the outset, we face a choice about how to think about either learning in games or games in learning. As I have insisted throughout preceding discussion, games—like any other technology—do not have effects, good or bad, all by themselves. Rather, they have different effects depending on the different uses we make of them, the different contexts in which we place them, and the different social systems that are built around them. When we are thinking about learning, what we must be concerned with is not just the game in the box, but the social and learning system that is built around the game. We might call the combination of the game in the box and the social and learning system built around it, the "Game" (the capital "G" or "big G" game).[5] Even children playing *Pokémon* on a *Game Boy* often are part of a social system in their communities, at school, and on the Web, a system that shares information, strategies, and cheats about the game and engages in co-play. When educators recruit games for learning, they build distinctive social and learning systems (e.g., curricula, mentors, connections to other activities, social interactions, and so forth) around the games, and we need to assess the effectiveness of the whole system, not the game alone.

The emerging field of video games and learning is built around a set of key questions, some of which we list below. In these questions, the term "learning" is used broadly to cover both processes of learning (how learning is happening) and the content of what is being learned. The term "content" is also used broadly to cover information, principles, forms of sociality, and values. Finally, remember when we talk about "games," in the end, we always must move on to talk about "Games" (game plus context, social system, and learning system):

1   What sorts of learning are connected to commercial video games?

2   How does this learning relate to learning in other aspects of people's lives?

3   How can so-called "serious games" enhance learning for schools, out-of-school programs (e.g., libraries), communities, and workplaces? Does learning through serious games (e.g., science) transfer to other learning activities where games are not used?

4   Can and should the types of learning (the models of learning or the learning principles) incorporated into good video games—commercial or serious—be implemented without using games, but, rather, by using other technological and non-technological devices and practices? How tightly tied to games as a vehicle are these learning principles?

5   Can games and game-based learning lead to new and better models of assessment?

6   How do games and game-based learning relate to demographic categories (e.g., race, class, and gender) and will games and gaming narrow or widen current equity gaps in learning and knowledge in schools and society? How can they be used to narrow such gaps?

7   What are the impacts of video games and gaming on our global society? What are their impacts on young people's lives, identities, and ways of learning and thinking? What future impacts can we expect from gaming?

2. Video Gaming as a New Literacy

Video Gaming is a new "literacy." By "literacy" we mean any technology that allows people to "decode" meanings and produce meanings by using symbols.[6] The alphabet is obviously such a technology, the one that gives rise to print literacy. The digital technologies by which games are made are another example of such a technology. Game design involves a "code"—a multi-modal one made up of images, actions, words, sounds, and movements—that communicates to players because players (conventionally) interpret aspects of that design to have certain meanings.[7] For example, players of real-time strategy games know that a "map" betokens a land mass that the player can build on in certain characteristic ways in competition with other builders.

Every literacy involves some set of relationships between consumption (reading) and production (writing). Gaming literacy is interesting in this respect, since consumption inherently involves certain forms of production on the part of the player. Gamers, of course, decode and comprehend ("consume") game design when they react effectively to that design in order to play the game. However, that game design doesn't really come into full existence until players make decisions and take actions in the game (otherwise the first screen of the game just sits there). If the game is open-ended enough, different players, by making different choices and taking different actions, produce somewhat different games. They enact the game designers' game design in different ways, in a sense, they design the game with the designers. Thus, production is inherently part of consumption in gaming, because gaming inherently involves taking action.[8]

This "productive" aspect of game consumption—the way in which players consume (read) games in part by producing (writing) them—goes further. Games are rule systems wherein players attempt to achieve goals, sometimes goals set by the game's designers and sometimes goals of their own, and sometimes a mixture of the two. To achieve these goals, gamers must reflect on the design of a game and how features of that design can serve to enhance or retard the achievement of those goals through specific strategies and actions. In this sense, at some level, to play a game successfully, gamers must think like game designers; they must at least think about how elements of game design work to help or hinder their goals as players. Questions like "Why is this virtual world (or this part of it) designed in this way?" and "What does this suggest about possible effective strategies?" are part and parcel of playing and winning a game (or achieving goals in games).

Thus, consuming and producing—reading and writing—are closely connected in gaming as a literacy. It is interesting to speculate on the question of how much of this is true also for print literacy. People have, of course, argued that reading, in the case of print literacy, involves thinking like a writer, reflecting on the design of the text from the writer's perspective, at least when people are reading "critically." This productive stance is pretty much forced, to some degree, for video games as a literacy, though we think this stance can and should be carried much further through good game design and good learning systems built around games. It can be carried further as a way of making learners deeply reflective about the design properties—the very design grammars—of the games they play.

But production in the case of gaming literacy—already caught up in the act of consumption—has another level, as well. Games often come with the software by which they are made, thereby allowing players to modify them in small or large ways. Players can build new maps, levels, and scenarios, and sometimes even change the rules of play. They can even design whole new games. Through such "modding" players become designers in their own right at an even higher level. Games like *Tony Hawk* allow players to build (design) many aspects of the game, from skate boards and skaters through skate board parks to the rules of play (e.g., the tricks and the points assigned to them).

Games, thus, inherently involve, at several different levels, a design stance even for their consumption. We believe this stance is a form of thinking that is important for the modern world.[9] The modern world is full of (sometimes risky) complexly patterned systems (e.g. government, markets, high-tech workplaces, environments, global flows of people and capital, and so forth). Such systems need to be understood as not just isolated elements, additively combined, but as complex wholes made up of sets of interacting relationships that take on the characteristics of a designed system, thanks to either the design work of people or the workings of physical or natural processes. We believe also that this stance can be taken further for a variety of educational goals by building good learning systems (mentoring and curricula) around good video games.

Video games are only one activity today where young people are stressing production and not just consumption. Indeed, modern digital technologies are leading us to an anytime, anywhere, anyone world of production. Young people today are producing their own websites, blogs, animation, machinima, music, fan fiction, video—and many other things—in massive amounts. Many of these activities—most certainly including modifying or redesigning or even designing games—involve art, technology, computation, and content in a very integrated fashion. Such production may be, for many young people, an important route for the acquisition of skills that are crucial for our modern, global, high-tech world. However, issues of equity arise here and it is to these we now turn.

3. Equity and Access Issues

Any literacy—traditional or otherwise—raises equity questions. Which groups in society have full access to it? Which groups master it? What is the social and economic payoff for different groups who use the literacy? Gaming literacy, even in the act of consumption, as we have seen, involves learning to think like a designer, to reflect on the ways in which the grammar of a game's design invites or retards the goals, choices, and actions one wants or needs to take. This is a stance that we believe is the heart and soul of being "media literate" for any medium, including print literacy.[10] When it is carried to its full extent, it is the heart and soul of "critical media literacy" for any medium: thinking like a designer, reflecting on design grammars for different media.

All games involve content: they build a virtual world of a certain sort. Media literacy in regard to a game's content means, then, being reflectively aware of how that content (world) is itself designed to facilitate or retard goals, choices, strategies, and actions. If that content, were, say, a branch of science—for example a certain type of biology—then the player would have to consider the content of biology not as a set of passive facts, but as a domain of facts, information, values, and practices that enhance or retard certain sorts of goals, choices, strategies, and actions, namely those of a certain type of scientist. This, then, would be science not as inert content, but as a "way of life," as a way of being in the world, one that leads to certain sorts of values, goals, and actions rooted in a body of facts, information, and practices.

So one contribution gaming literacy can make to young people is to help develop this productive reflective stance about design and how design works to facilitate or defacilitate actions, goals, and strategies and to do so from the perspective of certain sorts of values and ways of being in the world (virtual or real). We have argued that video games inherently encourage such a stance and that this stance can be taken much further through good game design and good learning systems built around games. This stance becomes also a productive and reflective stance towards the content (world) of the game and, thus, holds out rich potential for encouraging proactive and metacritical engagements with content like science or social studies.

But there is another contribution that gaming literacy can make to young people. Video games and their concomitant practices and ways of thinking are a gateway, for some young people, to the development of "tech-savvy" skills and identities. By "tech-savvy" we mean a mind-set in which people are comfortable and confident with modern digital technologies, as well as with technical languages and practices (e.g., computers, mathematics, programming, modeling, graphs, etc.).

If young people think like designers, mod the games they play, and extend their technological interests both socially—on the Internet, for instance—and cognitively to related technologies (e.g., machinima, graphic design, web sites, simulations, AI, level design, audio, computer science, etc.), they are developing particularly modern skill sets and mind sets. At the same time, video game technologies meld art and technology in ways that, for young people, make these areas much more closely related than they are for some older people. And, indeed, such a melding is another important modern skill.

So gaming literacy can lead—we believe—to both a productive reflective stance on design (including content) and to the formation of tech-savvy identities. We think both of these are particularly important for today's global, high tech world. But these things don't just happen all by themselves. They require guidance, in one form or another, from adults and more masterful peers.

We know that we face an equity crisis in the case of traditional literacy: poorer children do not learn to read and write as well as richer children. It is possible that gaming literacy—together with related digital literacies—will create yet another equity gap as richer children attain productive stances toward design and tech-savvy identities to a greater degree than poorer ones. This new equity gap will involve skills and identities that may be crucially tied to success in the contemporary world.

Evidence is already building that this new gap is, indeed, being created.[11] This evidence is beginning to show that just giving young people access to technologies is not enough. They need—just as they do for books—adult mentoring and rich learning systems built around the technologies, otherwise the full potential of these technologies is not realized for these children.

At the same time, a crucial question arises: Can we speak to the new gap (the tech-savvy gap) in such a way that we also address the old gap, the gap in regard to traditional print-based literacy? Since this is a crucial question, let's discuss, for a moment, the nature of the traditional literacy gap.

4. The Traditional Literacy Gap

We have known for some decades now about the phenomenon known as "the fourth-grade slump."[12] This is a phenomenon whereby many children, especially poorer children, pass early reading tests, but cannot later on in school read well to learn academic content. They learn early on to read, but don't know how to read to learn when they face more complex language and content as school progresses.

Early phonemic awareness and early home-based practice with literacy are the most important correlates with success in first grade, especially success in learning to decode print.[13] However, the child's early home-based oral vocabulary and early oral skills with the sorts of complex language associated with books and school are the most important correlates for school success—not just for reading, but for learning in the content areas—past the first grade, essentially for the rest of schooling.[14]

Decades of research in linguistics has shown that every normal child's early language development of their native language is just fine.[15] But when we say that children's early oral language—vocabulary and skills with complex language— are crucial correlates of success in school, we are not talking about children's everyday language. We are talking about their early preparation for language that is not "everyday," but for language that is "technical" or "specialist" or "academic."[16]

Let us give an example of what it means to get children ready for later complex language demands early on in life. Kevin Crowley has talked insightfully about quite young children developing what he calls "islands of expertise," which he defines as "any topic in which children happen to become interested and in which they develop relatively deep and rich knowledge."[17] Consider, then, a mother talking to her four-year-old son, who has an island of expertise around dinosaurs.[18] The mother and child are looking at a replica fossil dinosaur and a replica fossil dinosaur egg. The mother has a little card in front of that says:

- Replica of a Dinosaur **Egg**
- From the Oviraptor
- Cretaceous Period
- Approximately 65 to 135 million years ago
- The actual fossil, of which this is a replica, was found in the Gobi desert of Mongolia

In the transcript below, "M" stands for the mother's turns and "C" for the child's:

C: This looks like this is a **egg**.
M: Ok well this . . . That's exactly what it is! How did you know?
C: Because it looks like it.
M: That's what it says, see look *egg, egg* . . . . . . Replica of a dinosaur *egg*. From the oviraptor.
M: Do you have a . . . You have an oviraptor on your game! You know the **egg** game on your computer? That's what it is, an oviraptor.
M: And that's from the Cretaceous period. And that was a really, really long time ago. . . .
M: And this is . . . the hind claw. What's a hind claw? (pause) A claw from the back leg from a velociraptor. And you know what . . .

C: Hey! Hey! A velociraptor!! I had that one my [inaudible] dinosaur.

M: I know, I know and that was the little one. And remember they have those, remember in your book, it said something about the claws . . .

C: No, I know, they, they . . .

M: Your dinosaur book, what they use them . . .

C: Have so great claws so they can eat and kill . . .

M: They use their claws to cut open their prey, right.

C: Yeah.

This is a language lesson, but not primarily a lesson on vernacular ("everyday") language, though, of course, it thoroughly mixes vernacular and specialist language. It is a lesson on specialist language. It is early preparation for the sorts of academic (school-based) language children see ever increasingly, in talk and in texts, as they move on in school. It is also replete with "moves" that are successful language teaching strategies, though the mother is no expert on language development.

What are some of these "moves"? First, the mother uses elements of non-vernacular, specialist language (for example: "**replica** of a dinosaur egg"; "from the **oviraptor**"; "from the **Cretaceous period**"; "the **hind claw**"; "their **prey**"). Second, she asks the child the basis of his knowledge ("How did you know?). Third, she publicly displays reading of the technical text, even though the child cannot yet read ("That's what it says, see look *egg, egg* . . . . . . Replica of a dinosaur *egg*. From the oviraptor"). Fourth, her reading of the text also uses print to confirm the child's claim to know, showing one way this type of print can be used in an epistemic game of confirmation.

Fifth, the mother relates the current talk and text to other texts the child is familiar with ("You have an oviraptor on your game! You know the **egg** game on your computer? That's what it is, an oviraptor"; "And remember they have those, remember in your book, it said something about the claws"). Sixth, she offers a technical-like definition ("And this is . . . the hind claw. What's a hind claw? (pause) A claw from the back leg from a velociraptor"). Seventh, she points to and explicates hard concepts ("And that's from the Cretaceous period. And that was a really, really long time ago"). This signals to the child that "Cretaceous period" is a technical term and displays how to explicate such terms in the vernacular (this is a different move than offering a more formal definition).

Eighth, the mother offers technical vocabulary for a slot the child has left open (Child: "Have so great claws so they can eat and kill . . . Mother: They use their claws to cut open their **prey**, right"). This slot and filler move co-constructs language with the child, allowing the child to use language "above his head" in ways in line with Vygotsky's concept of a "zone of proximal development."[19]

All of these moves on the part of the mother are a good example of what we mean by building a learning system—with adult mentoring—around a child's activities. Here the learning system is informal and built in the service of getting the child prepared for the complex language demands of books and school. It is just the sort of interaction that we believe it is crucial to build around not only texts but other technologies, including video games, as well.

5. Complex Language in Popular Culture

If complex, specialist ("hard") language is the problem in terms of the traditional literacy gap, it is an irony, perhaps, that popular culture today speaks to just this issue in an interesting and important way. Something quite fascinating has happened in children's popular culture. It has gotten very complex and it contains a great many practices that involve highly specialist styles of language.[20] Young children often engage with these practices socially with each other in informal peer learning groups. And, some parents recruit these practices to accelerate their children's specialist language skills (with their concomitant thinking and interactional skills).

For example, consider the text below, which appears on a *Yu-Gi-Oh* card. *Yu-Gi-Oh* is a card game—played either via physical cards or as a video game—involving quite complex rules:

Armed Ninja
Card-Type: Effect Monster
Attribute: Earth | **Level:** 1
Type: Warrior
ATK: 300 | **DEF:** 300
Description: FLIP: Destroys 1 Magic Card on the field. If this card's target is face-down, flip it face-up. If the card is a Magic Card, it is destroyed. If not, it is returned to its face-down position. The flipped card is not activated.
Rarity: Rare

This "description" is really a rule. It states what moves in the game the card allows. This text has little specialist vocabulary (though it has some, e.g., "activated"), unlike the interaction we saw between mother and child above, but it contains complex specialist syntax. It contains, for instance, three straight conditional clauses (the "if" clauses). Note how complex this meaning is: First, if the target is face down, flip it over. Now check to see if it is a magic card. If it is, destroy it. If it isn't, return it to its face-down position. Finally, you are told that even though you flipped over your opponent's card, which in some circumstances would activate its powers, in this case, the card's powers are not activated. This is "logic talk," a matter, really, of multiple related "either-or"/"if-then" propositions.

Note, too, that the card contains a bunch of classificatory information (e.g., type, attack power, defense power, rarity). All of these linguistic indicators lead the child to place the card in the whole network or system of *Yu-Gi-Oh* cards— and there are over 10, 000 of them—and the rule system of the game itself. This is complex system thinking with a vengeance. We should point out, as well, that as complex as the language is on this card—a card borrowed from a seven year old—the language on *Yu-Gi-Oh* web sites devoted to the game's rules is yet much more dense and complex. Here is but one example:

> ***8-CLAWS SCORPION*** Even if "8-Claws Scorpion" is equipped with an Equip Spell Card, its ATK is 2400 when it attacks a face-down Defense Position monster.
>
> The effect of "8-Claws Scorpion" is a Trigger Effect that is applied if the condition is correct on activation ("8-Claws Scorpion" declared an attack against a face-down Defense Position monster.) The target monster does not have to be in face-down Defense Position when the effect of "8-Claws Scorpion" is resolved. So if "Final Attack Orders" is active, or "Ceasefire" flips the monster face-up, "8-Claws Scorpion" still gets its 2400 ATK.
>
> The ATK of "8-Claws Scorpion" becomes 2400 during damage calculation. You cannot chain "Rush Recklessly" or "Blast with Chain" to this effect. If these cards were activated before damage calculation, then the ATK of "8-Claws Scorpion" becomes 2400 during damage calculation so those cards have no effect on its ATK. http://www.upperdeckentertainment.com/ yugioh/en/faq_card_rulings.aspx?first=A&last=C

Let's consider for a moment what *Yu-Gi-Oh* involves. First and foremost it involves what we can call "lucidly functional language." The language on *Yu-Gi-Oh* cards, web sites, and in children's discussions and debates is quite complex, as we have seen, but it relates piece by piece to the rules of the game, to the specific moves or actions one takes in the domain. Here language—complex specialist language—is married closely to specific and connected actions. The relationship between language and meaning (where meaning here is the rules and the actions connected to them) is clear and lucid. The *Yu-Gi-Oh* company has designed such lucid functionality because it allows the company to sell 10, 000 cards connected to a fully esoteric language and practice. It directly banks on children's love of mastery and expertise. Would that schools did the same. Would that the language of science in the early years of school was taught in this lucidly functional way. It rarely is.

And, note, too, here that such lucidly functional language is practiced socially in groups of kids as they discuss, debate, and trade cards, where interactions with more advanced peers often play a major educative role. They learn to relate oral and written language of a specialist sort, a key skill for specialist domains, including academic ones at school. At the same time, many parents (usually, but not always, more privileged parents) have come to know how to use such lucidly functional language practices—like *Yu-Gi-Oh* or *Pokémon*, or, as we will see below, video games—to engage their children in informal specialist-language lessons.

6. Real Understanding: Another Gap

Beyond the traditional literacy gap—the literacy divide between rich and poor— there is another gap in education, one that implicates even the understandings of more privileged children in school. This is the gap between passing tests and really understanding. Lots of research has shown, for years now, that, in areas like science, a good many students, even those with good grades and passing test scores, cannot actually use their knowledge to solve problems.[21]

For example, many students who can write down, for a test, Newton's Laws of Motion cannot correctly say how many forces are acting on a coin when it is tossed into the air and at the top of its trajectory—and, ironically, this is something that can be deduced from Newton's Laws.[22] They cannot apply their knowledge, because they don't *see* how it applies. They don't see the physical world and the symbol system of physics (which includes language and mathematics) in such a way that it is clear to them how that system applies to that world. While the poor may do less well in school, even the well off seem not to understand what they learn all that deeply.

This lack of understanding is connected to language and other symbols. There are two ways to understand words. We will call one way "verbal" and the other way "situated."[23] A situated understanding of a concept or word implies the ability to associate the word with specific images, actions, experiences, or dialogue in such a way that one knows how to apply the word in specific contexts to solve problems or accomplish goals.[24] A general or verbal understanding implies an ability to explicate one's understanding in terms of other words or general principles, but not necessarily an ability to apply this knowledge to actual situations. Thus, while verbal or general understandings may facilitate passing certain sorts of information-focused tests, they do not necessarily facilitate actual problem solving.

Situated understandings are, of course, the norm in everyday life and in vernacular language. Even the most mundane words take on different meanings in different contexts of use. Indeed, people must be able to build these meanings on the spot in real time as they construe the contexts around them. For instance, people construct different meanings for a word like "coffee" when they hear something like "The coffee spilled, get the mop" versus "The coffee spilled, get a broom" versus "The coffee spilled, stack it again."[25] Of course, to assign such situated meanings to "coffee" here, one must have had experiences with coffee in different forms and contexts.

Verbal and general understandings are top-down. They start with the general, that is with a definition-like understanding of a word or a general principle associated with a concept. Less abstract meanings follow as special cases of the definition or principle. Situated understandings generally work in the other direction, understanding starts with a relatively concrete case and gradually rises to higher levels of abstraction through the consideration of additional cases.

Before discussing situated meanings in more depth, let us point out a phenomenon that all gamers are well aware of. This phenomenon gets to the heart and soul of what situated meanings are and why they are important: Written texts associated with video games are not very meaningful, certainly not very lucid, unless and until one has played the game. Let's take the small booklet that comes with the innovative game *Deus Ex* to use as an example of what I mean by saying this.

In the twenty pages of this booklet, there are 199 bolded references that represent headings and sub-headings. Each of these 199 headings and subheadings is followed by text that gives information relevant to the topic and relates it to other information throughout the booklet. Here is a typical piece of language from this booklet:

> Your internal nano-processors keep a very detailed record of your condition, equipment and recent history. You can access this data at any time during play by hitting F1 to get to the Inventory screen or F2 to get to the Goals/Notes screen. Once you have accessed your information screens, you can move between the screens by clicking on the tabs at the top of the screen. You can map other information screens to hotkeys using Settings, Keyboard/Mouse (p. 5).

This makes perfect sense at a literal level, but that just goes to show how worthless the literal level is. When you understand this sort of passage at only a literal level, you have only an illusion of understanding, one that quickly disappears as you try to relate the information in this passage to the hundreds of other important details in the booklet. Such literal understandings are precisely what children who fuel the fourth-grade slump have. First of all, this passage means nothing real to you if you have no situated idea about what "nano-processors," "condition," "equipment,,""history," "F1," "Inventory screen," "F2," "Goals/Notes screen" (and, of course, "Goals" and "Notes"), "information screens," "clicking," "tabs," "map," "hotkeys," and "Settings, Keyboard/Mouse" mean in and for playing games like *Deus Ex*.

Second, though you know literally what each sentence means, they raise a plethora of questions if you have no situated understandings of this game or games like it. For instance: Is the same data (condition, equipment, and history) on both the Inventory screen and the Goals/Notes screen? If so, why is it on two different screens? If not, which type of information is on which screen and why? The fact that I can move between the screens by clicking on the tabs suggests that some of this information is on one screen and some on the other. But is my "condition" part of my Inventory or my Goals/Notes—doesn't seem to be either, but then, what is my "condition" anyway? If I can map other information screens (and what are these?) to hotkeys using "Setting, Keyboard/Mouse," does this mean there is no other way to access them? How will I access them in the first place to assign them to my own chosen hotkeys? Can I click between them and the Inventory screen and the Goals/Notes screens by pressing on "tabs"?

Of course, all these terms and questions can be defined and answered if you closely check and cross-check information over and over again through the little booklet. You can constantly turn the pages backwards and forwards. But once you have one set of links relating various items and actions in mind, another drops out just as you need it and you're back to turning pages. Is the booklet poorly written? Not at all. It is written just as well or poorly, just like, in fact, any of a myriad of school-based texts in the content areas. It is, outside the practices in the domain from which it comes, just as meaningless, however much one could garner literal meanings from it with which to verbally repeat things or pass tests.

And, of course, too, you can utter something like "Oh, yeah, you click on F1 (function key 1) to get to the Inventory screen and F2 to get to the Goals/Notes screen" and sound like you know something. The trouble is this: in the actual game, you can click on F2 and meditate on the screen you see at your leisure. Nothing bad will happen to you. However, you very often have to click on F1 and do something quickly in the midst of a heated battle. There's no "at your leisure" here. The two commands really don't function the same way in the game—they actually mean different things in terms of embodied and situated action—and they never really *just* mean "click F1, get screen." That's their general meaning, the one with which you can't really do anything useful until you know how to spell it out further in situation-specific terms in the game.

But if you play the game for a while first and then read the book, then you can spell out such information in situation-specific terms and the relationships of this information to the other hundreds of pieces of information in the booklet becomes clear and meaningful. And, of course, it is these relationships that are what really count if you are to understand the game as a system and, thus, play it at all well. Now you can attach a situated meaning—images, actions, experiences, or pieces of dialogue from the game—to each word in the text. *Now* you can read the book if you need to piece in missing bits of information, check on your understandings, or solve a particular problem or answer a particular question you have. You can read it to enable problem solving,

So now we would make just the same claim about any school content domain as we have just said about the video game *Deus Ex*: Specialist language in any domain—games or science—has no situated meaning, thus no lucid or applicable meaning, unless and until one has "played the game," in this case the game of science, or, better put, a specific game connected to a specific science. Such "games"("science games") involve seeing the language and representations associated with some part of science in terms of activities I have done, experiences I have had, images I have formed from these, and interactional dialogue I have heard from and had with peers and mentors outside and inside the science activities. School is too often about reading the manual before you get to play the game, if you ever do. This is not harmful for kids who have already played the game at home, but it is disastrous for those who have not.

Good video games don't just support situated meanings for the written materials associated with them in manuals and on fan web sites—and these are copious—but also for all the language within the game. The meaning of such language is always associated with actions, experiences, images, and dialogue. Furthermore, players get verbal information "just in time," when they can apply it or see it applied, or "on demand," when they feel the need for it and are ready for it—and then, in some cases, games will give the player walls of print (e.g., in *Civilization IV*).

So our claim: what we will call "game-like learning" leads to situated and not just verbal meanings. "Game-like learning" need not involve an actual game—it simply requires learners to live and have (guided) experiences in the world from the perspective of the area being learned, for example, a particular branch of science. But actual video games hold out great potential to enhance and deepen this process—to offer learners a myriad of new experiences that can allow them to learn situated meanings and not just verbal definitions.

7. Video Games and the Human Mind

Just as children today often see complex specialist language in their popular culture activities like *Yu-Gi-Oh*, they also see complex and deep learning in their commercial video games. Modern video games set up a learning situation that is situated in the sense that meanings are situated, as we have just seen, and in the sense that skills and concepts are learned in an embodied way that leads to real understanding. There is a reason for this: Games place language and learning in a setting that fits very well with how the human mind is built to learn and think. Schools sometimes do not. Let us explicate what we mean.

Scholars have often viewed the human mind through the lens of a technology they thought worked like the mind. Locke and Hume, for example, argued that the mind was like a blank slate on which experience wrote ideas, taking the technology of literacy as their guide. Much later, modern cognitive scientists argued that the mind worked like a digital computer, calculating generalizations and deductions via a logic-like rule system.[26] More recently, some cognitive scientists, inspired by distributed parallel-processing computers and complex adaptive networks, have argued that the mind works by storing records of actual experiences and constructing intricate patterns of connections among them.[27] So we get different pictures of the mind: mind as a slate waiting to be written on, mind as software, mind as a network of connections.

Human societies get better through history at building technologies that more closely capture some of what the human mind can do and getting these technologies to do mental work publicly. Writing, digital computers, and networks each allows us to externalize some functions of the mind. Though they are not commonly thought of in these terms, video games are a new technology in this same line. They are a new tool with which to think about the mind and through which we can externalize some of its functions. Video games of the sort we are concerned with—games like *Half-Life 2*, *Rise of Nations*, *Full Spectrum Warrior*, *The Elder Scrolls III: Morrowind*, and *World of WarCraft*—are what we could call "action-and-goal-directed preparations for, and simulations of, embodied experience."

To make clear what we mean by the claim that games act like the human mind and are a good place to study and produce human thinking and learning, let us first briefly summarize some recent research in cognitive science.[28] Consider, for instance, the remarks below [in the quotes below, the word "comprehension" means "understanding words, actions, events, or things"]:

> . . . comprehension is grounded in perceptual simulations that prepare agents for situated action[29]

. . . to a particular person, the meaning of an object, event, or sentence is what that person can do with the object, event, or sentence[30]

. . . higher intelligence is not a different kind of process from perceptual intelligence[31]

What these remarks mean is this: human understanding is not primarily a matter of storing general concepts in the head or applying abstract rules to experience. Rather, humans think and understand best when they can imagine (simulate) an experience in such a way that the simulation prepares them for actions they need and want to take in order to accomplish their goals.[32]

Video games turn out to be the perfect metaphor for what this view of the mind amounts to, just as slates and computers were good metaphors for earlier views of the mind. To see this, let us now turn to a characterization of video games and then we will put our remarks about the mind and games together.

Video games usually involve a visual and auditory virtual world in which the player has micro-control (small scale control) over the movements of elements in the world (e.g., a virtual character in *Half-Life*, units in *Rise of Nations*, or shapes in *Tetris*). They often come with editors or other sorts of software with which the player can make changes to the game world or even build a new game world. The player can make a new landscape, a new set of buildings, or new characters. The player can set up the world so that certain sorts of actions are allowed or disallowed. The player is building a new world, but is doing so by using and modifying the original visual images (really the code for them) that came with the game. One simple example of this is the way in which players can build new skateboard parks in a game like *Tony Hawk Pro Skater*. The player must place ramps, trees, grass, poles, and other things in space in such a way that players can manipulate their virtual characters to skate the park in a fun and challenging way.

Even when players are not modifying games, they play them with goals in mind, the achievement of which counts as their "win state" (and it's the existence of such win states that, in part, distinguishes games from simulations). These goals are set by the player, but, of course, in collaboration with the world the game designers have created (and, at least in more open-ended games, players don't just accept developer's goals, they make real choices of their own). Players must carefully consider the design of the world and consider how it will or will not facilitate specific actions they want to take to accomplish their goals.

One technical way that psychologists have talked about this sort of situation is through the notion of "affordances."[33] An "affordance" is a feature of the world (real or virtual) that will allow for a certain action to be taken, but only if it is matched by an ability in an actor who has the wherewithal to carry out such an action. For example, in the massively multiplayer game *World of WarCraft* stags can be killed and skinned (for making leather), but only by characters that have learned the Skinning skill. So a stag is an affordance for skinning for such a player, but not for one who has no such skill. The large spiders in the game are not an affordance for skinning for any players, since they cannot be skinned at all. Affordances are relationships between the world and actors.

Playing *World of WarCraft*, or any other video game, is all about such affordances. The player must learn to **see** the game world—designed by the developers, but set in motion in particular directions by the players, and, thus, co-designed by them—in terms of such affordances.[34] Broadly speaking, players must think in terms of "What are the features of this world that can enable the actions I am capable of carrying out and that I want to carry out in order to achieve my goals?"

So now, after our brief bit about the mind and about games, let's put the two together. The view of the mind we have sketched, in fact, argues that the mind works rather like a video game. For humans, effective thinking is more like running a simulation than it is about forming abstract generalizations cut off from experiential realities. Effective thinking is about perceiving the world such that the human actor sees how the world, at a specific time and place (as it is given, but also modifiable), can afford the opportunity for actions that will lead to a successful accomplishment of the actor's goals. Generalizations are formed, when they are, bottom up from experience and imagination of experience. Video games externalize the search for affordances, for a match between character (actor) and world, but this is just the heart and soul of effective human thinking and learning in any situation.

As a game player you learn to see the world of each different game you play in a quite different way. But in each case you see the world in terms of how it will afford the sorts of embodied actions you (and your virtual character, your surrogate body in the game) need to take to accomplish your goals (to win in the short and long run). For example, you see the world in *Full Spectrum Warrior* as routes (for your squad) between cover (e.g., corner to corner, house to house) because this prepares you for the actions you need to take, namely attacking without being vulnerable to attack yourself. You see the world of *Thief* in terms of light and dark, illumination and shadows, because this prepares you for the different actions you need to take in this world, namely hiding, disappearing into the shadows, sneaking, and otherwise moving unseen to your goal.

When we sense such a match, in a virtual world or the real world, between our way of seeing the world, at a particular time and place, and our action goals—and we have the skills to carry these actions out—then we feel great power and satisfaction. Things click, the world looks as if it were made for us. While commercial games often stress a match between worlds and characters like soldiers or thieves, there is no reason why other games could not let players experience such a match between the world and the way a particular type of scientist, for instance, sees and acts on the world.[35] Such games would involve facing the sorts of problems and challenges that type of scientist does and living and playing by the rules that type of scientist uses. Winning would mean just what it does to a scientist: feeling a sense of accomplishment through the production of knowledge to solve deep problems.

We have argued for the importance of video games as "action-and-goal-directed preparations for, and simulations of, embodied experience." They are the new technological arena—just as were literacy and computers earlier—around which we can study the mind and externalize some of its most important features to improve human thinking and learning.

8. Distributed Intelligence and Cross-Functional Teams

Good video games have two other features that suit them to be good models for human thinking and learning externalized out in the world. These two additional features are: a) they distribute intelligence via the creation of smart tools, and b) they allow for the creation of "cross functional affiliation," a particularly important form of collaboration in the modern world.

Consider first how good games distribute intelligence.[36] In *Full Spectrum Warrior*, the player uses the buttons on the controller to give orders to two squads of soldiers. The instruction manual that comes with the game makes it clear from the outset that players, in order to play the game successfully, must take on the values, identities, and ways of thinking of a professional soldier: "Everything about your squad," the manual explains, "is the result of careful planning and years of experience on the battlefield. Respect that experience, soldier, since it's what will keep your soldiers alive" (p. 2).

In the game, that experience—the skills and knowledge of professional military expertise—is distributed between the virtual soldiers and the real-world player. The soldiers in the player's squads have been trained in movement formations; the role of the player is to select the best position for them on the field. The virtual characters (the soldiers) know part of the task (various movement formations) and the player must come to know another part (when and where to engage in such formations). This kind of distribution holds for every aspect of military knowledge in the game.

By distributing knowledge and skills this way—between the virtual characters (smart tools) and the real-world player—the player is guided and supported by the knowledge built into the virtual soldiers. This offloads some of the cognitive burden from the learner, placing it in smart tools that can do more than the learner is currently capable of doing by him or herself. It allows the player to begin to act, with some degree of effectiveness, before being really competent—"performance before competence." The player thereby eventually comes to gain competence through trial, error, and feedback, not by wading through a lot of text before being able to engage in activity.

Such distribution also allows players to internalize not only the knowledge and skills of a professional (a professional soldier in this case), but also the concomitant values ("doctrine" as the military says) that shape and explain how and why that knowledge is developed and applied in the world. There is no reason why other professions—scientists, doctors, government officials, urban planners[37]—could not be modeled and distributed in this fashion as a deep form of value-laden learning (and, in turn, learners could compare and contrast different value systems as they play different games).

Finally, let us turn to the creation of a form of collaboration we can call "cross-functional affiliation." Consider a small group partying (hunting and questing) together in a massive multiplayer game like *World of WarCraft*. The group might well be composed of a Hunter, Warrior, Paladin, Druid, and Priest. Each of these types of characters has quite different skills and plays the game in a different way.

Each group member (player) must learn to be good at his or her special skills and also learn to integrate these skills as a team member within the group as a whole. Each team member must also share some common knowledge about the game and game play with all the other members of the group—including some understanding of the specialist skills of other player types—in order to achieve a successful integration. So each member of the group must have specialist knowledge (intensive knowledge) and general common knowledge (extensive knowledge), including knowledge of the other members' functions.

Players—who are interacting with each other, in the game and via a chat system—orient to each other not in terms of their real-world race, class, culture, or gender (these may very well be unknown or, if communicated, made up as fictions). They must orient to each other, first and foremost, through their identities as game players and players of *World of WarCraft* in particular. They can, in turn, use their real-world race, class, culture, and gender as strategic resources if and when they please, and the group can draw on the differential real-world resources of each player, but in ways that do not force anyone into pre-set racial, gender, cultural, or class categories.

This form of affiliation—what we will call cross-functional affiliation—has been argued to be crucial for the workplace teams in modern "new capitalist" workplaces, as well as in modern forms of social activism.[38] People specialize, but integrate and share, organized around a primary affiliation to their common goals and endeavors, and use their cultural and social differences as strategic resources, not as barriers.

So video games, though a part of popular culture, are, like literacy and computers, sites where we can study and exercise the human mind in ways that may give us deeper insights into human thinking and learning, as well as new ways to engage learners in deep and engaged learning. What we see here—and it's the same message we saw with *Yu-Gi-Oh* and *Pokémon* before—is that areas of popular culture are beginning to organize thinking and learning in efficacious ways. The practices they recruit—lucidly functional language, situated meanings, and leveraging experiences to build simulations (in the mind and outside it), distributed intelligence, and cross-functional collaboration—are all ones that need not to be restricted to military games. They are key to deep understanding in any specialist domain, whether in school or at work.

9. Games as Games

So far much of what we have said about good video games and learning doesn't have much to do with the fact that they are games *per se*. The features we have looked at don't speak directly to video games as games and, indeed, these features all seem to be somewhat removed from the pleasures that games as games give us humans. However, it is certainly a leading question for research whether these features will work for learning well, or as well, if they are not embedded in video games that have these features and, moreover, are good games. What are the features that make a video game a game and a good game? What are the sources of the pleasures people draw from video games as games of a certain sort? How do these features relate to learning?

Hardly anyone has failed to notice how profoundly motivating video games are for players. Players focus intently on game play for hours at a time, solving complex problems all along. In an "attentional economy," where diverse products and messages, not to mention school subjects, compete for people's limited attention, video games draw attention in a deep way. It is clearly a profoundly important subject for research to understand the source or sources of this motivation. Such motivation is clearly foundational for learning.

Oddly enough, one hypothesis here is that it is problem solving and learning, as well as the display of mastery, that are themselves a key source of motivation in good video games. If this is true, then, we need to know why learning and mastery is so motivating in this context and not always as motivating in school.

Here another hypothesis would be that learning and mastery are motivating in good video games precisely because they use the sorts of deep learning principles we have just discussed above, as well as others.

But, of course, we need to know, as well, whether when the content of a video game is based on more academic or specialized learning goals the same sorts of effects can occur. Some people assume that things like science can never be made as enticing as fighting fictional wars in *America's Army* or running a family in *The Sims,* for example. At the same time, we know of few good scientists who do not find science, as a form of being in and seeing the world, motivating, entertaining, and life enhancing.

There are certainly features connected to video games as games that help explain both the motivation they recruit and the learning they enable. First, the role of failure is very different in video games from how it is in school. In good games, the price of failure is lowered—when players fail they can, for example, start over at their last saved game. Furthermore, failure—for example, a failure to kill a boss—is often seen as a way to learn the underlying pattern and eventually to win. These features of failure in games allow players to take risks and try out hypotheses that might be too costly in places where the cost of failure is higher or where no learning stems from failure.

Every gamer and game scholar knows that a great many gamers, including young ones, enjoy competition with other players in games, either one-on-one or team-based. It is striking that many young gamers see competition as pleasurable and motivating in video games, but not in school. Why this is so ought to be a leading question for research on games and learning. One thing seems evident; namely that competition in video games is seen by gamers as social, and is often organized in ways that allow people to compete with people at their own level or as part and parcel of a social relationship that is as much about gaming as it is about winning and losing. Furthermore, gamers highly value collaborative play, for example, two people playing *Halo* together to beat the game or the grouping in massive multiplayer games like *World of WarCraft.* Indeed, collaboration and competition seem often to be closely related and integrated in gaming, though not in school.

Beyond issues of motivation, failure, competition, and collaboration, the very ways in which games are designed as games seem to give them features that both enhance learning and a sense of mastery. This is a hypothesis that needs testing. Nonetheless, there are some features of the very design of video games that appear to be closely associated with well-known principles of learning. We list some of these design features below:

A   Interactivity: In a video game, players make things happen; they don't just consume what the "author" (game designer) has placed before them. In good games, players feel that their actions and decisions—and not just the designers' actions and decisions—are co-creating the world they are in and the experiences they are having. What the player does matters and each player, based on his or her own style, decisions, and actions, takes a somewhat different trajectory through the game world. The more open-ended a game is the more true this is, though in a more limited sense it is true of all games, since players must play them and play is, as we have seen above, a form of simultaneous "reading" (interpreting) and "writing" (producing). All deep learning involves learners feeling a strong sense of ownership and agency, as well as the ability to produce and not just passively consume knowledge.

B   **Customization:** In some games, players are able to customize the game play to fit their learning and playing styles, for example through different difficulty levels or the choice of playing different characters with different skills. In others, the game is designed to allow different styles of learning and playing to work (e.g., there are multiple ways to solve the problems in the game), for example, in the *Deus Ex* games and role playing games like *Arcanum*. Customization, in the sense of catering to different learning styles and multiple routes to success, is an important learning principle in many different areas.

C   **Strong Identities:** Good games offer players identities that trigger a deep investment on the part of the player. This identity is often connected to a specific virtual character, though sometimes it is attached to a whole "civilization" (as in *Civilization* or *Rise of Nations*). When gamers are playing characters, strong identities are achieved in one of two ways: Some games offer a character so intriguing that players want to inhabit the character and can readily project their own fantasies, desires, and pleasures onto the character (e.g., Solid Snake in the *Metal Gear Solid* games). Other games offer a relatively empty character whose traits the player must determine, but in such a way that the player can create a deep and consequential life history in the game world for the character (e.g., in role playing games like *The Elder Scrolls III: Morrowind*). Furthermore, in games, the identity of the character one plays is very clearly associated with the sorts of functions, skills, and goals one has to carry out in the virtual world. Many people have argued that identity (e.g., "being-doing a scientist" in order to learn science) is crucial for deep learning (see final section, as well, on this issue).[39]

D   **Well-ordered problems:** Problems in good games are well ordered. In particular, early problems are designed to lead players to form good guesses about how to proceed when they face harder problems later on in the game. In this sense, earlier parts of a good game are always looking forward to later parts. This is part of what good level design is all about. Work on the mind and learning which takes a connectionist approach has argued that such ordering is crucial for effective learning in complex domains.[40]

E   **Games are pleasantly frustrating:** Good games adjust challenges and give feedback in such a way that different sorts of players feel the game is challenging but doable and that their effort is paying off. Players get feedback that indicates whether they are on the right road for success later on and at the end of the game. When players lose to a boss, perhaps multiple times, they get feedback about the sort of progress they are making so that at least they know if and how they are moving in the right direction towards success. Andy diSessa[41] has argued that such pleasant frustration is an optimal state for learning things like science.

F   **Games are built around the cycle of expertise:** Good games create and support what has been called in the Learning Sciences the "cycle of expertise,"[42] with repeated cycles of extended practice, tests of mastery of that practice, then a new challenge that leads to new practice and new mastery at a higher level. This is, in fact, part of what constitutes good pacing in a game.

G   **"Deep" and "Fair":** These are terms of art in the gaming community. A game is "fair" when it is challenging, but set up in a way that leads to success and does not design in features that virtually ensure failure over which the player has little or no control. A game is "deep" when game play elements (e.g., a fighting system in a turn-taking game) that initially seem simple, and, thus, easy to learn and use, become more and more complex the more one comes to master and understand them. Such terms, it would seem, would make good terms of art in the Learning Sciences, as well.

These are all basic features of the way many games are designed. They also appear to be important features for effective learning. Thus, they raise the question as to whether the sorts of features we discussed earlier—the ones less connected to games as games *per se*—are rendered more effective when in the presence of these more directly game-like features.

10. Mentoring

Some enthusiasts for games and learning see games as a way to remove teachers from learning. They stress—as have many others in one branch of the progressivist tradition—immersion, experiential learning, inquiry, and learners setting their own agendas and goals. Similarly, some people in the field of artificial tutoring, as well, have held out the possibility that such tutors could replace human teachers.

On the other hand, Kirschner, Sweller, and Clark have recently published an attention-grabbing paper—"Why Minimal Guidance during Instruction Does Not Work: An Analysis of the Failure of Constructivist, Discovery, Problem-Based, Experiential, and Inquiry-Based Teaching"[43]—that argues:

> While unguided or minimally-guided instructional approaches are very popular and intuitively appealing, the point is made that these approaches ignore both the structures that constitute human cognitive architecture and evidence from empirical studies over the past half century that consistently indicate that minimally-guided instruction is less effective and less efficient than instructional approaches that place a strong emphasis on guidance of the student learning process. The advantage of guidance begins to recede only when learners have sufficiently high prior knowledge to provide 'internal' guidance. Recent developments in instructional research and instructional design models that support guidance during instruction are briefly described. (Abstract)

It is clear from our example of the mother and her four-year-old talking about dinosaurs—an example we took from Kevin Crowley's work—that in the sorts of effective home-based learning that prepares kids for school, the role of the adult is crucial. In this case the adult scaffolds a particular type of talk—talk that orientates towards school-based or academic language—and engages in what we might well refer to as informal language lessons; a form of overt—yes, even controlling—guidance. At the same time the child is immersed in an activity over which, as an "expert," he feels ownership and agency.

The dichotomy between overt instruction/guidance, on the one hand, and agentful immersion in experience is a false one. Good video games offer lots of guidance without taking away immersion or ownership: the game design structures the player's experience, setting up goals, constraining the problem space, and ordering the problems (level design); overt verbal information is offered—and often lots of it—"just in time" (when it is needed and can be used) or "on demand" (when the player is ready for it and knows why it is needed); tutorials, assessments, feedback, and practice abound in video games. Furthermore, gamers are most often members of social groups—communities of practice—where more advanced peers share information, guidance, modeling, and critique.

We stressed above that our focus should be, not on the game in the box, but on what we called "the big 'G' game," that is, the combination of the game in the box and the social and learning system built around the game. This learning system most certainly includes forms of overt guidance, instruction, and scaffolding, though these can take a variety of different forms.

One way to get at this issue is to return to our remarks about the human mind in Section 7. There we argued that people's embodied experiences in the world (experiences of action, interaction, and talk) are the foundations of their thinking and problem solving:

> For humans, effective thinking is more like running a simulation than it is about forming abstract generalizations cut off from experiential realities. Effective thinking is about perceiving the world such that the human actor sees how the world, at a specific time and place (as it is given, but also modifiable), can afford the opportunity for actions that will lead to a successful accomplishment of the actor's goals. Generalizations are formed, when they are, bottom up from experience and imagination of experience. Video games externalize the search for affordances, for a match between character (actor) and world, but this is just the heart and soul of effective human thinking and learning in any situation.

People form their simulations based on experiences they have had. But to do this successfully they have to have processed these experiences in certain ways.[44] They have to learn to interrogate their experiences (and they have to have the language capacities, in given domains, to do this). Interrogating one's experiences means, among other things, the following[45]:

1   In order to learn from and use their experiences for future problem solving, learners need to interpret their experiences. As we have seen, human experience works best for learning when it is goal-driven. Interpreting one's experience means thinking—both while in practice and later on after practice—about how one's goals relate to one's reasoning in the situation, and it means pulling out lessons learned and anticipating when and where those lessons might be useful.

2   Learners can learn best when they get immediate feedback in practice so they can recognize and assess their errors and situations where their expectations have failed, and when they are encouraged to explain why their errors and expectation failures happened, and what they could have done differently.

3   Learners need ample opportunities to apply their previous experiences—as interpreted—to new similar situations, so they can "debug" and improve their interpretations of these experiences, gradually generalizing them beyond specific situations.

4   Learners can and need to learn from the interpreted experiences and expla-
    nations of other people, most certainly including more expert people.
    This is best done through modeling and discussion.

When these four steps are carried out, learners' experiences become well
articulated "cases"[46] with which and from which they can reason. These four steps
obviously require the design of a learning system around a game (or other set of
activities generating experiences) that recruit very distinctive forms of individual action, interaction, participation, modeling, and discourse.

This framework also suggests a variety of roles for teachers or other adults
in young people's learning. Like game designers, teachers need to be designers
of learning systems that cause learners to process their goal-driven experiences
in the ways discussed in these four steps. They need to do this while still allowing a sense of agency and ownership on the part of the learners. Teachers must
offer overt information, modeling, worked examples, guidance at the appropriate level, often "just in time" and "on demand." They may very well need to offer
more such overt information, modeling, and guidance for beginners, just as good
games and good game tutorials do. Finally, teachers build and resource "communities of practice" where each learner can use the resources of good tools and technologies and other learners at different levels of expertise.[47] In such communities,
knowledge is distributed (spread across multiple people and their smart tools
and technologies) and dispersed (exists on site and off site with links).

One key thing teachers need to do is to build and resource certain forms of
talk, patterns of participation, and interaction.[48] This is so because (a) distinctive forms of content are connected (hopefully in lucidly functional ways) with
distinctive forms of language, connections rendered public in talk, (b) learners
need to learn to interpret, analyze, debug, and explain their experiences (and the
connections between goals and reasoning within experience)—and, again, all these
can be rendered public through talk, (c) learners need to learn from the interpreted experiences of others, their peers and more expert people in the domain,
and (d) communities of practice are, in part, formed through the sorts of talk that
allow for public sharing and joint modeling, building and problem solving.

Too often, though, people have celebrated learners talking and discussing without worrying enough about the type of talk in which they are engaged and the
cognitive foundations that give that talk situated meanings for (hopefully) everyone in the group. The Yu-Gi-Oh example above makes two things crystal clear.
First, learning Yu-Gi-Oh requires a very specific form of talk—a specific register
or social language[49]—a form that is deeply tied to the functions, meanings, and
purpose of Yu-Gi-Oh as an activity. Second, each young Yu-Gi-Oh player can discuss and debate with others in this language on common ground not because they

have done nothing but talk, but because they have played the game and that play has given them embodied, situated meanings for the language.

The same is true of science in the classroom: its language needs to be lucidly functional, kids need to get embodied, situated meanings of its words and concepts, and they need to use that language (not just the vernacular) in ways that are functional to "play the game" and accomplish meaningful goals (like winning in *Yu-Gi-Oh* or carrying out and defending a successful experiment). They hopefully do all these in the framework of the four points above. But note, crucially, *Yu-Gi-Oh* language goes hand in hand with certain forms of interactive participation (there are ways people relate to each other to play the game)—not just any old forms and certainly not "everyday" forms modeled on informal conversations. Those forms are related to the nature of the game and the requirements for being successful at it. The same is true of any type of science being taught in school.

If you actually study kids acquiring *Yu-Gi-Oh*, they are most certainly immersed in a rich set of multi-model experiences and activities (books, movies, TV shows, cards, games, trading, etc.), but they also usually have lots of overt teaching and modeling. In fact, the television show directly models how to play—and think about—the game. More advanced players—in the local community and at tournaments—offer lots of overt advice and guidance, sometimes gently, sometimes not. There is, in the end, no necessary opposition between guidance and immersion—we need lots of both, balanced differently at different points in the learner's trajectory—just as happens in any good video game.

11. Models and Modeling

If games are to be used in educational settings, there is another element beyond the role of mentors that needs to be discussed, namely the role of models and modeling in thinking, learning, and building knowledge. Models have not played an essential role in much of the mainstream educational literature, but they play a major role in current work in the Learning Sciences and in games.[50]

Specialist domains—like science and mathematics in academics or *Yu-Gi-Oh* or *Dungeons & Dragons* in popular culture—create tools and new ways with language in order to construct new worlds or new ways of looking at the real world. For science and math this involves looking at, talking about, and knowing the everyday world in new ways, ways that are often different from our everyday non-specialist ways. For the popular cultural activities like *Yu-Gi-Oh* and *Dungeons & Dragons* this involves constructing fantasy worlds with complex correspondences to the real world (though science and mathematics sometimes do this sort of thing as well)—e.g., by combining elements of the human, animal, natural, and textual-mythological domains. One of the key devices through which both science and popular culture construct new worlds, or new ways of looking at and acting on the real world, is the use of models.

I will be using the word "model" here in a somewhat extended sense from its everyday usage, so let's start with familiar territory. Consider a child's model air plane. Real planes are big, complex, and dangerous. A child can safely play with the model plane, trying out things, imagining things, and learning about planes. Of course, models are always simpler than the thing they model and, thus, different types of models capture different properties of the thing being modeled and allow different sorts of things to be tried out and learned. Even a child's toy plane may be more or less detailed, and a piece of folded paper can do in a pinch as a model of an airplane.

Model planes can, of course, be used by engineers and scientists, as well. They can use the model plane in a wind tunnel, for example, to test things that are too dangerous or too expensive to do with real planes. They can make predictions based on the model and see if they hold true for the real thing in real life (e.g., planes crash under certain conditions). They can use the model to make plans about how to build a better real plane. They can use it, as well, to test theories about planes and flight, to build explanatory ideas about new planes or not yet well-understood aspects of mechanical flight. They can even use the model to better understand, after the fact, problems like crashes that have already occurred in reality. The model plane is a tool for thought, learning, and action.

Models are just depictions of a real thing (like planes, cars, or buildings) or a system (like atomic structure, weather patterns, traffic flow, eco-systems, social systems, and so forth) that are simpler than the real thing, stressing some properties of the thing and not others. They are used for imaginative thought, learning, and action when the real thing is too large, too complex, too expensive, or too dangerous to deal with directly. It is also clear from our example of the model plane that models are embedded in distinctive sorts of activities (e.g., putting the model plane in a wind tunnel) that we can call "modeling."

A model plane closely resembles the thing it is modeling (a real plane). But models can be ranged on a continuum of how closely they resemble the thing they are modeling. They can be, in this sense, more or less "abstract." One model plane may have lots of details, right down to little decals designating the decorations on the plane. Another may be a simple balsa-wood wings and frame construction, no frills, meant to strip plane flight to its fundamentals. A folded piece of paper goes further away from a close resemblance to a real plane. Even more abstractly, the blue print of the plane, on a piece of paper, is still a model, useful for some purposes (e.g., planning and building) and not others. It is a model that resembles the plane very little, but still corresponds to the real plane in a patterned way. It's an abstract picture.

We can go even further and consider a model of the plane that is a chart with all the plane's different parts listed down a set of rows and a set of numbers ranged along the top in columns. The intersection of a part and number would stand for the amount of stress each part is under in flight. For each part we can trace along the row and see a number representing how much stress this part is under in flight. No resemblance, really, left here, but the chart still corresponds to the plane. We can still map from pieces of the chart to pieces of the plane. The chart still represents some properties of the plane, though this is a very abstract picture of the plane, indeed, and one useful for a narrow purpose.

However, this type of model—at the very abstract end of the continuum of resemblance—shows us another important feature of models and modeling. It captures an invisible, relatively "deep" (that is, not so readily apparent) property of the plane, namely how parts interact with stress. Of course, we could imagine a much more user-friendly picture (model) of this property, perhaps a model plane all of whose parts are color coded (say in degrees of red) for how much stress they must bear in flight. This is more user-friendly and it makes clear the mixture of what is readily apparent (the plane and its parts) and what is a deep (less apparent) property, namely stress on parts.

But, of course, the list-like model can probably list lots more parts than we can easily build into a small toy-like model plane, and it can give more accurate information through the use of numbers, rather than color shadings. As with all models, there are always trade offs in terms of what you want to know, learn, or represent, how user-friendly the model will be, and what the model will look like. In fact, one of the key intellectually interesting things about models and modeling is that it forces us to reflect on, explain, and defend such choices for specific purposes and goals.

These are very basic matters. Models and modeling are basic to human play. They are basic to a great many human enterprises; for example, science (a diagram of a cell), architecture (model buildings), engineering (model bridges), art (the clay figure the sculptor makes before making the real statue), video and film (e.g., story boards), writing (e.g., outlines), cooking (recipes), travel (maps), and many more. In fact, models and modeling are so basic to thought, learning, and action outside of school that it is odd children in school do not usually get a lot of time building, manipulating, transforming, thinking with, and discussing models as a way to understand things like science and society and to produce, and not just consume, knowledge.

Models are basic to video games, as well, and are another point where game design and the learning sciences intersect. However, thinking about models also keys us into two different large categories of commercial video games. Video games are simulations in which the player is inside the simulation. All simulations are models of what they are simulating. So *World of WarCraft* simulates (models) a world of mountains, lakes, roads, buildings, creatures, and so forth, that, while fantasy, is meant to resemble aspects of the real world. However, players for the most part pay very little attention to this modeling aspect of *World of WarCraft*, because it usually plays no important role in the game play. Rather, players concentrate on the embodied experiences of play, problem solving, and socialization that *World of WarCraft* offers them. By and large, the fact that it models environments does not matter all that much to the game play.

However, sometimes in *World of WarCraft* this is not true; sometimes the modeling aspect comes to the fore. For example, when I get stuck trying to walk up the inclines and crevices of a mountain in *World of WarCraft*, I begin to think about how the game's mountain is representing (modeling) gravity and resistance in the real world, sometimes with anger, because I realize that it did not model them well enough to ensure that I can get up an incline that in the real world I could, but in the game I can't.

However, there are other games in which the modeling aspect of the simulation is crucial. Players in these games are having experiences, just as they are in *World of WarCraft* or *Half-Life*, but the modeling aspect is also crucial at nearly all points, not just intermittently. In a game like *Civilization*, for instance, the depictions of landscapes, cities, and armies are not very realistic, not nearly as realistic as in *World of WarCraft*. For example, in *Civilization*, a small set of soldiers stands for a whole army and the landscape looks like a colorful map. However, given the nature of game play in *Civilization*, these are clearly meant to be models of the real things stressing only some of their properties. They are clearly meant to be used for quite specific purposes in the game; for example, modeling large scale military interactions across time and space and modeling the role of geographical features in the historical development of different civilizations. Models and modeling are integral to game play in *Civilization*—it's the point of the game, in one sense. Since a game like *Civilization* stresses modeling, it is not surprising that it is played with a top-down god's eye view, rather than the first person, world-internal view of *Half-Life*.

However, not all games that stress modeling as integral to game play have such a top down view, though other model-intensive games do; games like *Zoo Tycoon*, *Rise of Nations*, and *the Sims*. A game like *S.W.A.T.4* is played with a first person, world-internal view, but still, modeling is crucial to the game. The player is very well aware that it matters how and why the designers modeled the S.W.A.T. team members, their equipment, and the sorts of environments with which and in which they interact.

So we can distinguish between video games that stress player experiences, but not modeling, and other games that, while offering experiences, stress modeling, as well. However, even games where, at the big picture level, modeling is not integral to game play in terms of their overall virtual worlds—games like *World of WarCraft* or *Half-Life*—very often models appear ubiquitously inside the game to aid the player's problem solving. For example, most games have maps that model the terrain (and maps are pretty abstract models) and allow players to navigate and plan. The bottom of *World of WarCraft*'s screen is an abstract model of the player's abilities and skills. Lots of games allow players to turn on and off a myriad of screens that display charts, lists, and graphs depicting various aspects of game play, equipment, abilities, skills, accomplishments, and other things. In a first-person shooter, the screen that shows all the guns a player has, their firing types, and their ammunition is a model of the game's weapon system, an abstract picture of it made for certain planning, strategizing, predicting, and problem-solving uses.

Models inside games go further, much further. Players and player communities often build modifications of games that are models used to solve certain sorts of problems. For example, *World of WarCraft*'s players can download a mod that displays a chart (during actual fighting) that lists each player's class (e.g., Druid, Priest, Warrior, Mage, Paladin, etc.) and the amount of damage they are doing in a group raid inside a dungeon. This chart can be used to check—publicly—that each player is holding up his end of the group task (so Warriors had better be doing lots of damage and healing priests better not be—they had better be concentrating on healing rather than attacking). This is one of several tools, almost all of them made by players, that help players solve a very real-world problem, namely the problem of individuals attempting to take a free ride in a group or attempting to hide their lack of skill.

Models and modeling reach a new pitch in games like *Tony Hawk*. In these skateboarding games, first, the whole game is a model of the practices and culture of skateboarders. Within that larger model, there are a myriad of models of boards, dress styles, tricks, and parks. However, players can readily design their own skaters, clothes, boards, tricks, points for tricks, and skate parks. That is, they can build their own models. When they build a model skate park, they interact with a set of more abstract models of environments (screens made up of grids and rotatable objects) that help them build the more specific and realistic looking model skate park they want (like a toy plane). Furthermore, they can share their new skate parks with other players—who can even skate their parks—and thereby get feedback and critique, in turn revising their models, based on things like fidelity to skater culture, practices, and values; real-world properties like gravity; and player opinions about identity, fun, engagement, and the nature of skateboarding as a real activity and as a gaming activity. Indeed, as skating in the real world changes, the models in the game and those made by players change, each time trying to capture things that are seen as important or essential, all the while balancing a variety of criteria about fidelity to different things and systems. This is modeling with a vengeance. Here modeling is integral to game play at all levels.

So, why, in the end, are models and modeling important to learning—say, learning things like science or social science? Because, while people learn from their interpreted experiences—as argued above—models and modeling allow specific aspects of experience to be interrogated and used for problem solving in ways that lead from concreteness to abstraction. This is not the only way abstraction grows—it can grow, as well, from comparing and contrasting multiple experiences. But modeling is an important way to interrogate and abstract experience. This is readily apparent in a game like *Tony Hawk*. Surely, players of this game, if they have made skate parks and shared them, have both an embodied experiential understanding of skating (as least as an in-game simulated activity) and a more abstract take on properties and features of skating and skate parks. Indeed, these two forms of understanding can constantly interact with and feed off each other, wherein resides a real power for learning and innovation.

So, then, second, why are models and modeling important to game design? Because, in-game models are tools to facilitate, enrich, and deepen the problem solving the game designer is building. And because games like *Civilization*, *S.W.A.T.4*, *The Sims*, and *Tony Hawk*, games that stress modeling even at the larger level of the game-play experience, allow for a quite deep form of play—often connected in complicated ways with the real world—though this is not to say, of course, that such games are more "fun" than other games. They are, however, probably the key route to the making of so-called "serious games" (though, of course, models and modeling can readily be built into games whose overall game play does not stress modeling).

It may well be that when educators recruit games for learning in areas like science or social science the role of models and modeling will be a critical aspect. The fact that video games can give players rich experiences, allow them to interpret and reflect on these experiences, and, at the same time, get them to interact with models at various levels of abstraction as part and parcel of those experiences, both at the level of the game as a whole and within the game, may eventually be seen as one of the promising aspects of games in learning. It will be a crucial place at which mentors (teachers) will be able to guide and deepen learners' interactions with the game and with other people around the game.

12. A New Crisis?

Our discussion thus far leads to one of the deepest and most important issues in the field of games and learning. If we want to move games or game-like learning to school, will the structure of schooling have to change significantly or not? Can games or game-like learning adapt to schooling or will they demand major innovations and changes? It has been argued for some time that schooling as we know it is an antiquated institution, appropriate for an industrialized capitalism that is now passing in the developed world. Schools are out of kilter, it is argued, with our current fast-changing, information rich, knowledge intensive, high-tech, global world.[51]

Some have argued recently that the United States faces a new looming crisis in education.[52] The crisis, it is argued, resides in the fact that far too many young people in the United States today are being prepared—in school and at home—for standard jobs in a world that will very soon, in countries like the United States, reward people who can do "innovation work" and punish people fit only for standard jobs.[53] A standard job is a job—whether it be a call-center operator or a computer scientist, whether it be low or high status—that can be done more cheaply and just as efficiently, thanks to technologies like computers and the Internet, in low cost centers, often outside of the United States. Such jobs involve standardized skills that can now be trained efficiently almost anywhere.

Today, a country like India, to take just one salient example, has call-center operators, engineers, and computer scientists as well or better trained as those in the U.S., people able and willing to work for less, all the while staying in India. And in a connected world, it often does not matter where people are. In actual effect, time differences are an advantage, e.g., Indian radiologists can read American X-rays while American doctors and patients sleep at night and have them ready by morning in America.

Our government and our schools have made an effort to "leave no child behind" through the use of standardized testing and accountability. But standardized testing and the regime we have put in place to raise test scores produce standardized skills, skills that are now common across the world, even in counties like China that have massive numbers of poor people, but still, nonetheless, also have massive numbers of middle-class people, more, in fact, than the entire population of the United States.

Mastery of the complex technical languages (whether this be the language of chemistry or graphic design), complex symbol systems (whether this be non-linear mathematics or neural networks), and complex practices (whether this be socially engineering new workplaces or new eco-systems) that will be the basis for innovation in the coming world does not start in college. Such mastery starts in kindergarten and before—consider the discussion of young children's "islands of expertise."[54] Just as it is best to start learning a foreign language early—better to start learning Russian as a second language at home and school early on in life if you are to really master it—so too, today's technical languages, symbol systems, and practices are best based on learning that begins early in life and is sustained over the long haul.

A number of economically well-off people in the United States and elsewhere across the globe already realize this. They use modern technologies and a bevy of language and literacy practices in their homes to introduce their children early on to technical languages, skills, and knowledge. They create and support, as we have seen, "islands of expertise" in their children. These islands may be rooted in dinosaurs, mythology, computers, science, art, or video games, but their real import is the preparation they give these children for life-long learning as they face the ever-increasing demands of complex language, symbols, and practices at higher and higher levels of schooling.

We have argued above that some aspects of children's popular culture today are more complex than ever before, in the sense of demanding complex thinking, language, and problem solving. Indeed, the language on a Yu-Gi-Oh card or web site is often more complex—more technical—than the language children using the cards see in their school books or hear in their classrooms these days. Or consider the complex problem-solving and decision-making required to play a video game like *Age of Mythology*, a real-time strategy game with over 300 commands, a game played successfully by seven-year-olds (though not always by their parents).

As we have already pointed out, modern video games—like *Age of Mythology*—often come with the software by which they are made, so that players can "mod" (modify) the game, creating their own scenarios and maps. Often players trade these scenarios and maps with other players, via the web, to challenge and entertain them. When children have parents who help turn *Age of Mythology* into an "island of expertise," tying it to books, Internet sites, museums, and media about mythology, cultures, and geography, their children pick up a plethora of complex language, content, and connections that serve as preparation for future learning of a highly complex and deep sort. When children are encouraged to learn the technologies with which to modify video games and interact with others over them via the creation of web sites and new content, they pick up the beginnings of value-added technical skills preparing them for the long march up the value chain towards innovative work.

But what about the children who do not have these opportunities, ones now readily available to and sometimes put to good use by privileged families? Can they get this sort of modern learning system, directed towards preparation for future innovative work, in school? Today's popular culture, indeed, has great potential to be recruited into such high value learning systems. But this doesn't happen all by itself. Popular culture may be much less good for those children who do not have opportunities to have it actively leveraged for their long-term growth into complex thinking, complex language, complex content, and innovative work.

We believe that a new and massive equity gap is growing in just these terms—one not mitigated by and maybe even enhanced by today's technologically impoverished schools.[55] The solution to the looming crisis cannot reside in our schools alone. We must transform learning in and out of schools for children and adults. We need wholesale change. And the change we need is neither liberal nor conservative.

Liberals have too often advocated pedagogies that immerse children in rich activities and focus on the learners' own goals and backgrounds. This is empowering, but for many children it hides the "rules of the game," the skills, values, and assessments, not to mention the massive effort, that learners must overtly recognize if they are to succeed in a world that no longer rewards commodity jobs.[56] Some children, often from privileged homes, pick up the requisite understanding of the rules of the game at home and use liberal schooling as fruitful and empowering practice ground.

Conservatives have too often advocated pedagogies that stress overtly telling learners what they need to know and skilling-and-drilling them on factual knowledge, the sorts of knowledge standardized tests usually test. Decades of research have shown that while such learners can often pass paper and pencil tests, they cannot apply their knowledge—for example, their knowledge of Newton's Laws of Motion—to any real-world problem.[57] This is hardly a recipe for building expertise and innovation.

But liberal or conservative pedagogies are not our only choices. What we will call "post-progressive pedagogies" are neither liberal nor conservative.[58] As we discussed in the preceding section, such pedagogies stress immersion in practice (doing) supported by lots of structure, structure built into the design of learning systems meant to lead to expertise, higher-order skills, and the ability to innovate. These learning systems involve the sorts of immersion with guidance that one finds in good game design. Let us turn now to a consideration of what we can learn from game design about the design of learning in and out of classrooms.

13. Game Design and Education as a Design Science

We have talked thus far about how getting players to be reflective about their game play can lead to "media literacy" in the form of thinking like a designer, that is, becoming overtly aware of the design grammar by which effects are achieved and relationships established through digital game technologies. We have talked, as well, about how, if games were made around "academic" content—e.g., a branch of science—this process would allow learners to be reflective not just about the design grammar of a game, but of science as an active thinking-valuing-doing process itself.

But game design has another—much less remarked—contribution to make to education. Game design as an enterprise is, at a deep level, similar to education seen as a "design science." [59] How good game designers think about game design, we believe, has much to teach us about how educators ought to think about the design of learning in and out of classrooms. To see what this point amounts to, let's look at just one classic paper in the field of game design, Doug Church's "Formal Abstract Design Tools." [60]

Church starts by pointing out that a "modern computer game . . . fuses a technical base with a vision for the player's experience" (p.01). So, too, with the design of classroom learning systems or learning systems outside classrooms: the educator—often a reflective teacher, sometimes a researcher—must fuse technical knowledge about learning as a social and cognitive process with a vision of the learner's experience.

Church believes that the "primary inhibitor of design evolution is the lack of a common design vocabulary." And, indeed, this is a core problem in education as a design science, as well. In fact, game designers are more acutely aware of the problem than are educators. Church's notion of "Formal Abstract Design Tools" is an attempt to create a framework for such a vocabulary. Educators have something important to learn by watching how he goes about this task. But they have a great deal to learn, as well, from the outcome of Church's enterprise, due to the fact that both games and learning systems are ways of sociotechnically engineering people's social and cognitive experiences.

In Church's phrase "Formal Abstract Design Tools," he is using the term "formal" to mean precise definitions and the ability to explain them to someone else. "Abstract" is meant to focus on underlying ideas, not specific constructs specific to only one genre (e.g., role playing games as against real-time strategy games). This use of "abstract" would demand, in the educational sphere, that we focus first on core ideas about learning that hold across content areas, not just ones specific to a given area like math or literature. Church cautions, however, that abstract tools "are not bricks to build a game out of." He points out that "[y]ou don't build a house out of tools; you build it with tools" (p.02).

Before he offers examples of "Formal Abstract Design Tools" in his paper, Church offers an analysis of some of the game play features of the classic game *Mario 64*. Here is some of what he has to say about this game:

> *Mario 64* blends (apparent) open-ended exploration with continual and clear direction along most paths. Players always have lots to do but are given a lot of choice about which parts of the world they work on and which extra stars they go for. The game also avoids a lot of the super-linear, what's-on-the-next-screen feel of side-scrolling games and gives players a sense of control. In *Mario,* players spend most of their time deciding what they want to do next, not trying to get unstuck, or finding something to do.
>
> A major decision made in the design was to have multiple goals in each of the worlds. The first time players arrive in a world, they mostly explore the paths and directions available. Often the first star (typically the easiest to get in each world) has been set up to encourage players to see most of the area. So even while getting that first star, players often see things they know they will need to use in a later trip. They notice inaccessible red coins, hat boxes, strange contraptions, and so on, while they work on the early goals in a world. When they return to that world for later goals, players already know their way around and have in their heads some idea about how their goals might be achieved, since they have already visited the world and seen many of its elements.
>
> These simple, consistent controls, coupled with the very predictable physics (accurate for a *Mario* world), allow players to make good guesses about what will happen should they try something. Monsters and environments increase in complexity, but new and special elements are introduced slowly and usually build on an existing interaction principle. This makes game situations very discernable—it's easy for the players to plan for action. If players see a high ledge, a monster across the way, or a chest under water, they can start thinking about how they want to approach it.

This allows players to engage in a pretty sophisticated planning process. They have been presented (usually implicitly) with knowledge of how the world works, how they can move and interact with it, and what obstacle they must overcome. Then, often subconsciously, they evolve a plan for getting to where they want to go. While playing, players make thousands of these little plans, some of which work and some of which don't. The key is that when the plan doesn't succeed, players understand why. The world is so consistent that it's immediately obvious why a plan didn't work.

This involves players in the game, since they have some control over what they want to do and how they want to do it. Players rarely feel cheated, or like they wanted to try something the game didn't support.

This sounds a lot like an insightful analysis of a curriculum or a pedagogy. It is, in fact, as much an analysis of a learning situation as it is of a game. Church is talking about how design decisions impact the players' experience and how these design decisions "push the player toward deeper involvement in the game world." After offering this analysis, Church moves to abstract out some tools and define them well enough to apply them to other games, including games in other genres.

Church's analysis of *Mario* has made it clear that the game offers players many ways in which to form their own goals and act on them. Players "know what to expect from the world and thus are made to feel in control of the situation":

Goals and control can be provided and created at multiple scales, from quick, low-level goals such as "get over the bridge in front of you" to long-term, higher-level goals such as "get all the red coins in the world." Often players work on several goals, at different levels, and on different time scales.

Church argues that this process of accumulating goals, understanding the world, making a plan and then acting on it, is "a powerful means to get the player invested and involved." He calls this "intention," because in essence it allows and encourages "players to do things intentionally." Intention in this sense can operate at each level, from a quick plan to cross a river to a multi-step plan to solve a huge mystery. This leads Church to his first Formal Abstract Design Tool:

INTENTION: Making an implementable plan of one's own creation in response to the current situation in the game world and one's understanding of the game play options.

A second tool arises from Church's recognition that the "simplicity and solidity of *Mario*'s world makes players feel more connected to, or responsible for, their actions. In particular, when players attempt to do something and it goes wrong, they are likely to realize why it went wrong." This tool he calls "perceivable consequence." The key here is that not only does the game react to the player; its reaction is also apparent: "Any action you undertake results in direct, visible feedback":

PERCEIVABLE CONSEQUENCE: A clear reaction from the game world to the action of the player.

Church goes on to note how *Mario* uses these tools in conjunction: "[A]s players create and undertake a plan, they then see the results of the plan, and know (or can intuit) why these results occurred." Church then moves on to show how the tools of intention and perceivable consequence can be applied to other types of games and how they work out somewhat differently in different types of games.

While these are basic principles, what is striking is how centrally connected to efficacious learning they are. All of us would—at least if we accepted any remotely modern theory of learning supported by current research—applaud a science curriculum that was built not just by using the Intention tool and the Perceivable Consequence tool, but by deftly combining them. We would also applaud a design science of learning that carried out Church's task of building a common vocabulary around a set of shared and basic principles, principles that are abstract and yet are able to be practically implemented.

I believe that the deep compatibility of Church's game design enterprise and a design science of learning (implemented by researchers or teachers themselves) lies in the fact that games are learning systems (games draw some of their deepest pleasures from learning and mastery) and classrooms are, at their best, social/cognitive games played according to understandable and discoverable rules (otherwise learners are just lost, as they are in bad video games). In the end, then—though we are just at the bare beginnings of this enterprise—we believe that there can be very fruitful communication and learning between game design and educational design science (again, where we think of both researchers and teachers as designers).

14. Learning to Be

For years now we have attempted to speak to the literacy gap in our schools—
the fact that poorer children learn to read less quickly and less well than do better off children. But modern digital technologies are opening up possibilities for
new gaps on top of this old one, gaps in knowledge and in access to tech-savvy
skills and identities. This is happening at the same time as our country—along
with other developed countries—faces a looming creativity/innovation crisis, especially in technical areas. At the same time, fewer and fewer Americans are choosing to become scientists, engineers, or computer scientists.[61]

Deep learning—learning that can lead to real understanding, the ability to apply one's knowledge, and even to transform that knowledge for
innovation—requires that we move beyond "learning about" and move to
"learning to be."[62] It requires that learning be not just about "belief" (what
the facts are, where they came from, and who believes them) but also strongly
about "design" (how, where, and why knowledge, including facts, are useful and adequate for specific purposes and goals).[63]

Deep learning requires the learner being willing and able to take on a new
identity in the world, to see the world and act on it in new ways. Learning a new
domain, whether physics or furniture making, requires learners to see and value
work and the world in new ways, in the ways in which physicists or furniture makers do. One deep reason this is so is because, in any domain, if knowledge is to
be used, the learner must probe the world (act on it with a goal) and then evaluate the result. Is it "good" or "bad," "adequate" or "inadequate," "useful" or
"not," "improvable" or "not"?

Learners can only do this if they have developed a value system—what
Donald Schön calls an "appreciative system"[64]—in terms of which such judgments can be made. Such value systems are embedded in the identities, tools,
technologies, and worldviews of distinctive groups of people—who share, sustain, and transform them—groups like doctors, carpenters, physicists, graphic artists,
teachers, and so forth through a nearly endless list. A game like *S.W.A.T.4* is all
about such identities and values. In playing the game, the player comes to realize that S.W.A.T. team members look at and act on the world in quite distinctive ways because of their values and goals and that these values and goals are
supported by and integrally expressed through distinctive tools, technologies, skills,
and knowledge. So, too, with any type of science, for instance.

Good video games can offer people new experiences which can be interrogated inside good learning systems. They can offer problem sets integrated,
worked, modeled, and ordered in intelligent ways. They can offer identities—

new shoes to stand in from which to view the world, ready for action, in distinctive ways—connected to powerful tools, knowledge, and technologies. They can create new forms of collaboration and communities of practice. They can create new roles and enrich old ones for teachers. They can create new gaps and make old ones worse, or they can be one tool among many for us to close old gaps and forestall new ones.

Notes

1   Gee (2003, 2004, 2005); Shaffer, Squire, Halverson & Gee (2005); Squire & Jenkins (2005).

2   Gee (2003, 2004, 2005).

3   Brown & Thomas (2006); Castranova (2005); Steinkuehler (2006); Taylor (2006)

4   Juul (2005).

5   Shaffer (2007), Gee (2004).

6   Gee (1992, 1996, 2004); Kress (2003).

7   Kress (2003); Kress, Jewitt, Ogborn, & Tsatsarelis (2001); Kress & Van Leeuwen (2001, 2006).

8   Galloway (2006).

9   New London Group (1996).

10   GAPPS Group (2006).

11   Neuman & Celano (2006); Warschauer (2007).

12   American Educator (2003b); Chall, Jacobs, & Baldwin (1990).

13   Dickinson & Neuman (2006).

14   Dickinson & Neuman (2006); Senechal, Ouellette, & Rodney (2006).

15   Chomsky (1986); Labov (1979); Pinker (1994).

16   Gee (2004); Schleppegrell (2004).

17   Crowley & Jacobs (2002, p. 333).

18   The transcript is adapted from Crowley & Jacobs (2002, pp. 343–344).

19   Vygotsky (1978).

20   Gee (2004).

21   Gardner (1991).

22   Chi, Feltovich, & Glaser (1981).

23   Gee (2004) .

24   Brown, Collins, & Duguid (1989); Clark (1989, 1997); Gee (2004).

25   Clark (1993).

26   Newell & Simon (1972)

27   Clark (1989); Gee (1992).

28   Bransford, Brown, & Cocking (2000).

29   Barsalou (1999a: p. 77); see also Barsalou (1999b).

30   Glenberg (1997: p. 3; see also Glenberg & Robertson (1999).

31   Hawkins (2005, p. 96).

32   Barsalou (1999b); Clark (1997); Glenberg & Robertson (1999).

33   Gibson (1979).

34   Gee (2005).

35   Gee (2004).

36   Gee (2004); Hutchins (1995); Shaffer (2004).

37   Shaffer (2004, 2005).

38   Beck (1999); Gee (2004); Gee, Hull, & Lankshear (1996).

39   diSessa (2000); Gee (2004, 2005).

40   Elman (1991a, b).

41   diSessa (2000).

42   Bereiter & Scardamalia (1993).

43 Kirschner, Sweller, & Clark (2006).

44 Schank (1982, 1999); Kolodner (1993, 1997).

45 These points are adapted from Kolodner (2006, p. 227).

46 Kolodner (1993, 2006). "Case-based reasoning" is just one instantiation of the viewpoint that we primarily learn from reflections on the connections and patterns in our own embodied experiences and experiences we have learned about from media, discussion, and experts; see also Barsalou (1999a, b); Clark (1993); Gee (1992); Glenberg (1997).

47 Lave (1996); Lave & Wenger (1991); Wenger (1998).

48 See Greeno (2006) and Sawyer (2006b) for overviews. See also Rosebery, Warren, & Conant (1992); O'Connor & Michaels (1996).

49 Gee (2004); Halliday (1985).

50 Collela (2000); diSessa (2004); Lehrer & Schauble (2000, 2005, 2006); Stewart, Passmore, Cartier, Rudolph, & Donovan (2005); see also Nersessian (2002) on the cognitive basis of model-based reasoning in science.

51 Toffler & Toffler (2006).

52 Friedman (2005); Hagel & Brown (2005); National Science Board (2002).

53 Shaffer & Gee (2005).

54 Gee (2004).

55 Neuman & Celano (2006).

56 Delpit (1996); Gee (2001).

57 Bransford, Brown, & Cocking (2000); Chi, Feltovich, & Glaser (1981); Gardner (1991).

58 Gee (2001, 2004).

59 Cobb, Confrey, diSessa, Lehrer, & Schauble (2003).

60 Church (1999). All page references following are to this paper.

61 Committee on Prospering in the Global Economy of the 21st Century (2006).

62 Brown & Thomas (2006); Gee (1996).

63 Bereiter (2002); Scardamalia & Bereiter(2006).

64 Schön (1983, 1987).

References

American Educator (2003a). Spring Issue. http://www.aft.org/pubs-reports/american_educator/spring2003/index.html.

American Educator (2003b). The fourth-grade plunge: The cause. The cure. Special issue, Spring.

Anderson C. A. & Bushman, B. J. (2001). Effects of violent video-games on aggressive behavior, aggressive cognition, aggressive affect, physiological arousal, and prosocial behavior: A meta-analytic review of the literature. *Psychological Science* 12: 353–359.

Anderson, C. A. & Dill, K. E. (2000). Video games and aggressive thoughts, feelings, and behavior in the laboratory and in life. *Journal of Personality and Social Psychology* 78: 772–790.

Bakhtin, M. (1981). *The dialogic imagination*. Austin: University of Texas Press.

Bakhtin, M. (1986). *Speech genres and other late essays*. Austin: University of Texas Press.

Barsalou, L. W. (1999a). Language comprehension: Archival memory or preparation for situated action. *Discourse Processes* 28: 61–80.

Barsalou, L. W. (1999b). Perceptual symbol systems. *Behavioral and Brain Sciences* 22: 577–660.

Beck, U. (1999). *World risk society*. Oxford: Blackwell.

Beckett, K. L. & Shaffer, D. W. (2004). Augmented by reality: The pedagogical praxis of urban planning as a pathway to ecological thinking. Ms., University of Wisconsin-Madison. See: http://www.academiccolab.org/initiatives/gapps.html.

Bereiter, C. (2002). *Education and mind in the knowledge age*. Mahwah, NJ: Lawrence Erlbaum.

Bereiter, C. & Scardamalia, M. (1993). *Surpassing ourselves: An inquiry into the nature and implications of expertise*. Chicago: Open Court.

Bransford, J. D. & Schwartz, D. L. (1999). Rethinking transfer: A simple proposal with multiple implications. *Review of Research in Education* 24: 61–100.

Bransford, J., Brown, A. L., & Cocking, R. R., (2000). *How people learn: Brain, mind, experience, and school: Expanded Edition*. Washington, DC: National Academy Press.

Brown, A. L. (1994). The advancement of learning. *Educational Researcher* 23: 4–12.

Brown, J. S., Collins, A., & Duguid (1989). Situated cognition and the culture of learning. *Educational Researcher* 18: 32–42.

Brown, J. S. & Thomas, D. (2006). You play World of Warcraft? You're hired! *Wired Magazine* 14.04, April, http://www.wired.com/wired/archive/14.04/learn.html.

Bruner, J. (1986). *Actual minds, possible worlds*. Cambridge, MA: Harvard University Press.

Burke, K. (1973). *The philosophy of literary form*. 3rd. Revised Edition. Berkeley, CA: University of California Press [org. 1941].

Castranova, E. (2005). *Synthetic worlds: The business and culture of online games*. Chicago: University of Chicago Press.

Chall, J. S., Jacobs, V., & Baldwin, L. (1990). *The reading crisis: Why poor children fall behind*. Cambridge, MA: Harvard University Press.

Chi, M., Feltovich, P., & Glaser, R. (1981). Categorization and representation of physics problems by experts and novices. *Cognitive Science* 5.2: 121–152.

Chomsky, N. (1986). *Knowledge of language*. New York: Praeger.

Christie, F., Ed. (1990). *Literacy for a changing world*. Melbourne: Australian Council for Educational Research.

Church, D. (1999). Formal abstract design tools. *Gamasutra*, [online journal], viewed 1 July 2006, <http://www.gamasutra.com/features/19990716/design_tools_01.htm>.

Clark, A. (1989). *Microcognition: Philosophy, cognitive science, and parallel distributed processing*. Cambridge, Mass.: MIT Press.

Clark, A. (1993). *Associative engines: Connectionism, concepts, and representational change*. Cambridge: Cambridge University Press.

Clark, A. (1997). *Being there: Putting brain, body, and world together again*. Cambridge, Mass.: MIT Press.

Clark, A. (2003). *Natural-born cyborgs: Why minds and technologies are made to merge*. Oxford: Oxford University Press.

Cobb, P., Confrey, J., diSessa, A., Lehrer, R., & Schauble, L. (2003). Design experiments in education research. *Educational Researcher, 32*: 9–13.

Coles, G. (2003). *Reading the naked truth: Literacy, legislation, and lies*. Portsmouth, NH: Heinemann.

Collela, V. (2000).Participatory simulations: Building collaborative understanding through dynamic modeling. *The Journal of the Learning Sciences 9*: 471–500.

Committee on Prospering in the Global Economy of the 21st Century (2006). *Rising above the gathering storm: Energizing and employing America for a brighter economic future*. Washington, DC: National Academies Press.

Cope, B. & Kalantzis, M., Eds. (1993). *The powers of literacy: A genre approach to teaching writing*. Pittsburgh: University of Pittsburgh Press.

Crowley, K. & Jacobs, M. (2002). Islands of expertise and the development of family scientific literacy. In Leinhardt, G., Crowley, K., & Knutson, K., Eds., *Learning conversations in museums*. Mahwah, NJ: Lawrence Erlbaum, pp. 333–356.

Damasio, A. R. (1994). *Descartes' error: Emotion, reason, and the human brain*. New York: Avon.

Delpit, L. (1996). *Other people's children: Cultural conflict in the classroom*. New York: New Press.

Dickinson, D. K. & Neuman, S. B. Eds. (2006). *Handbook of early literacy research: Volume 2*. New York: Guilford Press.

Dickinson, E. (1924). *The complete poems*. Boston: Little, Brown.

diSessa, A. A. (2000). *Changing minds: Computers, learning, and literacy*. Cambridge, Mass.: MIT Press.

diSessa, A. A. (2004). Metarepresentation: Native competence and targets for instruction. *Cognition and Instruction 22*: 293–331.

Elman, J. (1991a). Distributed representations, simple recurrent networks and grammatical structure. *Machine Learning 7*: 195–225.

Elman, J. (1991b). *Incremental learning, or the importance of starting small*. Technical Report 9101, Center for Research in Language, University of California at San Diego.

Emergent Literacy Project. (n.d.). *What is emergent literacy?* [Online]. Available: http://idahocdhd.org/cdhd/emerlit/facts.asp.

Friedman, T. (2005). *The world is flat: A brief history of the twenty-first century*. New York: Farrar, Straus and Giroux.

Fukuyama, F. (1999). *The great disruption: Human nature and the reconstitution of social order*. New York: Free Press.

Galloway, A. R. (2006). *Gaming: Essays on algorithmic culture*. Minneapolis, MN: University of Minnesota Press.

Games-to-Teach Team. (2003). Design principles of next-generation digital gaming for education. *Educational Technology, 43*(5), 17–33.

GAPPS Group (2006). A productive approach to learning and media literacy through video games and simulations. Grant to the MacArthur Foundation. Madison: University of Wisconsin-Madison.

Gardner, H. (1991). *The unschooled mind: How children think and how schools should teach.* New York: Basic Books.

Gauntlett, D. (1998). Ten thing wrong with the "effects model." In R. Dickinson, R. Harindranath, & O. Linne, Eds, *Approaches to audiences—A reader.* London: Arnold.

Gee, J. P. (1992). *The social mind: Language, ideology, and social practice.* New York: Bergin & Garvey.

Gee, J. P. (1996). *Social linguistics and literacies: Ideology in Discourses.* Second Edition. London: Routledge/Taylor & Francis.

Gee, J. P. (1999). *An introduction to discourse analysis: Theory and method.* London: Routledge.

Gee, J. P. (2000–2001). Identity as an analytic lens for research in education. *Review of Research in Education* 25: 99–125.

Gee, J. P. (2001). Progressivism, critique, and socially situated minds. In C. Dudley-Marling & C. Edelsky, Eds., *The fate of progressive language policies and practices.* Urbana, IL: NCTE, pp. 31–58.

Gee, J. P. (2003). *What video games have to teach us about learning and literacy.* New York: Palgrave/Macmillan.

Gee, J. P. (2003a). Opportunity to learn: A language-based perspective on assessment. *Assessment in Education* 10.1: 25–44.

Gee, J. P. (2004). *Situated language and learning: A critique of traditional schooling.* London: Routledge.

Gee, J.P. (2005). *Why video games are good for your soul: Pleasure and learning.* Melbourne: Common Ground.

Gee, J. P., Hull, G., & Lankshear, C. (1996). *The new work order: Behind the language of the new capitalism.* Boulder, Co.: Westview.

Gibson, J.J. (1979). *The ecological approach to visual perception.* Boston: Houghton Mifflin.

Glenberg, A. M. (1997). What is memory for? *Behavioral and Brain Sciences* 20: 1–55.

Glenberg, A. M. & Robertson, D. A. (1999). Indexical understanding of instructions. *Discourse Processes* 28: 1–26.

Goldberg, K., Ed. (2001). *The robot in the garden: Telerobotics and telepistemology in the age of the Internet.* Cambridge, MA: MIT Press.

Goto, S. (2003). Basic writing and policy reform: Why we keep talking past each other. *Journal of Basic Writing.* 21: 16–32.

Greenfield, P. (1984a). *Mind and media: The effects of television, video games, and computers.* Cambridge, MA: Harvard University Press.

Greenfield, P. (1984b). *Media and the mind of the child: From print to television, video games and computers.* Cambridge, Mass.: Harvard University Press.

Greeno, J. G. (2006). Learning in activity. In R. K. Sawyer, Ed., *The Cambridge handbook of the learning sciences*. Cambridge: Cambridge University Press, pp. 79–96.

Hagel, J. and J.S. Brown (2005). *The only sustainable edge: Why business strategy depends on productive friction and dynamic specialization*. Boston, MA: Harvard Business School Press.

Halliday, M.A.K. (1985). *An introduction to functional grammar*. London: Edward Arnold.

Hawkins, J. (2005). *On intelligence*. New York: Henry Holt.

Hutchins, E. (1995). *Cognition in the wild*. Cambridge, MA.: MIT Press.

Jenkins, H. (2006). *Convergence culture: Where old and new media collide*. New York: New York University Press.

Jenkins, H., Squire, K., & Tan, P. (in press). Don't bring that game to school: Designing *Supercharged!* to appear in Laurel, B. (Ed.) *Design research*. Cambridge: MIT Press.

Johnson, S. (2005). *Everything bad for you is good for you: How today's popular culture is actually making us smarter*. New York: Riverhead.

Juul, J. (2005). *Half-real: Video games between real rules and fictional worlds*. Cambridge, MA: MIT Press.

Kelly, A. E., Ed. (2003). Theme issue: The role of design in educational research, *Educational Researcher* 32: 3–37.

Kelly, K. (1994). *Out of control: The new biology of machines, social systems, and the economic world*. Reading, Mass.: Addison-Wesley.

Kestenbaum, G. I. & Weinstein, L. (1985). Personality, psychopathology and developmental issues in male adolescent video game use. *Journal of the American Academy of Child Psychiatry* 24: 329–337.

Kirschner, P. A., Sweller, J., & Clark, R. E. (2006). Why minimal guidance during instruction does not work: an analysis of the failure of constructivist, discovery, problem-based, experiential, and inquiry-based teaching. *Educational Psychologist* 41: 75–86.

Kolodner, J. L. (1993). *Case based reasoning*. San Mateo, CA: Morgan Kaufmann Publishers.

Kolodner, J. L. (1997). Educational implications of analogy: A view from case-based reasoning. *American Psychologist* 52: 57–66.

Kolodner, J. L. (2006). Case-based reasoning. In R. K. Sawyer, Ed., *The Cambridge handbook of the learning sciences*. Cambridge: Cambridge University Press, pp. 225–242.

Koster, R. (2004). *A theory of fun for game design*. Scottsdale, AZ: Paraglyph Press.

Kress, G. (2003). *Literacy in the new media age*. London: Routledge.

Kress G., Jewitt, C., Ogborn, J., & Tsatsarelis, C. (2001). *Multimodal teaching and learning: The rhetorics of the science classroom*. London: Continuum

Kress, G. & van Leeuwen, T. (2001). *Multimodal discourse: The modes and media of contemporary communication*. London: Edward Arnold.

Kress, G. & Van Leeuwen, T. (2006). *Reading images: The grammar of visual design*. Second Edition. London: Routledge.

Labov, W. (1979). The logic of nonstandard English. In Giglioli, P., Ed., *Language and social context*. Middlesex, U.K.: Penguin Books, pp. 179–215.

Lave, J. (1996). Teaching, as learning, in practice. *Mind, Culture, and Activity* 3: 149–164.

Lave, J. and Wenger, E. (1991). *Situated learning: Legitimate peripheral participation*. Cambridge: Cambridge University Press.

Lehrer, R. & Schauble (2000). Modeling in mathematics and science. In R. Glaser, Ed., *Advances in instructional psychology: Educational design and cognitive science*. Vol. 5. Mahwah, NJ: Lawrence Erlbaum, pp. 101–159).

Lehrer, R. & Schauble, L. (2005). Developing modeling and argument in the elementary grades. In T. Romberg, T. P. Carpenter, & F. Dremock, Eds., *Understanding mathematics and science matters*. Mahwah, NJ: Lawrence Erlbaum, pp. 29–53.

Lehrer, R. & Schauble, L. (2006). Cultivating model-based reasoning in science education. In R. K. Sawyer, Ed., *The Cambridge handbook of the learning sciences*. Cambridge: Cambridge University Press, pp. 371–387.

Martin, J. R. (1990). Literacy in science: Learning to handle text as technology. In F. Christie (Ed.), *Literacy for a changing world* (pp. 79–117). Melbourne: Australian Council for Educational Research.

McFarlane, A., Sparrowhawk, A., & Heald, Y. (2002). *Report on the educational use of games: An exploration by TEEM of the contribution which games can make to the education process*. Cambridge.

National Science Board (2002). *Science and engineering indicators—2002 (NSB-02–01)*. Government Printing Office. Retrieved November 18, 2003 from http://www.nsf.gov/sbe/srs/seind02/start.htm: Washington, DC.

Nersessian, N. J. (2002). The cognitive basis of model-based reasoning in science. In P. Carruthers, S. Stich, & M. Siegal, Eds., *The cognitive basis of science*. Cambridge: Cambridge University Press, pp. 133–155.

Neuman, S. B. & Celano, D. (2006). The knowledge gap: Implications of leveling the playing field for low-income and middle-income children. *Reading Research Quarterly* 41.2: 176–201

Newell, A. & Simon, H. A. (1972). *Human problem solving*. Englewood Cliffs, NJ: Prentice Hall.

New London Group (1996). A pedagogy of multiliteracies: Designing social futures. *Harvard Educational Review* 66: 60–92.

O'Conner, M. C. & Michaels, S. (1996). Shifting participant frameworks: Orchestrating thinking practices in group discussion. In D. Hicks, Ed., *Discourse, learning, and schooling*. Cambridge: Cambridge University Press, pp. 63–103.

Pinker, S. (1994). *The language instinct: How the mind creates language*. New York: William Marrow.

Rehak, M. (2005). *Girl sleuth: Nancy Drew and the women who created her*. Orlando, FL: Harcourt.

Reeves, B. & Nass, C. (1996). *The media equation: How people treat computers, television, and new media like real people and places*. Stanford: CSLI Publications.

Rifkin, J. (2000). *The age of access: The new culture of hypercapitalism where all of life is a paid-for experience*. New York: Jeremy Tarcher/Putnam.

Rosebery, A. S., Warren, B., & Conant, F. R. (1992). Appropriating scientific discourse: Findings from language minority classrooms. *Journal of the Learning Sciences* 2: 61–94.

Salen, K. & Zimmerman, E. (2003). *Rules of play: Game design fundamentals*. Cambridge, MA: MIT Press.

Sawyer, R. K., Ed. (2006a). *The Cambridge handbook of the learning sciences*. Cambridge: Cambridge University Press.

Sawyer, R. K. (2006b). Analyzing collaborative discourse. In R. K. Sawyer, Ed., *The Cambridge handbook of the learning sciences*. Cambridge: Cambridge University Press, pp. 187–204.

Scardamalia, M. & Bereiter, C. (2006). Knowledge building: Theory, pedagogy, and technology. In R. K. Sawyer, Ed., *The Cambridge handbook of the learning sciences*. Cambridge: Cambridge University Press, pp. 97–115.

Schank, R. C. (1982). *Dynamic memory*. New York: Cambridge University Press.

Schank, R. C. (1999). *Dynamic memory revisited*. New York: Cambridge University Press.

Schön, D.A. (1983). *The reflective practitioner: How professionals think in action*. New York: Basic Books.

Schön, D.A. (1987). *Educating the reflective practitioner: Towards a new design for teaching and learning in the professions*. San Francisco: Jossey-Bass.

Schleppegrell, M. (2004). *Language of schooling: A functional linguistics perspective*. Mahwah, NJ: Lawrence Erlbaum.

Senechal, M., Ouellette, G., and Rodney D. (2006). The misunderstood giant: Predictive role of early vocabulary to future reading. In Dickinson, D. K. & Neuman, S. B. Eds., *Handbook of early literacy research: Volume 2*. New York: Guilford Press, pp. 173–182.

Shaffer, D. W. (2004). Pedagogical praxis: The professions as models for post-industrial education. *Teachers College Record* 10: 1401–1421.

Shaffer, D. W. (2005). Epistemic games. *Innovate* 1.6 http://www.innovateonline.info/index.php?view=article&id=81.

Shaffer, D. W., & Gee, J. P. (2005). *Before every child is left behind: How epistemic games can solve the coming crisis in education*. Madison: University of Wisconsin-Madison.

Shaffer, D.W., Squire, K.D., Halverson, R., & Gee, J.P. (2005). Video games and the future of learning. *Phi Delta Kappan* 87, 2: 105–111.

Sherry, J. L. (2006). Would the great and might Oz play Doom?: A look behind the curtain of violent video game research. In P. Messaris & L. Humphreys, Eds., *Digital media: Transformations in human communication*. New York: Peter Lang, pp. 225–236.

Sherry, J. L., Curtis, J., & Sparks, C. (2001). Arousal transfer or priming? Individual differences in physiological reactivity to violent and non-violent video games. International Communication Association Annual Convention, Washington, D.C.

Snow, C. E., Burns, M. S., & Griffin, P., Eds. (1998). *Preventing Reading Difficulties in Young Children*. Washington, DC: National Academy Press.

Squire, K. (2003). Video games in education. *International Journal of Intelligent Games & Simulation*, *2(1)*. Last retrieved November 1, 2003: http://www.scit.wlv.ac.uk/~cm1822/ijkurt.pdf.

Squire, K. & Jenkins, H. (2004). Harnessing the power of games in education. *Insight* 3.1: 5–33.

Steinkuehler, C. A. (2005). Cognition & learning in massively multiplayer online games: A critical approach. Unpublished doctoral dissertation, University of Wisconsin-Madison.

Steinkuehler, C. A. (2006). Massively multiplayer online videogaming as participation in a Discourse. *Mind, Culture, & Activity* 13: 38–52.

Sternheimer, K. (2003). *It's not the media: The truth about pop culture's influence on children.* Cambridge, MA: Westview Press.

Stewart, J., Passmore, C., Artier, J., Rudolph, J., & Donovan, S. (2005). Modeling for understanding in science education. In T. Romberg, T. Carpenter, and F. Dremock, Eds., *Understanding mathematics and science matters.* Mahwah, NJ: Lawrence Erlbaum, pp. 159–184.

Squire, K., Barnett, M., Grant, J. M., & Higginbotham, T., (2004). Electromagnetism Supercharged! Learning physics with digital simulation games. In Kafai, Y. B., Sandoval, W. A., Enyedy, N., Nixon, A. S., & Herrera, F., Eds., *Proceedings of the Sixth International Conference of the Learning Sciences*, pp. 513–520. Mahwah, NJ: Lawrence Erlbaum.

Taylor, T. L. (2006). *Play between worlds: Exploring online game culture.* Cambridge, MA: MIT Press.

Toffler, A. & Toffler, H. (2006). *Revolutionary wealth: How it will be created and how it will change our lives.* New York: Knopf.

Vygotsky, L. S. (1978). *Mind in society: The development of higher psychological processes.* Cambridge, Mass.: Harvard University Press.

Warschauer, M. (2007). *Laptops and literacy: Learning in the wireless classroom.* New York: Teachers College Press.

Wenger, E. (1998). *Communities of practice: Learning, meaning, and identity.* Cambridge: Cambridge University Press.

Wenger, E., McDermott, R., & Snyder, W. M. (2002). *Cultivating communities of practice.* Cambridge, MA: Harvard Business School Press.

Name Index

Subject Index

Colin Lankshear, Michele Knobel,
Chris Bigum, & Michael Peters
*General Editor*s

New literacies and new knowledges are being invented "in the streets" as people from all walks of life wrestle with new technologies, shifting values, changing institutions, and new structures of personality and temperament emerging in a global informational age. These new literacies and ways of knowing remain absent from classrooms. Many education administrators, teachers, teacher educators, and academics seem largely unaware of them. Others actively oppose them. Yet, they increasingly shape the engagements and worlds of young people in societies like our own. The *New Literacies and Digital Epistemologies* series will explore this terrain with a view to informing educational theory and practice in constructively critical ways.

For further information about the series and submitting manuscripts, please contact:

> Michele Knobel & Colin Lankshear
> Montclair State University
> Dept. of Education and Human Services
> 3173 University Hall
> Montclair, NJ 07043
> michele@coatepec.net

To order other books in this series, please contact our Customer Service Department at:

> (800) 770-LANG (within the U.S.)
> (212) 647-7706 (outside the U.S.)
> (212) 647-7707 FAX

Or browse online by series at:

> www.peterlang.com